Tourism Research

Tourism Research:
An Interdisciplinary Perspective

Edited by

Nazmi Kozak and Metin Kozak

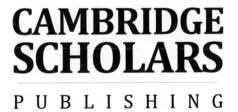

Tourism Research: An Interdisciplinary Perspective,
Edited by Nazmi Kozak and Metin Kozak

This book first published 2013

Cambridge Scholars Publishing

12 Back Chapman Street, Newcastle upon Tyne, NE6 2XX, UK

British Library Cataloguing in Publication Data
A catalogue record for this book is available from the British Library

ISBN (10): 1-4438-4861-1, ISBN (13): 978-1-4438-4861-9

TABLE OF CONTENTS

INTRODUCTION

Though tourism academicians widely view tourism as an independent discipline (Kozak & Kozak, 2011), there is much debate concerning the interdisciplinary position of tourism research and teaching. For instance, as tourism can be hardly described as a discipline in its own right (Tribe, 1997; Xiao & Smith, 2005) and also lacks a substantial theoretical underpinning (Barca, 2012), it has progressed as a multi-disciplinary field (Jafari, 2003; Xiao & Smith, 2006; Tribe & Xiao, 2011). As a result, tourism research has become a part of social-oriented disciplines that requires an emphasis both on industrial training and academic education. From the perspective of education, giving a practical example from both undergraduate and graduate programs, it is clear to see that there are many courses integrating tourism with many others, e.g. sociology, psychology, geography among others. Also, the quality of tourism education has progressed well under the leadership of non-tourism oriented researchers (*outsiders*) in order to lecture and supervise the future's tourism researchers (*insiders*). As to the research perspective, we have no doubt that the capacity of tourism literature has significantly grown both qualitatively and quantitatively with the contribution of these outsiders over the past four or five decades.

On the basis of this debate, there lies the fact that many disciplines play a significant role in the production of knowledge in tourism. In this respect, tourism research seems to have an interdisciplinary identity. Taking this consensus as a reference point, as being its first kind in tourism research worldwide, we felt the significance of introducing another academic event but from a different perspective. In saying so, with its specific name called as the *2nd Interdisciplinary Tourism Research Conference* (its first series was held in Turkish, Cappadocia, 25 - 30 May 2010), the purpose of this conference was to emphasize the interdisciplinary nature of such a specific field as tourism to create an academic platform to bring together those scholars doing research directly or indirectly in these fields and also to create harmony within the standard of tourism research. The conference aimed to fulfil this purpose by attracting a selected list of participants in two categories. First, it was open for those faculty members and/or graduate students who had a background in a different discipline (outsiders), but had the willingness to expand their research interests into tourism and related disciplines. This category welcomed the submission of papers with single or multiple authors. Second, for those contributors with a background in tourism (insiders), papers were expected to be complete by the cooperation of at least two multiple authors and each author represented a different discipline.

With this in mind, the conference was successful attracting over one hundred submissions representing various fields of tourism research such as planning, geography, economics, management, marketing, architecture, culture and communication among others. It also received the interests of interdisciplinary scholars affiliated with a large academic and geographic diversity, e.g. South Africa, Canada, USA, UK, Australia, Malaysia, Portugal, Poland, Iran, China, New Zealand, UAE, and Turkey etc. We are truly thankful and blessed to have had all the participants whose contributions made this academic event possible and a reference point for future discussions.

The conference program was also enriched with the participation of four distinguished scholars who were internationally well-known with their long standing contribution to the dissemination of tourism research and with their representations of different fields and institutions. John Urry, affiliated with the University of Lancaster (UK), represented the field of sociology and his contribution to the sociology of tourism is outstanding. Next, Jafar Jafari, University of Wisconsin-Stout (USA), has a background in anthropology and one of the prominent leaders of tourism research in its history. Third, with his specific contribution to consumer behaviour and marketing, Arch Woodside, Boston College (USA), has a background in psychology. Finally, Allan M. Williams, University of Surrey (UK), has published much to approach the debate from a geography perspective. We would very much appreciate their significant contribution to make the conference such a remarkable success as well as sharing their thoughts with such a diversified academic community.

Having said this, the book is compiled of 19 chapters altogether, selected among those papers presented at the Interdisciplinary Tourism Research Conference hosted in Fethiye, Turkey, 24-29 April 2012. With a diversified background of its authors, the overall of this book is enriched by including those chapters that have had a significant potential to address wider coverage of subjects such as geography, recreation, architecture, archaeology, and culture etc. The selected countries as case studies are also diverse including USA, Australia, France, Canada, New Zealand, India, Poland, Spain, Portugal, South Africa, Croatia, Italy, and Turkey. Therefore, its target readership includes both faculty members and postgraduate students around the world whose research expertise is the field of tourism (both in tourism and other disciplines).

In sum, we hope that the output of this book would be of help to provide prosperity for scholars to expand their horizons and understand the significance of tourism research as the catalyst of other research fields.

Nazmi Kozak, Ph.D.
Metin Kozak, Ph.D.
Co-editors

References

Barca, M. (2011). Third academic tourism education conference: The scientific state of tourism as a discipline. *Anatolia*, 22(3), 428-430.

Jafari, J. (2003). *Encyclopedia of Tourism*. NY: Routledge.

Kozak, M., & Kozak, N. (2011). *Summary report of the search conference on academic tourism education: The scientific state of tourism as a discipline*. Ankara: Detay.

Tribe, J. (1997). The indiscipline of tourism. *Annals of Tourism Research*, 24, 628–657.

Tribe, J., & Xiao, H. (2011). Development in tourism social science. *Annals of Tourism Research,* 38(1), 7-26.

Xiao, H., & Smith, S.L.J. (2005). Source knowledge for tourism research. *Annals of Tourism Research*, 32(1), 272-275.

—. (2006). The making of tourism research: Insights from a social science. *Annals of Tourism Research*, 33(2), 490-507.

CHAPTER ONE

CULTURAL HERITAGE AND TOURISM: ECONOMIC, SOCIAL AND POLITICAL PERSPECTIVES

METIN KOZAK

Abstract

Taking its departure from a close relationship between cultural heritage and tourism, the primary objective of this chapter is to stimulate the debate on cultural heritage from three major perspectives. First, the economic part of cultural heritage management is mostly taken in the context of national or international tourism activities in which cultural resources and values are seen as a source of revenue, contributing to the local or national economy. Second, the social perspective of heritage management is often neglected, although it is expected to make a greater contribution to the social development of a community that holds the heritage in their own hands or on their land. Finally, the political perspective should be cautiously considered by political instruments or public agencies as an important element in taking formal action to protect heritage sites in their original style. **Keywords:** Cultural heritage, heritage management, sustainable tourism, heritage tourism.

1. Introduction

Cultural heritage is a popular term featuring frequently in contemporary culture, and is defined as the legacy of physical artifacts and intangible attributes of a group or society that are inherited from past generations, maintained in the present and bestowed for the benefit of future generations (see e.g. Staiff, 2003). This definition refers to the classification of cultural heritage into two categories: tangible and intangible (Zeppel & Hall, 1991). Tangible or physical cultural heritage encompasses buildings and historic places, monuments, artifacts, etc., which are considered worthy of preservation for the future (Greffe, 2004). These include objects significant to the archaeology (e.g. ancient cities), architecture (e.g. palaces, churches, and mosques), science, or technology (e.g. industrial factories) of a specific culture. Intangible aspects of a particular culture include social values and traditions, customs and practices, aesthetic and spiritual beliefs, artistic expression, language, and other aspects of human activity. Naturally, intangible cultural heritage is more difficult to preserve than tangible objects.

The primary objective of this chapter is to stimulate the debate on cultural heritage from three major perspectives. First, the economic part of cultural heritage management is mostly taken in the context of national or international tourism activities in which cultural resources and values are seen as a source of revenue, contributing to the local or national economy, for example, the Great Wall in China. Second, the social perspective of heritage management is often neglected, although it is expected to make a greater contribution to the social development of a community that holds the heritage in their own hands or on their land, for instance, the Pyramids in Giza, Egypt. Finally, the political perspective should be cautiously considered by political instruments or public agencies as an important element in taking formal action to protect heritage sites in their original style, e.g. the Heritage Site in Evora, Portugal. The political perspective also involves developing positive relations between different national or geographical regions sharing a similar or having a different historical or cultural background, but which all have a cultural connection with the heritage site, e.g. the Anzac monuments in Gallipoli, Turkey.

2. Link between Cultural Heritage and Tourism

From the general perspective discussed above, one may see that the term "heritage" is diverse with regard to the resources and attractions it covers, including natural heritage (e.g. national parks and biosphere reserves), built heritage (e.g. monuments and structures), and intangible heritage (e.g. culture and literature). Different countries may have distinctive features and strengths in different types of heritage. For instance, the US and Turkey are popular countries in terms of natural heritage, whereas the Czech Republic is a unique destination for built heritage. On the other hand, Russia and France have become popular for their intangible heritage resources. Findings of previous empirical studies have shown that, as enabling factors to tourism development, culture and nature are the major reasons for tourists choosing a destination to visit (e.g.

Kozak, 2001; Weber, 1997; Mao, Howard, & Havitz, 1993; Biran, Poria, & Reichel, 2006; Zeppel & Hall, 1991). Therefore, each country may have similar or distinct natural or cultural attractions that can be utilised to promote itself in international tourism.

As a result, over decades, it has become a necessity to establish a public organization which is in charge of promoting national culture both at the national and international level. Many countries have therefore launched a Ministry of Culture, e.g. Canada, Sweden, Spain, etc. The governments of various countries have tended to establish a link between culture and its minor or major fields, e.g. the Ministry of Culture, Arts and Heritage in Malaysia, the Ministry of Culture and Education in Finland, the Ministry of Culture and Communication in France, and the Ministry of Culture and Heritage in New Zealand, etc. More specifically, the link between culture and tourism has been established in official institutions. Heritage is also becoming an important part of the tourism industry and society as a whole, which is evident in some developing countries with the establishment of public organizations at the Ministry level, e.g. the Ministry of Culture and Tourism in Turkey, Malta, Moldova, Ukraine, and Azerbaijan. Whether initially seen as allies or enemies to each other, this interrelationship has led to greater integration of cultural heritage and tourism.

From an optimistic point of view, this development shows the government's recognition of this sector's role in generating income via the tourism industry and in maintaining the national legacy. Heritage resources are irreplaceable; they are non-renewable resources of conservation and tourism. Heritage provides a tangible link between the past, present, and future. Thus, maintaining sound management of heritage is crucial to sustaining these resources. If there is something wrong or misunderstood in the way that heritage is included as part of societal or economic values, the potential risk is that a significant portion of our heritage may be lost forever. There are many issues and challenges that threaten the sustainability of heritage assets, including modernization and tourism. Unfortunately, from a pessimistic point of view, tourism itself also poses a threat to heritage.

3. Three Perspectives on Cultural Heritage

This chapter argues that the stability of cultural heritage arises from the three major perspectives discussed above: economic, social, and political. The current debate claims that cultural heritage has become a commodity of national economies exploited in order to satisfy contemporary consumption. When cultural heritage is taken into consideration within the perspective of tourism development in a specific location or country, it is possible to see the promotion of cultural heritage as a main source of revenue generation, through its ability to attract visitors from all over the world (e.g. Strauss & Lord, 2001; Richards, 1996; Peleggi, 1996), and and thereby to create new job opportunities (e.g. Greffe, 2004). Although this is considered to be a positive impact from the economic perspective, there may also be negative side effects from the social perspective. Local people or visitors may perceive all such cultural values as economic assets, while neglecting their significance in terms of reflecting the cultural and historical background of the society. Especially in a number of developing countries, tourism organizations or governments take decisions or develop policies to motivate local people to protect such resources solely because of their positive contribution to the local economy. Although this tactic would be taken as a positive case from the political perspective, more examples can be given as evidence supporting the negative side, for instance the destruction of cultural monuments in Iraq or in Afghanistan due to political conflicts, either at the intra-national or international level.

Currently, from the social perspective, there have been tremendous efforts to promote awareness by local citizens or service providers of their cultural resources, and to encourage them to increase their short-term and long-term revenues by displaying such resources as of economic value to those people visiting the location. This increases the spread of knowledge among local people as well as the transfer of knowledge to people travelling all over the world. The widespread nature of such knowledge capacity development leads us to talk about the domino effect of tourism which brings not only economic, but also additional, benefits for societal development. The main problem appears at the stage where the balance between economic and social benefits is not maintained for mutual benefit according to the social perspective. As long as economic benefits are given priority, then the economic perspective obtains more power to control or limit the social benefits of such resources.

From the political perspective, due to the sensitive structure of cultural heritage, when it is gone, there is no way of reinstating it to its original setting. In order to protect this cultural heritage, as indicated above, in many countries political institutions have had to take several political and legal actions, e.g. the Ministry of Environment and Heritage in Australia and the Ministry of Culture and Tourism in Turkey, etc. In addition, further actions have been taken on a broader scale. For example, various macro organizations have been established to take a more active role in the international arena by forcing local and national authorities to give utmost consideration to protecting their cultural heritage, e.g. the Council on Monuments and Sites (ICOMOS), UNESCO, and so on. At the country level, similar types of agencies have been developed at the local or national level to control both the local people and the responsible authorities in terms of their ability to comply with the laws and regulations in this respect, e.g. the Council for Protection of Natural and Cultural Heritage in Turkey, and the Directorate for Cultural Heritage in Norway. Such micro organizations are responsible for developing strategies and policies within the entire field of cultural heritage.

As a result of the global understanding of conservation being ahead of that in various individual countries, many organizations now promote the principle that natural and particularly cultural heritage is not specific to a country; instead it is a global principle under the responsibility of all human beings, and pertains to their common values. Such social and environmental associations as UNESCO, ICOMOS, the EU Culture Commission, and UNEP, developed within the concept of a worldwide conservation framework, have carried the issue of conversation into the international arena. Such associations, with their internationalist approach, manage the attention from the public at cultural sites not only by protecting a particular site or location, but by putting all similar places that are at risk on the agenda, with reports entitled "Heritage at Risk"; by responding to their problems; and/or by releasing obligations to include or exclude their names in the worldwide heritage list. Such punishments have forced the local and central governments to take further steps to reserve a place in the list. For example, the Governorship of İstanbul is currently desperate to find a solution to keeping the city in UNESCO's world heritage list.

4. Relationship between Economic, Social and Political Perspectives

Figure 1 illustrates how the relationship between economic, social, and political perspectives is taken into consideration in this study. As indicated in Figure 1, the interaction between three of these perspectives is very intense. Firstly, both social and political instruments should be reinforced to protect cultural heritage and to obtain more economic benefits from such a relationship in the future, e.g. encouraging cultural tourism activities etc. (see aspect "a"). Secondly, recalling the memory of the past and the greater intention of experiencing nostalgia, both economic and political roles should be encouraged for local people to see the value of their cultural heritage and to pay more attention to its conservation, e.g. opening museums, restoring historical buildings, demonstrating local traditions etc. (see *"b"*). Finally, the political side could be better organised to maintain the economic prosperity associated with cultural heritage and to encourage people to become more aware of such resources and their value for the future of their own community, e.g. giving financial and moral support and taking action to support cooperation etc. (see *"c"*).

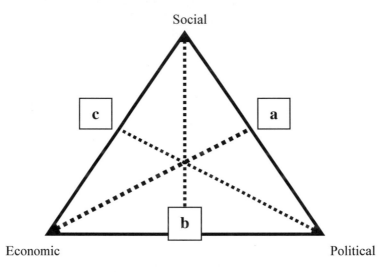

Figure 1 - Interdependence of Economic, Political, and Social Perspectives

The link between the economic perspective and the political perspective does not operate in a straightforward way (see *"a"* in Figure 2). As a direct consequence of tourism development, some tourist locations in Turkey, for example, have become more successful at attracting investment either from other sectors within the country, or from foreign capital. Such a development has led to an increase in the economic value of cultural sites or resources within the relevant areas. In this case, the main problem has appeared to be to find the best way to keep the balance between the economic perspective and the political perspective. In some cases, both the political authorities and the local people may agree to open these places for tourism development for the sake of economic growth in the local or national economy. In so doing, the political perspective will support the economic perspective, which will then manipulate the development of the social perspective in order to take a further step. In those places where the political perspective holds the power to support tourism, cultural heritage has become a significant marketing tool, or sometimes a brand name. A number of governments, for instance in Hong Kong and Singapore, have begun giving strong support to the tourism industry and promoting their locations in terms of cultural tourism (Li, 2003).

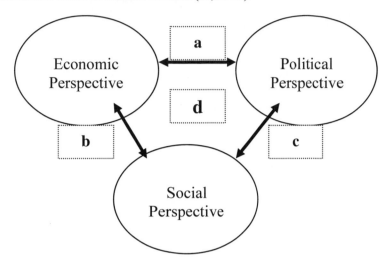

Figure 2 - Interrelationship between Economic, Political, and Social Perspectives

Looking at aspect *"b"* in Figure 2, the interdependence between cultural heritage and tourism makes these two terms sometimes allies, and at other times enemies to each other, depending on the context in which they are seen (McKercher, Ho, & du Cross, 2005; Staiff, 2003; Zeppel & Hall, 2003). Such interdependence brings some advantages to the local community from the economic side, as well as leading to several problems from the social side (Nuryanti, 1996). From the negative point of view, the literature has numerous examples of studies dealing with the side effects of tourism development, including the transformation of social values and the degrading of cultural heritage in many countries. Both in the literature and in practice, it is also possible to see many descriptions of how things change under the influence of tourism activities, a process that has been referred to as "tourismification" (Jansen-Verbeke, 1998) or "commodification" (McIntosh & Prentice, 1999; Urry, 1995). In particular, the challenge lies in the fact that the development of cultural tourism in historical cities initiates an irreversible form of change (Jansen-Verbeke, 1998). This will become a prime concern for local residents and service providers on how to keep the life of such places for the future. As noted, "the desire to earn more money will only increase with the possibility of developing tourism in the area and some inhabitants are bound to be more interested in earning short-term gains from speculation rather than in the long-term development of their town" (Greffe, 2004, p. 309).

The locations where cultural heritage is demonstrated to visitors have become the centre of social transformation, which essentially means the degradation of local customs and social values. For instance, it is possible to observe people harassing foreign visitors to force them to buy their products and services in Turkey, Jamaica, and China. One may see people sitting in front of the Notre Dame Cathedral in Paris and asking visitors for money. In some cases, it is evident that people are carrying out trade in fake products of lower quality to be sold as gifts for international visitors in front of major cultural and historical attractions. From an ethical point of view, some shopkeepers or local agencies may charge at least twice the normal price for local visitors as an entrance fee or for products or services for those people visiting a cultural attraction as foreign tourists. The reason for all such cases is very simple: to obtain economic benefit from the advantages of the cultural heritage in their neighborhood through the business of tourism. Such a practice may also convey a risk for the positive development of social well-being within a community.

Examining the relationship between the social and political perspectives (see *"c"* in Figure 2), the benefit of demonstrating cultural heritage is to allow the people, either as locals or as visitors, to explore the differences or similarities between the past and "now (McIntosh & Prenctice, 1999). This process includes numerous activities such as renovating historical buildings, opening museums, and organising festivals, in order to make a contribution to the promotion of their cultural heritage and the social values generated from the past. As a way of demonstrating one's cultural heritage or social identity to outsiders, this would be a good example of how interdependence between the political and social perspectives could and should work together to prevent the disappearance of such resources in the future. For example, Ondimu (2002) notes that, in the case of the Gusii heritage in Kenya, people have become concerned about the future of their cultural heritage because they have failed to get enough support from the government. In short, due to the risks involved in developing cultural tourism, including the degradation of cultural heritage itself, the political perspective should be in charge of developing ways to enhance the awareness of communities of the significance of protecting the resources that are crucial to the success of heritage tourism at present and to its sustainability in the future.

Istanbul, recently accepted as European Capital of Culture for 2010, is a fitting example to showcase the importance of benefiting from cultural heritage from these three perspectives (see *"d"* in Figure 2). As outlined on the city's website, "Istanbul, one of the most popular metropolises of all times, with its long and impressive history, is being transformed with the construction of universities, art galleries, museums, etc. In addition to suffering from massive flows of migration, the city still welcomes everyone". The chairman of the Executive Committee of Istanbul's bid for the title of Cultural Capital of Europe for 2010 is convinced that Istanbul's long history has enabled the city to 'design a sui generis concept of cosmopolitanism.' In being named as a European Cultural Capital, the city serves as a showcase of living together. To gain both the social and economic benefits as given in Table 1, from the political perspective, the central government has put forward an amendment in law by bringing together the Ministry of Culture and Tourism, Municipality of Istanbul, and Governorship of Istanbul to cooperate on this fruitful project.

5. Conclusion

This chapter has firstly emphasized the advantages of heritage management from the economic, social, and political perspectives, as well as the main problems faced in several countries in today's world. Then, it has attempted to provide various practical examples identifying how the relationship between these perspectives operates in the context of tourism development. The social part of the triangle encompasses the preparation of strategies for identifying, conserving, and promoting cultural heritage. The political side includes providing a partnership between local authorities, landowners, and businesses for the protection of significant sites of cultural heritage. The role of such partnerships in cultural heritage is manifested in the processes of establishing museums and art galleries, publishing literature in book or journal form, making film documentaries, protecting the culture within its original setting such as local lifestyles, monuments, and buildings etc. The outputs will lead to benefits for all three perspectives of heritage management, increasing revenues and thereby enhancing local peoples' quality of life from the economic perspective, strengthening their social values, and testing the effectiveness of political decisions.

From a comparative perspective to examining cultural heritage management versus natural heritage management, as outlined in this chapter, the authorities in some cases have a tendency to consider cultural heritage together with natural heritage. In practical terms, the globalization discourse is more prone to considering natural heritage as more important, due to its close relationship with economic growth. This is due to the impact of the environmentalist movement on the development of industrialization at the international level. However, cultural heritage management does not receive enough attention, at least not economically, because it is very difficult, especially for developing countries, to fund cultural heritage management for either social or economic reasons. The protection of natural heritage appears to be easier and less expensive, and requires less time because the attractiveness of natural resources has become the number one reason for the majority of people to visit different destinations around the globe.

Conservation as an idea is generally applied to natural heritage sites and benefits from the environmentalist discourse, whereas the idea can also be used in a broader sense to encompass the conservation of cultural heritage sites. Although there has been a consensus within the communinty on the definition and specific meaning of cultural heritage as the aspects of our past that (1) we want to keep, appreciate, and enjoy today, and (2) to pass on to future generations, we mainly focus our efforts on the first part of this meaning, neglecting the second part. In other words, we just think about how to enjoy today by providing a link between the economic and political perspectives. Such an approach leads to the avoidance of the role of the social perspective for the future of cultural resources. The challenge lies in the fact that the development of cultural tourism in historical cities initiates an irreversible form of change (Jansen-Verbeke 1998). To achieve our objective, which is to pass cultural heritage on to future generations, the development of effective marketing and management strategies to control cultural heritage and to support heritage tourism will probably maximize the economic, social, and political returns to those interested bodies within the community.

References

Biran, A., Poria, Y., & Reichel, A. (2006). Heritage site management: The link between visitors' prei-visit perceptions, motivations and expectations. *Anatolia*, 17(2), 279-304.

Greffe, X. (2004). Is heritage an asset or a liability? *Journal of Cultural Heritage*, 5(3), 301-309.

Jansen-Verbeke, M. (1998). Tourismification of historical cities. *Annals of Tourism Research,* 25(3), 739-742.

Kozak, M. (2001) Comparative analysis of tourist motivations by nationality and destinations. *Tourism Management*, 23(3), 221-232.

Li, Y. (2003) Heritage Tourism: The Contradictions between Conservation and Change, *Tourism and Hospitality Research*, 4(3), 247-261.

Mao, C., Howard, D.R., & Havitz, M.E. (1993). Testing an international tourist role typology. *Annals of Tourism Research,* 20(2), 319–335.

McKercher, B., Ho, P.S.Y., & du Cros, H. (2005). Relationship between tourism and cultural heritage management: Evidence from Hong Kong. *Tourism Management,* 26(4), 539-548.

McIntosh, A.J., & Prentice, R.C. (1999). Affirming authenticity: Consuming cultural heritage. *Annals of Tourism Research,* 26(3), 589-612.

Nuryanti, W. (1996). Heritage and postmodern tourism. *Annals of Tourism Research,* 23(2), 249-260.

Peleggi, M. (1996). National heritage and global tourism in Thailand. *Annals of Tourism Research,* 23(2), 432-448.

Richards, G. (1996). Production and consumption of European cultural tourism. *Annals of Tourism Research,* 23(2), 261-283.

Staiff, R. (2003). Cultural and heritage tourism: Whose agenda? *Journal of Tourism and Hospitality Management,* 10(2), 142-156.

Urry, J. (1995). *Consuming Places.* London and New York: Routledge.

Weber, K. (1997). Assesment of tourist satisfaction using the expentancy disconfirmation theory: A study of German travel market in Australia. *Pacific Tourism Review,* 1, 35–45.

Zeppel, H., & Hall, C.M. (1991). Selling art and history: Cultural heritage and tourism. *The Journal of Tourism Studies,* 2(1), 29-45.

CHAPTER TWO

CULTURE OF TOURISM

MAURO DUJMOVIĆ AND ALJOŠA VITASOVIĆ

Abstract

In the context of globalisation and migration, tourism acquires new dimensions. It is our aim to reveal new trends in tourism and encourage readers to question the assumptions inherent in much writing about tourism. The chapter begins by defining the culture of tourism within the framework of contemporary society. Subsequently, the chapter considers some elements involved in the production of tourist places and the last part of the chapter highlights new trends in tourism related to embodied tourist practices. The central argument is that the traditional notions of tourism experiences and practices have been modified because of a range of contradictory socio-cultural developments occurring in the field of contemporary tourism. **Keywords:** Post-modernism, place, space, consumption, change.

1. Introduction

Tourism is of central importance to social, cultural and economic lives in the twenty-first century and it is one of the most exciting and relevant phenomenon in today's times of great mobility. In the context of a fast changing world and forces of geographical transformation, globalisation and international migration, tourism undoubtedly acquires new dimensions, properties and directions. Therefore, our intention is to question and challenge the overt rationality that pervades many tourism texts, and argue that there are many competing interpretations of the contemporary world. By utilising critical theory, it is our aim to reveal and indicate new trends and tendencies in tourism and encourage readers not just to understand contemporary tourism from the binary of supply and demand perspectives, but also to encourage them to begin to think critically and question the assumptions inherent in much writing about tourism. We draw inspiration from Franklin's (2003) *Tourism* book and this chapter includes information and ideas from disciplines as diverse as human geography, literary criticism, history, archaeology, sociology, cultural studies and media studies.

Our understanding of tourism is premised upon the notion of the social construction of reality asserting that appearances of reality are influenced by thinking, writing, gazing and experiencing. It is clear that there are objective facts about the things in the world, but the meanings we place upon these things are socially constructed. Therefore, understandings and mental representations of a product or service may acquire new meanings as time goes by and as they are circulated between individuals, in the media and in society. As Franklin and Crang (2001, p.3) argue: "tourism has broken away from its beginnings as a relatively minor and ephemeral ritual of modern national life to become a significant modality through which transnational modern life is organised". Writers such as Lash and Urry (1994) argue that a significant change has taken place within contemporary societies, involving a shift from organised to disorganised capitalism or from Fordism to post-Fordism, that is a shift from mass consumption to more individuated patterns of consumption. These changes have been characterised by Poon (1993) as involving the shift from old tourism, which involved packaging and standardisation, to new tourism, which is segmented, flexible and customised. It is essential to point out that during organised capitalism tourism and culture were relatively distinct social practices in both time and space.

Tourism as practice and discourse involved clear specification in time (the week and the fortnight) and space (the specialised resorts and spas). It particularly involved the centrality of clock-time to its organisation. The holiday experience was remarkably regulated. It was almost impossible to book mid-week. Visitors were informed when they were to eat, what they would eat and exactly when they could use different facilities. 1990s marked a shift from the organised tourism to a much more differentiated and fragmented pattern of mobility. Tourism and culture now plainly overlap and there is no clear frontier between the two and they cannot be kept apart. This is because culture has come to occupy a more central position in the organisation of present day societies. Tourism fits in with trends in economic development towards service based, consumer oriented industries associated with the production of symbolic or cultural capital rather than material goods. The role of culture in this process is multi-faceted: culture is in the same time a resource, a product, an experience and an outcome. In addition, place marketing, the use of imagery and the selling of places have become central theming, and components of the economy of tourism.

Contemporary society has experienced a remarkable time-space compression as people travel more conveniently and cheaply than ever before. As Celia Lury indicates: "both objects and people are increasingly mobile and such mobilities are culturally encoded". (Lury 2000, p. 79). What John Urry (2002) has termed the tourist gaze is still a part of contemporary tourist experience and practices. However, the more recent interest in human body has focused attention on the other senses (smell, touch, sound, taste) and other embodied activities, which cannot be separated from wide structural and cultural developments within contemporary societies.

This chapter thus reviews some of the recent engagements with theory in tourism research from the interdisciplinary point of view. It begins by reviewing the global prominence of tourism and its postmodern paradigm characterised by the dominance of the global media sphere and spectacle as the most influential features of the contemporary tourism. Subsequently, the chapter considers some elements involved in the production of tourist places giving rise to the so called new economy of space and the last section of the chapter highlights new trends in tourism related to embodied tourist practices. The central argument of this chapter is that the traditional notions of tourism experiences and practices have been modified as a result of a range of contradictory cultural developments occurring in the field of contemporary tourism. If disorganised capitalism involves the predominance of culture, consumption, the global, that is, the dominance of non material forms of production, then all these characterise contemporary tourism as well.

2. Global Prominence of Tourism

We are much less rooted in time and space than were people in previous times. Huge numbers of people and places now are caught up within a more globalised tourism that is characterised by flow of images, people, objects and communications (Hannam, 2008). Tourism and more importantly travel is increasingly seen as a process that has become integral to social life. Everything seems to be in perpetual movement throughout the world and most people travel. Tourism is less the privilege of the rich few, but something involving and affecting many people. The amount of traffic along the infrastructures of the global travel industry including virtual travel through the Internet, imaginative travel through phone, radio and television, and corporeal travel has expanded and intensified over the last decade. Although there are complex intersections between these different modes of travel, there is no evidence yet that virtual and imaginative travel is replacing corporeal travel. Nevertheless, it must be acknowledged that the current conditions of globalisation, with mobility and transience to the fore, allow for a much greater degree of mixing and interchange than was possible in the past, which clearly involves the transient mobility of tourism (Reiser, 2003)..

As a consequence of all these trends place after place is reconfigured as a recipient of such flows of tourists who mediate almost all societies across the globe (Burns, 1999.). Mobility is therefore responsible for the ways in which people experience the contemporary world, influencing and altering both their forms of subjectivity and their aesthetic appreciation of nature, landscapes, townscapes and other cultures and societies across the world. The proliferation of many forms of real and simulated mobility has contributed to the development of an aesthetic cosmopolitanism (Lury, 2000), defined as the ability to experience different cultures and societies historically and geographically, favouring transnational relations, organisations and exchanges, in which process the social organisation of travel and tourism has facilitated and structured such cosmopolitanism. Aesthetic reflexivity and cosmopolitanism are concerned with identifying a particular place's location within the contours of geography, history and culture that circulate the globe as well as identifying that place's actual and potential material and semiotic resources indispensable for the development of tourism.

Tourism's growth has coincided not only with the de-industrialisation of mature western economies, but also with the phenomenon known as postmodernism. As a movement postmodernism is perhaps most commonly known within the fields of architecture, literature and the visual arts, but it also has a number of prominent features which should outline any discussion of tourism as it has developed since the 1970s. Next section elaborates the complex notion of the changing culture of tourism by briefly analysing some prominent features of postmodernity and postmodern tourism brought about by the changes in contemporary tourism and travel and the cosmopolitan attitude.

3. Postmodern Tourism

Postmodernism is a popular theoretical perspective and it is often and easily applied to tourism. The fact is that there are profound differences among the major practitioners of postmodern social theory such as Baudrillard, Foucalt, Lyotard, Jameson etc. (Brooker, 1992). The term is often used in relatively loose and ill defined ways, leading to much confusion and contestation. Since the discussion about the nature and character of this term goes way beyond the scope of this chapter it is important to point out that under this term we imply a historical phase that follows modernity characterised by a set of cultural developments or what Urry has named "a new cultural paradigm" (Urry 2002, p.75). Postmodernism is a social consciousness organised around the economy of sign rather than an economy of commodities.

Postmodernism is marked by the breakdown in the distinctiveness of various cultural fields. Each merges with the other and most involve visual spectacle and play. This is seen most clearly in multi-media events where cultural production, especially via the central role of television, is difficult to categorise and place within any particular field (Pavlić, 2004). The real and the mediated, fact and fiction, document and spectacle irrevocably merge and implode. French sociologists and philosopher Jean Baudrillard (2005) argues that we live in the age where we consume signs and images rather than real things. These signs and images are copies of an original, but increasingly the idea of what the original actually was is lost. He thinks of the ways in which in the contemporary world we can produce copies of places and objects that may seem better or more real than the original (caves at Lascaux in France, replicas of Paris and Venice in Hangzhou in China, etc.). Everything is a copy of something that does not exist, or a simulacrum. This world of sign and spectacle is one in which there is no real originality, only what Eco (1986) terms travels in hyperreality (Disneyland, Las Vegas, Dubai, etc.). Tourism has always involved spectacle. Many professionals participate in the process of image creation: photographers, writers of travel books and guides, local councils, experts in the heritage industry, travel agents, hotel owners, designers, tour operators, TV travel programmes, tourism development officers, architects, planners, tourism academics etc. In contemporary tourism, these technical, semiotic and organisational discourses are combined to construct and sell visitor attractions. In the early twenty-first century almost all environments across the globe have been transformed, or are being transformed into diverse and collectable spectacles as local and national governments chase after tourist dollars. Tourism as an industry or cultural activity is thus very much tied up with the presentation of place, culture, heritage or events, and these presentations could be said to take place on stages that are created out of the interaction between destinations or attractions and their staff and visitors. The stages on which tourism takes place are created by the tourism industry itself, the media and the behaviour of tourists.

Every surface has been rendered consumable in a touristic way and there is a tendency to market almost every conceivable place, past, nature, culture and activity to tourists (Meethan, 2003).. The once singular activity of the tourist, seeking authenticity and an authentic experience away from the work has been replaced by the whole series of experiences, knowledges, anticipations, activities and performances that constitute a postmodern tourism mixing texts into an elaborate wave of leisure practices distinct from a pre-packaged holiday. Authenticity was an "archaic tourist desire related to an impossible belief in the real and the original experience now clearly altered and enhanced by the omnipresence of the media in all its forms" (Rojek & Urry, 2000, p. 202). The quest for authenticity has lost its primacy, as a culturally legitimising principle of tourism; the hedonistic enjoyment and fun tends to take its place in post-modern tourism. Post-modern tourists or post-tourists comply with this assertion, turning from the serious quest for experiences of the authentic, to a playful enjoyment of surfaces imagining that simulated and otherwise contrived attractions are the real thing (Cohen, 1995).

We live in the hyperreal world where everything has a unique cultural content, even fakes. The so called landscapes of consumption including contrived attractions, such as theme parks, amusement centres, malls, reconstructed environments, and touristic festivals increasingly become the principal attractions of post-modern mass tourism. Post-tourists often seek familiar experiences on their trip (Ritzer 1999), deriving enjoyment from the quality of the offerings, rather for fun and of a playful attitude to the world. Therefore, tourism has become a series of simulations from which we build our own package. The post-tourist combines the imagined (dream of a destination, media representations, screen cultures), the real (actual travels, guides) and the virtual (myths, media, Internet) into a package that together construct their tourist experience. This view is supported by Chris Rojek who advocates the idea that with new communication technologies the individual is an active participant using computer technology to combine elements from fictional and factual representations into new practice described as collage tourism. That is, fragments of cultural information are assembled by the network user to construct a distinctive orientation to a foreign sight. Through television, radio and especially Internet we can practise collage tourism at home, which could even replace the necessity physically to visit the sight (Rojek & Urry, 2000). Post-tourist is creative rather than passive in receipt of the defined and pre-packaged experience propelled by the media.

Tourism is infused into the everyday and has become one of the ways in which our lives are ordered, in which consumers orientate themselves or take a stance to a globalised world. Besides, most of the things we like to do in our leisure time double up as touristic activities and are shared spaces (fashionable cafes, local art exhibitions, museums, beaches, sporting activities, etc.) Many leisure investments made for tourists and tourism rely on the fact that local people will visit them too. Much of our everyday lives are spent doing what tourists do, alongside tourists and in a touristic manner. In a globalised world where old certainties and differences have disappeared and where new mixes and hybrids seem to be an increasing part of our experience, we draw on our experience and skills as a tourist to make sense of it and to consume it. Tourism is simply one manifestation of the spectacle and in the context of tourism, spectacles are more dramatic manifestations of images, ideas, events, cultures, people and behaviours with which tourists are already familiar.

The above discussion has demonstrated that there are many ways in which a holiday is not necessarily dramatically different from life at home, but that it could be seen to be a spectacular manifestation of the everyday or every week familiar in which people engage at home with often the same friends, in the same venues, listening to the same kinds of music, or visiting the same kinds of museums and galleries, eating the same kinds of foods, etc. It is clear then that boundaries between tourism and everyday life are being blurred. The line between home and away, between work and rest, between novelty and routine, between safety and danger, between the exotic and the ordinary, between the expected and unusual is gradually fading. These facts undermine the confidence in a theory that places the need for difference and the unusual as the principle motive for tourism. We have argued that in the contemporary world almost everywhere has been mantled with touristic properties and that our stance to the world we live in whether at home or away, has become increasingly touristic. It is obvious then that subjective intangible factors such as dreaming and the play of imagination remain central to the formulation of desire and place attraction and serve as a source of perpetual tourist yearning and fantasy.

4. Changing the Gaze

If all stated above might seem rather controversial and too abstract let's once again take into consideration a more plausible socio-cultural view which argues that demand for tourism results from a need to escape from the ordinary (work, domestic arrangements, etc.) into the extraordinary (what we seek when we go on holiday), and that this act of escape by tourists is driven and structured by culturally-determined notions of what is extraordinary and therefore worth viewing. It is true that tourism involves travelling long distances and that people travel in order to be tourists. It is true that they look for pleasure and difference and that they need relief from the monotony of the ordinary life, but in doing so they are not passive and driven by forces external to and greater than them. Tourism does not exist externally to the individual, but the question is how an individual constructs and gives meaning to it. Tourist do more than just being pleasured by the new and the unusual, they seek some sense of personal change, growth or transition and self-realisation. Travel and the knowledge and experience that come from travel became an important source of cultural capital (the concept was developed originally by Bourdeau (1978, 1984), and denotes the consumption and collection of commodities, social networks and cultural values intended explicitly to demonstrate taste, style, and status). However, tourism does not require us to travel very far in order to find objects, cultures, music, food, styles and people relevant for the acquisition of the cultural capital, because they all flow back into the origins of western tourism. There is no need to travel abroad, since abroad is travelling to you.

Therefore, functionalist explanations of tourism, which describe how tourism contributes to or relates to a social order, may be abandoned and tourism should be conceived as heterogeneous clusters of humans and non-humans comprised of touring humans and tourism objects. The mass tourism of cheap package tours, which characterised escape from the modern economy of Fordist industrial production, has given way to tourism based on the consumption of a broad palette of sights, attractions and, above all, experiences. The paradigm has shifted from the modern notion of mass tourism to the post-modern notion of lifestyle experience tourism.

Tourists consume signs and the media as a primary source of destination images. Our point is that post tourism in this manner contests traditional notions of tourist experience offering more than physical travel and the destination is inescapably bound up in very modern image markets. It is implicated in the society of the commodity and the society of the spectacle, and is a social and cultural construct, which is subject to a constant flux of production, consumption, reproduction, representation, commodification and transformation (Rojek & Urry, 2000). John Urry and Chris Rojek are notable innovators of what might be called visual theories of tourism, but in recent years, more emphasis is being given to embodied perspectives on tourism. This is a reaction to concerns that important aspects of the body were being ignored and despite the new virtual world a new tourism of the body has been emerging which has nothing to do with the limitations of the tourist gaze. It could be said that as the 1990s faded into 2000s more people wanted to get their hands on the world, to taste it, feel it, smell it and do things with it instead of just looking at it. Before the further elaboration of this notion, in the next section, we are going to establish a connection between tourist places and embodied social practices implying that tourist places are produced spaces and that tourist are co-producers of such places.

5. Consuming Places and Consuming Spaces

Tourism destinations need to create unique identities and selling points as the basis of survival in an increasingly competitive capitalist global tourism marketplace. Such local competitiveness of place stems from globalisation, from time space compression of capital and travel, which forces many places to compete to attract investment, workers and visitors.

The spaces and places where consumption occurs are as important as the products and services consumed. Zukin (1990) states that cultural capital is not just of symbolic importance; it plays a real, material role in moving financial capital through both economic and cultural circuits. It is integrally involved in real investment and production. It creates real economic value. In addition, it influences trends in physical infrastructure as well as shaping new demands for labour. According to Jennifer Craik (1997) there are four main forms of cultural capital: built environments (amusement and theme parks; cultural centres, casinos, shopping centres); spectacles (events and festivals), property markets (internationalisation of real-estate speculation and development) and festival markets (dock redevelopments; tourist-oriented malls and entertainment centres) which do not only share a trend towards large-scale developments, multiple facilities and attractions but entail a blurring between tourist and everyday leisure activities. Sites and sights are increasingly used and planned for mixed purposes and diverse groups of users. Thus, the continued growth of tourism must be placed in the context of new forms of consumer development and in particular the convergence between patterns of consumption, leisure and tourism (Verbeke, 2007). This convergence creates destinations where cultural production, in the form of cultural industries, thrives and where cultures of production and consumption, more generally, predominate in ways both actual and symbolic. All these transformations and trends concerning the production of a destination have given rise to a new economy of space characterised by the following:

1. Compression of time and space, which includes collapse of geographical barriers and boundaries in the effort to create competitive poles of tourism attraction. The substantiation involves all human faculties in the tourist experience: bodily/sensual, emotional and cognitive.
2. Dissolution of geographical particularity and distinctiveness due to globalising forces and place homogenisation. Its outcomes are often described in terms of inauthenticity and placelessness or in terms of the loss of the geographical sense of home.
3. Creation of fictitious, commercialized, ephemeral, disposable, staged inauthentic worlds as a direct outcome of the processes of touristification, commercialisation and cultural banalisation, often described as "Disneyfication" (Terkenli, 2002).
4. Instantaneous replication, dissemination and communication of place images around the world electronically or through travel literature.

Tourism is not a one way process and tourism places are not produced only by the industry or the tourists. These places receive their meanings only through concrete production processes that connect people to the world by contextualising one's experiences (Selby, 2004). There are more general shifts in consumption and culture such as the growth of slow food, dining out in ethnically diverse settings, the heritage industry, niche shopping, cultural tourism, themed parks and environments that affect the possibilities of transforming a place and its image. Tourism places are complex mixtures of the tangible and the non-tangible, tourism and non-tourism, hosts and guests, and authorities at different levels. Thus, places do not exist as such but are active socio-cultural constructions that change over time due to internal and external processes.

Tourist consumption involves the sense of performing routines reflexively in another place. Tourist places are simultaneously places of the physical environment, embodiment, sociality, memory and image. Almost all places across the world are toured and the pleasure of place derives from the emotion of movement, movement of bodies, images and information, moving over, under and across the globe and reflexively monitoring places through their abstract characteristics. Those mobilities have produced a capacity for the judgement of places. Indeed places only emerge as tourist places when they are appropriated, used and made part of the memories, narratives and images of people engaged in embodied social practices (Baerenholdt, Haldrup, Larsen, & Urry, 2004).

6. Embodied Tourism

In the 1990s, tourism research was particularly inspired by the visual dimension of tourism in Urry's *The Tourist Gaze*, tourism behaviour was explained as the pleasurability of seeing or gazing upon the different and unusual, as a contrast to the familiarity of everyday life. Tourism was conducted in precisely constructed and decoded semiotic fields: tourists were held to be collectors of views and gazes on objects and landscapes that symbolise something else (the Eiffel Tower – Frenchness, etc.). Such tourism developed in the late nineteenth century in the British practice of the mass movement of the working class of an industrial city to a particular seaside resort to which the city was connected by railway. It was a mass activity because all the factories would close for the same holiday period. The activity would be organised so that people tended to do the same sorts of things and to gaze on the same sights.

The decline of the seaside resort from the 1970s onwards has led to a greater range of tourist and leisure experiences, as well as the development of an extensive and increasingly global tourist industry. A key aspect of Urry's work is his argument that the gaze is central to the tourist experience. Thus, he maintains that practices of looking, such as the taking of photographs and the purchasing of postcards, are at the core of the tourist activity. Urry has been criticised for his emphasis on the visual, tourism is not confined to visual repertoires of consumption, rather it is characterised by sensuality; it is an embodied experience. Taste, smell, touch, sound are all key to tourism indeed, it has been suggested that Urry is in danger of writing the body and pleasure out of tourism (Franklin & Crang, 2001, Franklin, 2003).

Urry (2002) subsequently revised some of these ideas and pointed out that his intention was not to play down other aspects of the tourist experience. He highlights that corporeal movement and forms of pleasure are central to tourism nevertheless, he argues that it is the visual that is dominant or organises this range of experience. Franklin (2003) argues that as the 1990s faded into the 2000s the focus has shifted to activity and active bodies and their senses and there is a trend towards more active, muscular and sensual tourism related to embodied objectives such as fitness, thrill, taste, sensual connection, sexuality. Visualism is still very much a part of the tourist experience but the essentially passive nature of visual consumption in tourism is now in decline and more fully embodied modes of tourism are increasingly sought after. It is consistent with the view that contemporary tourism is a way of life, an everyday experience and it is characterised by activity (performance, taste and smell, excitement, acquiring new things especially through shopping, dance, sex and music). The embodied tourism is related to a range of technologies of the body that have appeared within the tourism industry in recent years and have begun to appear regularly in tourism brochures, such as yoga, meditation, body building, weight loss, physical exercises of any kind, diving, skiing, gliding, fishing, etc. The therapeutic benefits of contagion with nature have extended from natural foods, diets and medicines, fabrics and births to many overlapping spheres of leisure and tourism in and with nature. Franklin (2003) thinks that there are at least five reasons for such a dramatic shift in relationship with nature in recent years:

1. The consequence of deindustrialisation as 1980s faded into 1990s, when many regions lost their industries and become more reliant on income from tourism
2. Muscular tourisms became dominant as part of a generalised awareness of the importance of a physical activity as a treatment of non-disease problems such as obesity, stress, depressive and allergenic disorders, etc.
3. Congestion of scenic tourism by large numbers of people, queues, rising prices at iconic sites, etc.
4. Globalisation of information and reduced costs of transport - although many of embodied forms of tourism may be undertaken close to home, they have expanded into the principal purpose for travelling
5. Environmentalism which has created a reflexive tourist as opposed to the anthropocentric tourist focused purely on entertainment and spectacle. The reflexive environmentally sensitive tourist is concerned about such issues as sustainability, impact on local species and habitats, issues to do with protection and conservation.

Tourism of the contemporary world is tempered by the position people occupy in global modernity. Wanting to get away is still a feature of contemporary tourism. With the exception of those who are poor or tied in some other way to a restricted space, where nothing ever happens, for most people now life is hectic and things change so rapidly that most people want to escape the stresses and strains of fast time living. Activities such as surfing, climbing, strolling or sunbathing take the body to points of concentration and skill where it appears to lose its separation from the natural world and fuses with it in brief moments of ecstasy. There is no doubt that the growth of these nature-based and high adrenalin tourisms marks out stages in the trend towards a more active and performative tourism related to changing conditions in the contemporary culture.

7. Conclusion

The contemporary world is in a state of flux. It is a world of motion and complex inner connections. A myriad of processes operating on a global scale constantly cuts across national boundaries integrating different cultures. It is also a world of mixtures of cultural flows – respectively, of capital, people, commodities, images, and ideologies. To understand culture is to understand tourism and, to understand tourism, is to provide us with at least a glimpse of our own humanity and inconsistent place in the world.

We have tried to explain many of the changes occurring in the nature of tourism in terms of notions of post-Fordism, postmodernism and consumerism associated with the production of symbolic or cultural capital rather than material goods. Understanding that the tourist is an embodied individual is crucial for providing tourists with a total experience resulting from the inclusion of all five senses in the tourist product or service.

We believe that the relationship between nature and body are important themes of the contemporary tourism and that they are connected in interesting touristic ways. Although the visual gaze is still an important part of tourism, tourists are increasingly doing things with their own bodies and there is a trend towards more active, muscular and sensual tourism. Since one of the most prominent competitive advantages of the Croatian tourism is the seaside, which is still a dominant form of tourism, and since Croatia boasts with numerous natural beauties and nature has become a major tourism resource, it is our opinion that the national tourism and hospitality strategy should be focused on the promotion and development of these specialist active tourisms. This is especially viable in the contemporary world. The tyranny of the present is not boredom or the lack of excitement in our lives but the opposite: we are over excited, bombarded by stimulation, information, possibilities, connections and access. We suffer from lack of time to commit to things we consider important like family relationships, careful planning and leisure. The phrase stressed-out belongs to this period and not to periods before. That's why many of the new forms of tourism and hospitality might be considered rituals of slow time and slow food, activities designed to slow down the body and to maximise the present (Franklin, 2003).

In case of Croatian tourism the beach is central to this metaphor and a place of diverse embodied practices. It remains one of the most important aspects of tourism because it has retained its ritual devotion to the sea, the sun and the body, outside normal time, where the moment is suspended and held. When people think of an ideal holiday or break, in their imagination seaside is still a dominant evocation. It constitutes an aesthetic reflexivity that enables sensual and emotional experiences to be recognised as inherently worthwhile. They are worthwhile because they generate pleasurable effects, carving a liminal space away from the cruelties of fast time.

The complexity of the tourism product and its development process require more in-depth study of the tourism industry from a socio-cultural perspective and, therefore, rethinking the modern approach, which has been mainly based on traditional management and marketing theories with an emphasis on economic transactions and exchange and customer satisfaction.

References

Baudrillard, J. (1983). *Simulations*. NY: Semiotext.

—. (2005). Iznad istinitoga i neistinitoga. *Europski glasnik*, 10(10), 189 – 199.

Berenholdt, J., Haldrup, M., Larsen, J., & Urry, J. (2003). *Performing Tourist Places*. Bodmin, Cornwall: Ashgate.

Brooker, P.(1992). *Modernism/Postmodernism*. Harlow: Longman.

Bourdieu, P. (1978). Sport and social class, *Social Science Information*, 17(6), 819-840.

—. (1984). *Distinction: A Social Critique of Judgement of Taste*, London: Rutledge & Kegan Paul.

Burns, M.P. (1999). *Tourism and Athropology*. London: Routledge.

Cohen, E. (1995). Contemporary tourism – trends and challenges: sustainable authenticity or contrived post-modernity? in R.Butler, & D. Pearce, *Change in Tourism. People, Places, Processes,* London & NY: Routledge.

Craik, J. (1997). *The Culture of Tourism*, In C. Rojek, & J. Urry (Eds.), *Touring Cultures; Transformations of Travel and Theory* (pp.113-137). London: Routledge.

Crouch, D. (2007). The Media and the Tourist Imagination in *Culture, Tourism and the Media,* Christel DeHaan Tourism and Travel Research Institute, Nottingham University Business School, 1, 67-79.

Eco, U. (1986). *Travels in Hyper-Reality*. London: Picador.

Franklin, A. (2003). *Tourism: An Introduction.* London: Sage.

Franklin, A., & Crang, M. (2001). The trouble with tourism and travel theory, *Tourist Studies,* 1, 5-22.

Hannam, K. (2008). Tourism geographies, tourist studies and the turn towards mobilities. *Geography Compass,* 2(1), 127–139.

Lash, S., & Urry, J. (1994). *Economies of Signs and Space.* London: Sage.

Lury, C. (2000). The objects of travel in C. Rojek, & J. Urry (Eds.), *Touring Cultures.* London: Routledge.

MacCannell, D. (1999). *The Tourist: A New Theory of the Leisure Class.* London: University of California Press.

Meethan, K. (2003). Mobile cultures? Hybridity, tourism and cultural change. *Tourism and Cultural Change,* 1(1), 10-27.

Pavlić, I. (2004). Modern tendencies in the development of global tourism and globalisation processes. *Naše more,* 51(5-6), 214-226.

Poon, A. (1993). *Tourism, Technology and Competitive Strategies.* Wallingford: CABI.

Reiser, D. (2003). Globalisation: An old phenomenon that needs to be rediscovered for tourism?. *Tourism and Hospitality Research,* 4(4), 306–320.

Ritzer, G. (1999). *Mc Donaldizacija društva.* Zagreb: Naklada Jesenski i Turk.

Rojek, C., & Urry, J. (2000). *Touring Cultures: Transformations of Travel and Theory.* London: Routledge.

Selby, M. (2004, May). Consuming the city: Conceptualizing and researching urban tourist knowledge. *Tourism Geographies,* 6(2), 186–207.

Terkenli, T.S. (2002). Landscapes of tourism: Towards a global cultural economy of space?. *Tourism Geographies,* 4(3), 227–254.

Urry, J. (2002). *The Tourist Gaze.* London: Sage.

Verbeke, M. (2007, July). Cultural resources and the tourismification of territories. *Acta Turistica Nova,* 1, Zagreb, 21-43.

Zukin, S. (1990). Socio-spatial prototypes of a new organisation of consumption: The role of real cultural capital, *Sociology,* 24, 37-55.

Chapter Three

The Importance of the 19th and 20th cc. Architecture in Developing Cultural Tourism in Cities

Alicja Gonia, Monika Kozłowska-Adamczak, Hanna Michniewicz-Ankiersztajn and Anna Dłużewska

Abstract

Cultural Tourism benefits from such qualities like those presented by the presence of 19th & 20th cc. buildings, which constitute an indispensable element of the local history and culture. Unfortunately, more often than not, architectural monuments from those two centuries are unappreciated and as a result not promoted. This is clearly visible when in the neighbourhood one can find older landmarks dating back to Baroque, Renaissance, or even Gothic styles. The following chapter's goal is to discuss the role of the 19th & 20th cc. architecture in the creation of cultural tourism in urban areas. **Keywords:** Cultural tourism, architecture, urban tourism.

1. Introduction

Solid, useful, and beautiful are the three key elements described in *De architectura* by Vitrivius (Basista, 2000, p. 8), which are perceived and appreciated by tourists all over the world. This may be verified by the number of tourists visiting cradles of architectonic styles, e.g., Aachen (Carolingian) and Florence (Renaissance), or cities renowned for their masterpieces of architecture like Rome and Paris. It comes as no surprise that architecture seems to possess an undeniable potential that can easily be utilised in marketing and tourism. Observing and contemplating works of art and architecture enables tourists to learn the history of the place with its unique culture. In the case of cities, the layout of streets interplaying with architecture may be read like a diary depicting city's changing functions, its development with all ups and downs, as well as various roles played in a wider network of settlements. They may also be perceived as a chronicle of traditions and everyday life of a community. Therefore, the hidden potential of architecture should play an important role in creating educational tourism or cultural tourism defined as "all activities performed by tourists in relation to their genuine interest in cultural heritage … and in participating in contemporary cultural life in a broad sense" (Kowalczyk, 2008, p. 13).

However, it must be stressed that architectonic beauty is not always appreciated, especially in the case of monuments dating from later periods or located in smaller towns. Relatively often, areas with numerous buildings dating back to the 19th and 20th cc. generate only a small proportion of tourist movement. For this reason, the authors decided to take a closer look at the relation between the development of urban cultural tourism and monuments of architecture from the last two centuries. It has been noticed that tourists' interest in cities is often directly related to the age of monuments, and not to their artistic value. The older the monuments, the larger tourist movement. However, after analysing various cases, the authors conclude that it is possible to increase the product of cultural tourism based on the architectonic appeal of 19th and 20th cc. monuments. Unfortunately, most of those buildings remain unnoticed and unused in tourism despite the fact that their promotion and exposition allows enlivening and enriching tourism in locations previously deemed unattractive.

It became possible to conduct the research and formulate the aim of the investigation due to field studies after which a number of historical monuments was identified and listed. The collection encompasses various sites dating from 1800 to 1939 which are located in Kujawsko-Pomorskie Voivodeship (Bydgoszcz, Chełmno, Inowrocław, Grudziądz, Toruń, and Włocławek). The list was compiled on the basis of data collected from town halls, the Heritage Conservator of Bydgoszcz, and various documents reflecting the history of the above mentioned towns and cities, and describing the history of art and architecture. During the field studies all sites were described from the perspective of their current function as well as their share in tourism. The investigation culminated in conducting a survey among the students of Tourism and Recreation at Kazimierz

Wielki University in Bydgoszcz. Finally, it was possible to take into consideration artistic and historic qualities, current functions, as well as the level of attractiveness of those buildings and monuments in order to determine their potential in the creation of cultural tourism in the selected towns and cities.

1.1. The Development of Urban Cultural Tourism

Cultural tourism is becoming to dominate over other trends in tourism at the beginning of the 21st century. Already in the 1990s up to 20% of visitors coming to Europe were described as cultural tourists, and as many as 60% of tourists claimed that culture was at the root of their travels (Buczkowska, 2008, p. 5 after WTO *Cultural Heritage and Tourism Development*, 2001). The future development of cultural tourism around the world is also very promising. It is estimated that in 2020 it will remain as one of seven most important pillars of tourist movement (Buczkowska, 2008, p. 6 after UNWTO). Taking into consideration the amount of tourists around the world, the number rose from 565 mln in 1995 to above 1bln in 2010, and finally to 1.5bln estimated for 2020 (Buczkowska, 2008, p. 6 after *City Tourism*, 2005, p. VII, IX, 37-38). A lion's share of those tourists will be motivated by cultural reasons.

Moreover, areas with large cities dominate over other regions characterised by the increase in tourist movement. For example, in 2011 Ile de France, together with Paris, accommodated 35mln travellers, Prague was visited by 11mln, and Vienna by ca. 8mln (EUROSTAT). Cities are becoming the major arena in the development of cultural tourism due to a high quantity of historic and cultural sites, and due to robust cultural life (Górczyńska, 2008; Kowalczyk, 2010; Kurek, 2007). M.J. Thomas (1997) stresses the impact of the so called 'cultural capital' of cities, which, in his terms, is currently defined by the level of knowledge and also by the number of locations and institutions involved in education, scientific research, and artistic activities. According to Thomas all those factors are important when considering the development of tourism within a city. Consequently, it seems reasonable to conclude that there is a strong relation between urban tourism and cultural tourism.

Therefore, it comes as no surprise that urban tourism is far from decreasing. Actually, whenever social trends and tendencies are answered, whenever active and adequate promotion is applied, a number of cities perceives tourism as the chance safeguarding optimal development. International advertising of such actions as "Tourism to cities" helps in developing this additional urban function. Cultural tourism as such is also strengthened by a number of formal motions, e.g., in various EU actions like ART. CITY in EUROPE describes rules under which cultural tourism should be developed. Additionally, *the Charter for Sustainable Tourism* signed in Lanzarotte, also in 1995, devotes many passages to the issue at question (Przybyszewska-Gudelis, 1997, p. 15). Hence, in the time of spatial changes and socio-economic fluctuations, there is a strong tendency to enliven the historical background of urban areas in accordance with sustainable development. In order to carry out those modern programmes aiming at the renewal of both cities and towns, specific districts, previously left unattended and often falling into decay, are met with large scale actions collectively grouped under the umbrella of revitalisation.

Skalski (1994) defines revitalisation as "a component of the whole town planning policy, when one takes into account both material substance – houses, public space, architectural monuments – as well as the needs of local communities populating particular city districts" (p. 102). As a result, the application of sustainable growth policy applied to tourism translates into decreasing the pressure on most frequented sites, while districts and towns relatively forgotten enjoy the growing appeal, and the development of infrastructure and services (Przybyszewska-Gudelis, 1997, p. 15). Such towns and districts can eventually become the so-called 'city breaks,' typical holiday or weekend destinations. According to P. Przybyszewska-Gudelis (1997, p. 16) the data supplied by Polish tourist information centres in London and in Rome suggests that such visits constituted the bulk of trips booked to Poland, although the majority concerned Warsaw, Cracow, and Danzig (Warszawa, Kraków, and Gdańsk).

The basis of the cultural product in terms of cultural tourism in cities can be listed as follows: language, beliefs, customs, fashion, building types, tradition, history, monuments, art masterpieces, regional cuisine, dialects, songs and dances among others (Gołembski, 2002). These together comprise material and immaterial cultural values. They encompass all human creations, which may become of interest to tourists. When investigating material cultural values, the spotlight falls on architectural and construction monuments. In relation to their past and/or present function it is possible to differentiate between sacral sites: churches, monasteries, chapels, and shrines; military: castles, fortifications; urban: town halls, public buildings; dwellings: tenement houses, cottages, huts; residential: palaces and mansions; and farm buildings (Jarowiecka, Sacha, 1973). However, their appeal cannot be equalised. The interest in cultural values depends on a number of factors, which are usually listed as follows (Kruczek, 2003; Rogalewski, 1977):

1. age – the older, the more interesting
2. rank of qualities
3. uniqueness
4. concentration of sites and/or their size – the larger (the number), the greater the interest
5. accessibility – level of preservation, technical standard, exposition
6. representative for a particular group or style
7. aesthetic values reflecting the adequate interplay between the site and landscape
8. approachability – easy access and well developed transport
9. spatial arrangement in relation to roads and tourist areas, as well as additional advantages of the surrounding area

There seems to be a large discrepancy between the academic evaluation of a site's appeal (objective approach), and tourists' estimates. It is a direct consequence of a non-academic, subjective approach on the part of tourists, who evaluate everything from a personal perspective basing their likes and dislikes on previous trips, education, interests, etc. (Kruczek, 2003)

2. The Role of the 19th & 20th cc. Urban Architecture

The architecture of the 19th & 20th cc. mirrored transformations of the contemporary world which was being re-shaped by the industrial revolution. Such traces could be easily found in meanings, forms or the choice of materials. These, in turn, reflected new social divisions and emerging classes, and new ideologies. The 19th century art started recalling previous era, it returned to past architectural styles. This happened in accord with deep social, political, and economical changes noticeable in whole Europe, which led to the inability to create a new and different style in art (Koch, 1996, p. 264). At the beginning everyone receded to the rules of Roman Antiquity. They were closer to the styles utilised by secular constructions, and at the same time reflected national ideologies. As could be seen in the cases of Turin or London, the function of sacred buildings was often limited to that of "viewing points" in the classical layout of streets (Koch, 1996, p. 267).

Numerous architects of the 19th century Europe returned to a variety of previous styles, Antiquity being just one of those. Revivalism was becoming more and more popular by applying modern materials to older forms of previous era in art and architecture, e.g., Romanesque, Gothic, Renaissance, and Baroque. Eclecticism was also gaining in popularity by combining various styles in one building. A typical trend of the time could be found in redefining everything Gothic. This could be explained by aesthetic values on one hand, and national ideology on the other (Ller, 2008, p. 180), as Gothic style seemed to "respect national tradition" (Koch, 1996, p. 268). English architects may be blamed for this Gothic supremacy; they were returning to a centuries-long tradition. European architecture became a mirror in which national values and ideologies were clearly reflected. Such nations as Poles, Hungarians, and Fins, who struggled with cumbersome situations, opposed regimes and cultivated their identities via architectural statements. In the case of Russia and Germany architectural styles were supposed to strengthen the image of international superpowers (Jastrzębska-Puzowowska, 2009, p. 192). However, Gothic style played one more important role by becoming a national and cultural statement, a beacon of independence (Jędrzejczyk, 2004).

At the beginning of the 20th century, European art ceased to simply repeat past motifs and forms. Architects strived to undertake projects which "were aiming at designing buildings in which they could express the wealth of artistic achievements encompassing the abundance of human life" (Koch, 1996, p. 275). New materials and methods of production, fixation on the Gothic style and a growing interest in Japanese art culminated in the creation of a completely new style known as Art Nouveau, *Jugendstil, Modern, Secession* or *Stile Liberty*. The first half of the 20th century was also characterised by the emerging Modernism, which shed the previously glorified styles and forms of the past by concentrating on functionality and modern technologies (Jastrzębska-Puzowska, 2009, p. 196).

From the perspective of a common tourist, the value of 19th and 20th cc. buildings is of lesser importance in comparison to previous architectural eras. Such conclusions are only strengthened by surveys conducted among students of Tourism and Recreation. For the purpose of this investigation 117 students from Kazimierz Wielki University answered a selection of questions. The group consisted of 81% women. More than 50% lived in cities, and 80% of those city-dwellers came from Kujawsko-Pomorskie Voivodeship. It was clearly visible from the answers of those future tourists and also employees of tourist agencies and institutions that the most popular and interesting are Gothic – 75%, and Romanesque – 30% eras. As most attractive European sites they enumerated the Leaning Tower of Pisa, Gothic cathedral of Notre Dame, Arc de Triomphe, and the Louvre in Paris, the Acropolis of Athens, the Brandenburg Gate at Berlin, and finally St Peter's Basilica in Rome. In Poland they tended to favour

Cracow, an immensely rich city in terms of international tourism, with its Gothic St Mary's Church (92%) often referred to as the *Mariacki* Church, Gothic Wawel Castle (83%), and the centrally located Cloth Hall (30%) known as the *Sukiennice*. Among other holiday destinations the students listed the Malbork brick castle (59%) and the Royal *Łazienki* park in Warsaw (25%). In terms of the 19th and 20th cc. architecture students recalled only such landmarks like the Eiffel Tower in Paris (70%), the Houses of Parliament and Big Ben in London (38%), and the still unfinished church designed by Antoni Gaudi, the Sagrada Familia in Barcelona (19%).

Generally speaking tourists appreciate Revivalism and Eclecticism in architecture by visiting churches in Vienna, the Museum Island (*Museumsinsel*) in Berlin, or numerous residential buildings and the whole layout of Saint Petersburg. From the perspective of urban tourism, Eclecticism, Modernism, and Art Nouveau determine an area's success as buildings following these styles interplay with modern forms. For example, Paris is visited by more than 25mln tourists every year. The capital of France can boast a very unusual character thanks to the urban layout and buildings dating back to the 19th and 20th cc. The still present system of roads, the boulevards, squares, and vantage points like the Eiffle Tower, Sacré-Cœur Basilica, or the Palais Garnier, they all are well recognisable facets of Paris, and also function as the living proof of successful engineers, town planners, and architects of the 19th and 20th cc. Nevertheless, it must be clearly stated that the popularity of Paris among tourists originates both from its fame and from the international promotion. Also the Parisian lifestyle seems more than appealing with bistros and restaurants resembling those of *fin de siècle*, with street markets, numerous market halls, and rich cultural life. The ambience of the turn of the century, of *la Bohème*, is omnipresent.

In Poland, three cities are usually connected to the architecture of the last two centuries, namely Lodz (Łódź), Breslau (Wrocław), and Gdynia. The first in this list, Łódź, was founded during the industrial revolution; hence, most of its architecture reflects 19th century styles. One of the main streets, Piotrowska, is an unquestionable example. Wrocław can boast the modernistic Centennial Hall which entered UNESCO's World Heritage Site list. Till present times, the hall functions as a cultural and recreational place, as well as an exhibition centre. Finally Gdynia, the youngest, was established in 1920s following Modernistic approach. Among other interesting architectural sites it is possible to enumerate various, mainly industrial, constructions: the first European cantilever bridge in Tczew, the match factory in Częstochowa, the radio station in Gliwice, or the inclined planes of the Ostróda-Elbląg water canal.

3. The Importance of the 19th & 20th cc. Architecture

As it is virtually impossible to present the wealth of Polish heritage and architecture dating back to the 19th and 20th cc. the following sub-chapter will focus on the examples found in the Kujawsko-Pomorskie Voivodeship. It is also interesting to notice the fact that the towns and cities described below are mostly known for their medieval architecture, while the 19th and 20th cc. sites are on the road to oblivion. This unfavourable condition was confirmed by the monitoring of tourist movement in the voivodeship (Badanie ruchu turystycznego, 2011).

As a result of this monitoring conducted in 2009 and 2010, a selection of towns and cities in Kujawsko-Pomorskie Voivodeship can be properly assessed. It is also possible to confirm the earlier hypothesis that the bigger the town and the richer its monuments and their promotion, the more cultural tourists visit them. Among the studied locations, Toruń can boast the largest group of tourists with cultural motivations. The birthplace of Nicholas Copernicus was enlisted as the World Heritage Site in 1997. Also Chełmno, a small town often described as 'Cracow of the North', is frequently visited due to possessing the longest medieval city walls encircling the old town with the medieval layout of streets. In the total number of 2009 tourist movement, the visitors with cultural motivations – visiting monuments and museums – exceeded 50% both in Toruń and in Chełmno. In 2010 those numbers amounted to 48% and 37% respectively. A large number of cultural tourists also visits Bydgoszcz: 8.5% in 2009 and 19.5% in 2010. This may be partly due to the additional function of this largest city in the region, namely the seat of local authorities. In comparison the figures describing Grudziądz, a small town with many interesting sites, are relatively low. Mere 21% in 2009 and 11% in 2010 do not do justice to its landmarks. Also in the case of Inowrocław, a well known Polish spa, with its 19th century parks and buildings, only 5% of culturally motivated tourists were interested in its beauty spots. The least amount of tourists visited Włocławek, where only 2% of tourists with cultural interests decided to go. The general and false preconception holds Włocławek as an unkempt industrial city with no monuments of any sort.

3.1. Overview of architectural sites

Objectively speaking, **Bydgoszcz** can be proud of possessing the largest amount of 19th and 20th cc. architecture (Tab. 1). According to the Heritage Conservator of Bydgoszcz, in 2010 there were 181 architectural sites dating from the investigated period. Most of them can be found in the heart of the city, which was mostly erected between 1865 and 1915. In Bydgoszcz, the 19th century architecture directly reflects the changes in the European art. However, as a result of belonging to the Prussian Partition (1772-1919), this area was under the influence of strong Germanisation processes in various spheres of life: political, social (colonisation), economic (stimulating the economic growth with investments), as well as cultural. Germanisation was also manifested in the promotion of those artistic movements which were favoured in Prussia, and which in turn were supposed to make Bydgoszcz look like other German towns and cities (Biskup, 1991, p. 557).

The influence of the well-off German citizens of Bydgoszcz, who were fond of traditional architecture, was so great that German authorities funded most of public buildings and hired architects from Berlin, e.g., Friedrich Adler and Heinrich Seeling. They remained true to the styles popular in their motherland. At the beginning of the 19th century, architecture was often dominated by Classicism, which can still be seen in Regent's House and Governor's Office. In the second half of the 19th century those tendencies transformed into Revivalism. Both in the city as well as in its surroundings, numerous sacred and secular buildings were erected with the Gothic Revival at the helm: Evangelic churches, post offices and schools. Romanesque Revival was represented by St Peter and St. Paul's Church, while Baroque and Renaissance revival by the Court House. Palaces and parks in the vicinity of Bydgoszcz usually followed Eclectic style while retaining some Classical forms or elements.

During the first decades of the 20th century, as a result of visible German influence and the work of famous German architects, Bydgoszcz was often referred to as "small Berlin" (*kleine Berlin*). Most buildings of this period were built in accordance with the rules of Art Nouveau (*Jugendstil*) and Modernism. Art Nouveau especially is well seen in the excess of details adorning façades of tenement houses and public buildings like schools, hotels, and administrative buildings. New trends were also visible in urban concepts, e.g., the 'city garden' project of E. Howard put to practice in Sielanka, a district of Bydgoszcz. The majority of secular architecture erected in Bydgoszcz is constituted by detached houses and tenement houses or by villas. Most of those dwellings still retain their purpose (53.8%), while others function as seats of various institutions:

administrative (5.6%), scientific (3.8%), and educational (3.1%). Among other items of secular architecture one can list fences, parks and green areas, walls, gates, and gardens.

Table 1 - Types of Historical Monuments in Selected Locations of Kujawsko-Pomorskie Voivodeship in 2010

sites		Bydgoszcz		Chełmno		Grudziądz		Inowrocław		Toruń		Włocławek		Total	
		l	%	l	%	l	%	l	%	l	%	l	%	l	%
19th & 20th cc.	sacred	21	11,3	5	15,6	8	17,0	4	20,0	14	5,5	5	7,7	57	9,4
	secular	160	86,0	13	40,6	10	21,3	11	55,0	81	31,6	41	63,1	316	52,1
	other	0	0,0	1	3,1	3	6,4	0	0,0	2	0,8	5	7,7	11	1,8
Sites pre-dating the 19th c.		5	2,7	13	40,6	26	55,3	5	25,0	159	62,1	14	21,5	222	36,6
total		186	100,0	32	100,0	47	100,0	20	100,0	256	100,0	65	100,0	606	100,0

Source: Authors' studies conducted on the basis of the Register of Monuments (Rejestru Zabytków Województwa Kujawsko-Pomorskiego, 2010)

So far **Toruń** has been mainly renowned for its Gothic architecture and monuments; however, more and more tourists start to notice later eras in its architecture, which actually constitute 38% of its historical buildings. Since 2009, the so called 'Bydgoskie Przedmieście' is on the list of Toruń's architectural heritage. This residential district was planned and erected in the 19th and 20th cc., south of the old medieval centre. This urban complex incorporates such major forms and styles as bricks, Eclecticism, Art Nouveau, and Modernism. One can find there tenement houses, villas, public houses, and a massive 19th century park with adjoining botanical gardens. Another characteristic feature visible everywhere around is the timber framing construction of walls – a relic of the times when the whole city was turned into a Fortress during the 19th century. Large parts of Toruń bear the mark of various Prussian fortifications and military buildings. The series of constructions was started in 1818 and lasted for nearly 60 years. There are two major rings of forts, the inner and the outer ring. However, there is a plethora of supplementary buildings like barracks, warehouses, gunpowder magazines, etc. Presently some of those sites are open to visitors, others function as places of commerce, while still others remain in the custody of the Armed Forces.

Włocławek with more than 100,000 inhabitants is unfairly believed to lack in interesting monuments. The city can surprise tourists with sites proving its rich history and rapid development especially in the period of the industrial revolution. The residence of Hugon Mühsam may function as a perfect example. This large house, locally known as Mühsam's Palace, was built in 1894 by a factory owner who invested extensively in the city. Also the fire station, with its tall clock tower, erected in 1909 is a splendid example of Gothic revival. This building belonged to a local fire brigade for many decades and a reconstructed painting "Firemen on their way" remains at the first floor. Revivalism is not only present in public and industrial buildings as numerous tenement houses date back to the 19th century, and still retain their residential function. Actually, nearly all monuments found in Włocławek originated in the 19th century or the first half of the 20th century (Table 1). The most prominent architecture sites still are:

1. A wooden granary known as the 'Black Granary' (*Czarny Spichlerz*) built with massive logs at the beginning of the 19th century. It functioned as a warehouse at a chicory factory complex designed by two brothers, Ferdynand and Filhelm Bohm, around 1816.
2. The city park established in 1870 – one of the oldest Polish urban green areas.

Grudziądz, is relatively under-represented in terms of the 19th and 20th cc. monuments, which constitute only 45% of its assets (Table 1). The church following the Gothic Revival is worth mentioning. It was built in 1898 according to the design of August Menken, an architect responsible for over 60 constructions in Germany. The same style is well visible in the imperial post office erected in 1883 or in the Higher Vocational School from the 1890s, which was designed by Martin Witt. At present the building still retains its educational function as a part of the Nicolaus Copernicus University based in Toruń.

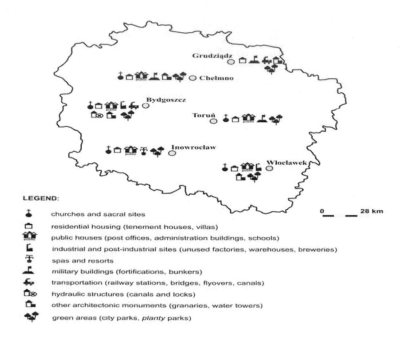

Picture 1 - Types of Architectural Monuments from the 19th and 20th cc. in the Selected Locations of Kujawsko-Pomorskie Voivodeship.
Source: Authors' studies on the basis of the registry of historical monuments in Kujawsko-Pomorskie Voivodeship and of official webpages of selected towns and cities.

Other interesting remains of the 19th and 20th cc. architecture can still be found in **Inowrocław**, where the health resort and the residential district with beautiful villas are nearly intact. In the 1870s a very modern spa was constructed with a number of buildings covering the area of 55 ha: a main health resort, saline baths, saunas, pump rooms, a concert hall, and the 1930s sanatorium. At present the spa is visited by ca. 20,000 patients and 10,000 of tourists annually. Besides, there are other interesting 19th and 20th cc. sites located in Inowrocław: the Cooperative Bank designed in Modern fashion by Zdzisław Mączeński, a Warsaw architect, in 1923; the similarly styled Higher Secondary School for girls; and also the seat of local authorities erected in 1907-1908, which follows Gothic Revival.

Finally, **Chełmno** is the last of the investigated cities. It is an old, medieval town located at the Vistula River. Despite its long history 59% of its monuments dates back to the 19th century. Still the most popular among tourists are medieval fortifications, numerous sacral buildings, and the Renaissance town hall. The grandeur of the mentioned monuments renders the 19th century architecture uninteresting to most tourists. And there are such pearls like the 19th century houses encircling the main square, buildings at Grudziądzka Street, military church in Romanesque Revival style, the monastery of the Daughters of Charity, the military school for cadets, or the old seat of local authorities built at the turn of the 19th century using timber framing. One could also mention the water tower, the construction of which began in 1898, functioning until the mid 1980s.

3.2. Architectonic Monuments at Roots of Cultural Tourism

Baring in mind the number and quality of various monuments from the 19th and 20th cc. still present at the selected towns and cities, it seems only fair to conclude that cultural tourism can be developed in those locations on the basis of the following: placement, architectonic features, equipment and furnishing, as well as cultural and religious events (Table 2). First, in terms of architecture, the features to consider are connected to façades: forms, decorations, details of architectonic value; surrounding green areas: gardens, parks, and graveyards or their remains; and finally forms and architectonic details that belong to the interior. In some cases the personality of the architect itself can be a spellbinding factor. The mentioned qualities and features may belong both to educational tourism and to religious tourism.

Still another set of features important from the perspective of creating the products of cultural tourism is found in the collections of works of art and memorabilia related to local history. It must be mentioned here that sacred sites can boast the possession of varied collections, hence, a greater potential. Most of them retain the original interior and decorations, e.g., pipe organs, cult objects, and the relics of saints. Secular buildings can rarely display original interior and decorations, e.g., "Pod Orłem" Hotel ("Under the Eagle"), Copernicanum building belonging to the Kazimierz Wielki University, and Secondary Schools Nr. 1 and Nr. 2 all found in Bydgoszcz. The majority of remaining art, interior decorations from the turn of the century, photographs depicting everyday lives of city dwellers and the development of Bydgoszcz can be found at numerous exhibitions and museums, e.g., at Leon Wyczółkowski District Museum in Bydgoszcz, Bydgoszcz Canal Museum, the Pharmacy Museum open next to the oldest pharmacy in Bydgoszcz, and at the Chamber of Railway Traditions (*Izba Tradycji Kolei*) at the main railway station in Bydgoszcz.

Table 2 - Possible Paths of Developing Cultural Tourism

19th & 20th Century Architecture		
Secular Monuments		**Sacred Monuments**
Inaccessible	**Accessible**	**Accessible**
Tenement houses mansions palaces and parks industrial sites	Public buildings palaces and parks industrial sites	Temples chapels graveyards morgues
Location surrounding exterior features of architecture	**Location surrounding exterior features of architecture**	**Location, surrounding features of architecture interior events**
Educational Tourism	**Educational Tourism Event Tourism**	**Educational Tourism, pilgrimages Religious Tourism**
Cultural Tourism		

Source: Authors' studies conducted on the basis of Kaczmarek, Liszewski, Włodarczyk 2006; Małek 2003; Rohrscheidt 2008; and Różycki 2009

Third, cultural events may create products of cultural tourism as they reflect local history at the turn of the century, e.g., anniversaries of some streets (Gdańska and Cieszkowskiego in Bydgoszcz). Organisers revive history and make it accessible to city dwellers and tourists by presenting traditions, culture, and architectural designs from pre-WW2 times. Sacred buildings rely on other cultural events, e.g., festivals and pipe organs concerts, and religious celebrations, which may easily stimulate pilgrimage tourism.

The possibility to create the product of tourism and to utilise the mentioned locations while developing cultural tourism depends on such factors as ownership and on the condition of particular sites. Many locations remain in private hands, and as a result are inaccessible to tourists despite their immense value. In such cases only educational tourism may thrive, when only façades are visible, when only the vicinity and some architectonic features may be appreciated. On the other hand, most public buildings, e.g., temples and graveyards, are easily accessible; they can support the development of tourism, especially in its educational, event, pilgrimage and religious forms.

4. Conclusion

Cultural Tourism is gaining in importance in the 21st century. More and more tourists are not that much interested in the quantity but rather in the quality of information. Also in terms of J. Urry, the 'tourist gaze' translates into the ability to perceive and isolate those places that are somehow different from other every-day locations. The source of pleasure or gratification lies in the direct contact with the unusual, with something unique, or something typical for the visited location, or still in finding the interesting facet in something that so far was regarded as normal and dull (Buczkowska, 2008, p. 29).

The development of cultural tourism may also safeguard the restoration and re-creation of those less known sites, which belong to later periods in the history of art and architecture. In the case of Polish monuments, this usually means re-discovering sites that have been neglected, underfunded, but still possessing unique charm and value. Revitalisation is gaining in importance and is becoming more common thanks to UE structural funds. Sustainable development functions as a guiding rule while reviving forgotten buildings, falling into decay due to the lack of adequate care. As a result it is possible to list some major tendencies in restorations of Polish towns and cities:

1. whole segments of public space in urban areas, e.g., markets, squares, streets, and buildings dating back to the 19th and 20th cc.: Bydgoskie Przedmieście in Toruń, parks belonging to the health resort in Inowrocław, Bohaterów Monte Casino Street in Sopot, or Sielanka district in Bydgoszcz;
2. residential houses, e.g., Art Nouveau tenement houses from the 1920s and 1930s that nowadays provide lodgings and services, hotels and shops: Gdańska and Cieszkowska Streets in Bydgoszcz, and Piotrowska Street in Łódź;

3. public buildings, e.g., seats of administrative bodies, schools, libraries, post offices, water towers: the former secondary school for boys in Bydgoszcz, the building housing local authorities in Chełmno, the former court house in Inowrocław, post offices in Bydgoszcz and Toruń which follow Gothic Revival, the Stary Teatr (Old Theatre) in Cracow;
4. industrial and post-industrial sites, e.g., old factories, warehouses, breweries: Wyspa Młyńska (Mill Island) in Bydgoszcz, former factory buildings in Łódź, Stary Browar (Old Brewery) in Poznań, former carpet factory in Kowary, former administrative buildings of the slaughterhouse in Bydgoszcz;
5. former military buildings and constructions utilised in educational tourism, e.g., bunkers and fortification: Twierdza Toruń (Toruń Fortress), and Twierdza Kraków (Cracow Fortress);
6. hydraulic structures and waterways, which constitute a new trend, e.g., old water power plants, canals, and locks; also sites connected to transportation, e.g., rail stations, flyovers, and bridges: Ostróda-Elbląg Canal, the cantilever bridge in Tczew, railway brick bridges in Bydgoszcz;
7. sacred buildings and monuments, e.g., churches of various creeds, chapels, necropolises, parks – often unkempt and underfunded, palace gardens funded by wealthy nobility and factory owners: palaces of Izrael and Maurycy Poznański, of Alfred Biderman, or of Juliusz Heinzel in Łódź.

The results of the 2012 survey conducted among the students of Tourism and Recreation at Kazimierz Wielki University confirmed authors' hypothesis. All students unanimously concluded that architecture does influence the tourist movement. Also 19th and 20th cc. monuments seem to favour tourism; however, due to the fact that many of those buildings are very common in Poland, but also because they still retain their original functions and are not incorporated in tourism and promotion, they tend to be less appreciated than older sites. The architecture of the 19th and 20th cc. seems to be problematic for another reason. Such buildings and constructions are often located in a considerable distance from other sites, or, as it is in the case of Polish monuments, they are usually underfunded and unkempt. There seems to be an ongoing struggle towards finding their appropriate 'touristy character.' In some EU countries the solution was found to the problem of promoting various sites to a wider group of tourists by creating thematic trails, which are not solely based on the already known and appreciated locations. Cultural tourism takes part in an interplay with material and spiritual culture. It finds linkages between cultural heritage (heritage tourism) and contemporary culture (arts tourism) (Buczkowska, 2008, p. 8).

References

Anszperger, A., Radkiewicz A. (Eds.). (2012). *Badania ruchu turystycznego w województwie kujawsko-pomorskim w latach 2009-2010, tom 1* [Studies of tourist movement in Kujawsko-Pomorskie Voivodeship in 2009-2010. Vol. 1]. Bydgoszcz: Kujawsko-pomorska organizacja turystyczna.

Basista, A. (2000). *Architektura. Dlaczego jest jaka jest* [Architecture. Why it is what it is.]. Kraków: Znak.

Biskup, M. (1991). *Historia Bydgoszczy, Tom I, do 1920 roku* [History of Bydgosz. Vol. 1. Since 1920]. Bydgoszcz: BTN.

Buczkowska, K. (2008). *Turystyka kulturowa. Przewodnik metodyczny* [Cultural Tourism. Methodological Guidebook]. Poznań: Akademia Wychowania Fizycznego im. Eugeniusza Piaseckiego w Poznaniu.

Dłużewska, A. (2009). *Walory sakralne a społeczno-kulturowe dysfunkcje turystyczne* [Sacral values and socio-cultural tourist dysfunctions]. In K. Obodyński , M. Ďuriček, A. Nizioł [Eds.]. Dziedzictwo kulturowe szansą rozwoju turystyki w regionie [Regional tourism as an element of the global processes] (139-146]). Rzeszów: EACE.

European Commision. Eurostat. http://epp.eurostat.ec.europa.eu/portal/page/portal/eurostat/home/

Gołembski, G. (2002). *Kompendium wiedzy o turystyce* [Companion to Tourism]. Warszawa: PWN.

Górczańska, M. (2008). Rewaloryzacja przestrzeni miejskiej a rozwój turystyki kulturowej, na przykładzie miasta Cork (Republika Irlandii) [Revitalisation of urban space in relation to cultural toursim. Case study on the basis of Cork, Republic of Ireland] In A. Kowalczyk (Ed.), *Turystyka Kulturowa – spojrzenie geograficzne, Geografia turyzmu, t.1* [Cultural Tourism – geographical perspective. Geography of tourism Vol. 1]. Warszawa: Wydawnictwo Uniwersytetu Warszawskiego.

Jarowiecka, T., Sacha. S. (1973). Walory krajoznawczo-turystyczne Polski In J. Podolski (Ed.) *Turystyka szkolna. Poradnik dla nauczycieli – kierowników wycieczek krajoznawczo-turystycznych młodzieży szkolnej* [Tourism at school. Handbook for teachers and organisers of educational trips], Wydawnictwo Sport i Turystyka, Warszawa

Jastrzębska-Puzowska, I. (2009). Architektura polska i niemiecka w Bydgoszczy przed 1945 rokiem [Polish and German architecture in Bydgoszcz before 1945]. In K. Grysińska, W. Jastrzębski, A.S. Kotowski (Eds.), *Bydgoszcz miasto wielu kultur i narodowości* [Bydgoszcz. A city of many cultures and nationalities]. Bydgoszcz: LOGO.

Jędrzejczyk, D. (2004). *Geografia humanistyczna miasta* [Human geography of urban areas]. Warszawa: Wydawnictwo Akademickie Dialog.

Kaczmarek, J., Liszewski S., & Włodarczyk, B. (2006). *Strategia rozwoju turystyki w Łodzi* [The Strategy of developing tourism in Łódź]. Łódź: ŁTN.

Koch, W. (1996). *Style w architekturze. Arcydzieła budownictwa europejskiego od antyku po czasy współczesne* [Styles in architecture. European musterpieces from Antiquity to present times]. Warszawa: Świat Książki.

Kowalczyk, A. (Ed.) (2008). *Turystyka Kulturowa – spojrzenie geograficzne, Geografia turyzmu, t.1* [Cultural Tourism – geographical perspective. Geography of tourism Vol. 1]. *Warszawa: Wydawnictwo Uniwersytetu Warszawskiego.*

—. (Ed.) (2010). *Turystyka zrównoważona* [Sustainable tourism]. Warszawa: Wydawnictwo Naukowe PWN.

Kruczek, Z., Kurek, A., & Nowacki, M. (2003). *Krajoznawstwo. Zarys teorii i metodyki* [Tourism. Introduction to theory and methodology]. Kraków: PROKSENIA.

Kurek, W. (2007). *Turystyka* [Tourism]. Warszawa: Wydawnictwo Naukowe PWN.

Llera, R.R. (2008). *Historia architektury* [Brief History of Architecture]. Warszawa: Buchmann.

Małek, J. (2003). *Turystyka kulturowa jako czynnik rozwoju lokalnego* [Cultural tourism. A factor in local development]. A. Kowalczyk (Ed.), *Prace i studia geograficzne, tom 32, Geografia Turyzmu* [Works and studies in geography. Vol. 32. Geography of tourism] (13-34). Warszawa: Wydawnictwo Uniwersytetu Warszawskiego.

Przecławski, K. (1997). Turystyka a kultura na przełomie XX i XXI w. [Tourism and culture at the turn of the 19th century]. In A. Gotowt-Jeziorska (Ed.), *Kulturowe aspekty turystyki i gospodarki turystycznej* [Cultural aspects of tourism and tourist economy]. Warszawa: Polskie Stowarzyszenie Turystyki.

Przybyszewska-Gudelis, R. (1997). Problemy rewitalizacji miast przez turystykę [Problems with revitialising urban areas with tourism]. In A.

Gotowt-Jeziorska (Ed.), *Kulturowe aspekty turystyki i gospodarki turystycznej* [Cultural aspects of tourism and tourist economy]. Warszawa: Polskie Stowarzyszenie Turystyki.

Rogalewski (1977). Zagospodarowanie turystyczne [Tourist management, Wydawnictwo Szkolne i Pedagogiczne, Warszawa.

Rohrscheidt, A.M. (2008). *Turystyka kulturowa. Fenomen, Potencjał, perspektywy* [Cultural Tourism. Phenomenon, potential, perspectives.]. Poznań: AWF.

Różycki, P. (2009). *Turystyka religijna i pielgrzymkowa* [Religious tourism and pilgrimages]. In K. Buczkowska, A. M. Rohrscheidt (Eds.), *Współczesne formy turystyki kulturowej* [Contemporary forms of cultural tourism] (157-173). Poznań: AWF.

Skalski, K. (1994). Francuski model rehabilitacji zasobów mieszkaniowych. Propozycja zastosowań w Polsce [French model of revitalising housing estates. Possible Polish applications]. In *Sprawy Mieszkaniowe, nr 4* [Housing issues. Vol. 4] (102-111). Warszawa: Instytut Gospodarki Mieszkaniowej.

Rejestr zabytków województwa kujawsko-pomorskiego, 2010 [Register of Monuments in Kujawsko-Pomorskie Voivodeship, 2010].

Thomas, M.J. (1997). Rewitalizacja miast a rozwój kulturalny [Revitalisation of cities and cultural development]. In K. Broński, J. Purchla, & Z.K. Zuziak (Eds.), *Miasto historyczne. Potencjał dziedzictwa* [Historical cities. Potential of Heritage] (74-87). Kraków: Międzynarodowe Centrum Kultury.

Tołłoczko, Z. (2011). Z kart dziejów historyzmu europejskiego na przykładzie architektury rezydencjonalno-reprezentacyjnej na Łotwie w XIX wieku [The annals of European historizm. The 19th century residential and representative architecture in Latvia]. In *Czasopismo Techniczne z. 16. Architektura z. 5-A.* [Technical Magazine 16. Architecture 5A] (225-270). Kraków: Wydawnictwo Politechniki Krakowskiej.

Tuan, Y.F. (1987). *Przestrzeń i miejsce* [Space and Place: The Perspective of Experience]. Warszawa: PIW.

CHAPTER FOUR

A NEW TROJAN HORSE:
THE HIDDEN INFLUENCE OF ART AND MEDIA
ON THE ARCHAEOLOGICAL TOURIST

KRISTIN M. BARRY

Abstract

Stories of the Trojan War have captivated audiences for millenia, and today draw thousands of visitors to the Archaeological Site of Ancient Troy at Hişarlik, Turkey. However, despite the international notoriety, Hişarlik itself has always lacked any visual reference to the famous stories. This "problem" that was rectified with the construction of both ancient and modern monuments for the specific purpose of Trojan War tourism, including the Hellenistic "tomb" of Ajax and Achilles and *Trojan Horse* (1975) by Turkish architect Izzet Senemoglu. This chapter discusses how the construction of these false monuments has affected the visitor interpretation and understanding of the archaeological site to suggest a history that has never been definitively proven. **Keywords:** Heritage Management, archaeology of tourism, Trojan War, Hişarlik.

1. Introduction

Identified as The Archaeological Site of Troy by UNESCO in 1998, Hişarlik has survived for thousands of years as a testament to ancient fortification and architectural construction. Consisting of at least nine identifiable occupation layers, the site today is popular with tourists, averaging 350-500,000 visitors annually (Riorden, 2009, p. 19). Although the archaeological material excavated at the site over the course of 130 years is extensive, it cannot help but be overshadowed by the shared public perception of what the name "Troy" suggests. Part of the association can be attributed to the visual culture established by books on the subject and the popular Wolfgang Peterson movie, "Troy" (2004), but the geographic area and archaeological site also have a long history of creating visual culture for the purposes of tourism, dating back over 2000 years. The purpose of this chapter is not to debate the possible existence of either Ancient Troy or the Trojan War (for a comprehensive summary of sources on this, please see Wood, 1996), but to instead investigate the history of visual culture associated with the archaeological site and the name Troy to understand how various types of media, either controlled by the site or not, affect the interpretation of the archaeological evidence by the general public.

This chapter draws from a collection of media types that are available to tourists before or at the Archaeological Site of Troy, including photographs, cinema, brochures, sculpture and tourist arts, as well as literature associated with each of these media groups. Along with the analysis of the individual objects and literature, history in this case in particularly significant because the Troad surrounding Hişarlik boasts some of the oldest "tourist traps" in the world, as established by archaeologist Manfred Korfmann in the course of his investigation of Başik Tepe (1982). The importance of the study, therefore, is not to criticize the how the site is presented through various media outlets, but instead to bring awareness to the history of tourism to the area and how the associated visual culture impacts the public perception of archaeological remains.

2. Archaeology through the Tourism Lens

In recent years, many studies have been done on the impact of visual media specifically on tourism (Brent Ritche & Hudson, 2006; Jenkins, 2003; Larsen, 2006), from photographs to motion pictures to brochures. The analyses describe both positive and negative results from the perspectives of the tourism industry, as well as from the world of marketing. Archaeological tourism is often overlooked in these types of studies, because it has traditionally represented a small sector of the tourism community, and site interpretations were considered insular, developed locally with little analysis from the outside world. However, with a constantly increasing number of tourists visiting historic sites *as* leisure tourism, a reanalysis of archaeological sites as modern tourism destinations is necessary to further the discourse in the changing role of the historic site and its interpretation through artistic media. This chapter, therefore, seeks to bridge the gap between traditional tourism studies and art historical and archaeological research by examining visitor interpretation of the modern presentation of Ancient Troy together with a historical analysis of the role of the site as a tourism destination.

As part of this interdisciplinary exploration, a number of references are critical to the understanding of destination interpretation. Tourism research is particularly important areas to cite because it assists in the understanding of *why* people visualize and understand tourism sites as they do. John Urry's iconic book, *The Tourist Gaze* (1999), is one of the modern icons of tourism analysis and subsequently crucial to the study of site interpretation, as it defines a tourist phenomenon that was previously difficult to identify. Although the book discusses the "gaze" as applied to leisure tourism not educational tourism, many of the characteristics apply to both as parallel, constantly-modernizing phenomena. All types of tourism require constant local, regional, and national development. Archaeological sites are not exception to this, especially if they are actively excavated. The discovery of new material dictates an update to the interpretation, potentially creating more visitors as the site adapts to new knowledge.

Using Troy acting as a case study, this chapter will investigate the various types of media that have historically influenced the public's perception of the archaeological site at Hişarlik through the "tourist gaze," as conceptualized by John Urry (1999, 2002, 2011). However, In the case of this particular site, the gaze is not only present, but the associated visual media was necessary to the survival of the site as a tourist destination. The gaze itself may be a modern concept, but the theory of Trojan War representation impacting the number of visitors at the site has a history of several thousand years. Therefore, the study will also address Stuart Hall's "Circle of Representation" (1997) and establish how each of the visual media components individually or as a group affect the way that tourist visualize the history of the archaeological site, and especially, how the interpretation perpetuates itself.

Perhaps most importantly, this paper will draw from an art historical approach, using both ancient and modern scholarship to establish the role of Troy as a historic tourism destination. The geography and historical background of the site is almost as important to establishing the gaze as any modern media influence, because in a way, it helps authenticate the association with the Trojan War, through extensive historical precedent. This historical discourse is combined with an architectural analysis of the modern interpretation from the perspective of both site organizers and tourists, which will help to establish not only what is perceived before visitors arrive, but also what is visually available to them on-site. These types of case studies are integral to the development of archaeological tourism facilities, because they often reveal that the impact that all types of visual culture have on visitors' tourist gaze, a concept that is not often considered after the presentation is finished. Although the intended interpretation may be understandable to researchers, archaeologists, and other stakeholders, a less specialized audience is inclined to view the site through the gaze, often resulting in a discrepancy in how developers see the site and how the public experiences the site.

3. Ancient Trojan War Tourism and Iconography

The area surrounding Ancient Troy has been experiencing documented tourism specific to the Trojan War for thousands of years. The first believed descriptions of the geographic region around Hişarlik as the site of the Trojan War begin with Homer in his iconic *Iliad*, which most modern scholars agree was composed in the 8th century BCE (Luce, 1998; Raaflaub, 1998; Rose, 1998). The *Iliad* mentions a number of geographic features, including the Scamander and Simoeis Rivers, the proximity of the coastline, and Kallikolonê, a feature known today as Kara Tepe (Luce, 1998). These geographic indicators surrounding the Troad pointed to Hişarlik as the location that Homer was describing, and also helped lead to the modern rediscovery of the site by Heinrich Schliemann in the 19th century. However, well before Schliemann's time, they could have also played a role in the reestablishment of the region by ancient Greek colonists in the late 8th century BCE (Wood, 1996, p. 29). Because the site was never truly abandoned, as evidenced in the archaeological record (Rose, 1998), it is possible that the place-memory of Hişarlik as Troy remained until the arrival of the Greek colonists, who so believed in the site as the city of Priam that they named/renamed the city Ilion after the repeated reference to Ilios in Homer's poems (Luce, 1998, p. 55; Wood, 1996). This was the name of the city when Xerxes, the first documented Trojan War tourist, arrived at the site in the 480 BCE (Rose, 1998). His march through area is described in Herodotus' *Histories* (5th century BCE), as is his intentional visit to Hişarlik because of its Trojan War association. Herodotus writes:

> Then when the army had come to the river Scamander…when I say Xerxes had come to this river, he went up to the Citadel of Priam, having a desire to see it all; and having seen it and learnt by inquiry of all the events of the Trojan War, he sacrificed a thousand heifers to Athene of Ilion, and the Magian poured libations in honour of the heroes. *Histories*, 7.43.1-2[1]

Certainly the association was enough to draw Xerxes in to pay homage to the great military heroes and goddess who came before him. However, beyond the reference to the Citadel of Priam, presumably the remains of an architectural feature at the site, the description does not mention any additional Trojan War visual culture that would have been available to Xerxes. The archaeological record suggests that during the period of Xerxes visit, the city was in economic decline but inhabited, meaning that the local population must have pointed Xerxes in the direction of the supposed citadel. But, there does not appear to be any evidence to suggest that the inhabitants of the city were profiting from the ancient association beyond the occasional visit from a conqueror (Rose, 1998). Even if travelers familiar with the stories came through, there was essentially nothing to see as a tourist, beyond the ruins of a city that could not be visually tied to the ancient fortress of Priam, as the city had since progressed in architectural style. In a sense, the "tourist gaze" was still present enough to draw some visitors to the area, but it was based largely on ancient literary descriptions and associated geographic features and not any type of available visual culture.

The mentality of the later Troy inhabitants seems to have changed by the Late Classical, Early Hellenistic Period when the local population developed a way to promote and profit from ancient Trojan War tourism (Rose, 1998: 407), meaning that potentially, the site was seeing enough visitors to necessitate providing something for them to see. By the time Alexander the Great famously came to the site in 334 BCE, Plutarch describes him making sacrifices at an identifiable architectural feature dedicated to Achilles:

> Then, going up to Ilium, he sacrificed to Athena and poured libations to the heroes. Furthermore, the gravestone of Achilles he anointed with oil, ran a race by it with his companions, naked, as is the custom, and then crowned it with garlands, pronouncing the hero happy in having, while he lived, a faithful friend, and after death, a great herald of his fame. As he was going about and viewing the sights of the city, someone asked him if he wished to see the lyre of Paris. 'For that lyre,' said Alexander, 'I care very little; but I would gladly see that of Achilles, to which he used to sing the glorious deeds of brave men.' *Alexander*, 15: 4-5[2]

The description also alludes to a 'lyre of Paris,' which seems to be another feature at the city intended specifically for tourism. As there is no archaeological proof that the family of Priam as described by Homer ever existed at the site, the idea of a lyre surviving for a thousand years and being attributed to a member of the Trojan royal family is suspect enough, but it is very clear that despite the lack of authenticity of the object, the local people were promoting individual objects and places associated with the Trojan War for tourists to see. However, like any description by an ancient author, it must be read with a number of caveats. Plutarch is writing nearly 300 years after Alexander's visit, so there is a possibility that he padded the story with these types of fabricated details as rhetorical exercise to accentuate certain personality traits placing Alexander's in a better light. Certainly Achilles is seen as a hero in the stories, whereas Paris is often seen as a coward, so Alexander's casual attitude to Paris could be read as promoting the hero worship of Achilles and dismissing Paris as relevant. Plutarch will occasionally betray a political agenda in his writing, making this a distinct possibility. Or maybe a guy really did have lyre and wanted to make some money off of Alexander the Great.

All literary introspection aside, by the Hellenistic period the Troad featured several new architectural constructions: a series of tombs each dedicated to a Trojan War hero, including individual tombs for Ajax and Patroclus, among others [Figure 1]. The features were built to resemble Bronze Age beehive tombs, making them appear to have been constructed at the time of the Trojan War, though in reality they were the work of local peoples. Visually, the tombs must have been believable, because even Alexander was fooled by the design, believing the Tomb of Achilles to actually possess the remains of the hero. Modern excavations by Manfred Korfmann later revealed that the so-called tomb (modernly referred to as Beşik Tepe) had, in fact, been built in the Hellenistic Period. He writes: "Thus the ancient visitor to the port of Troy was confronted with a gleaming white cone in the midst of the landscape" (1987: 193). Presumably, the site was already experiencing significant Trojan War tourism, something that Alexander's visit would further encourage, and the Hellenistic inhabits felt that having one or more iconographic monuments would encourage the visual association, as the rest of the site was lacking in identifiable Trojan War architecture.

The tumuli were essentially acting as some of the earliest tourist traps in the world, encouraging visitors to leave goods as offerings to the heroes, and acting as a concrete reference to a believed shared heritage that was previously not established architecturally. Following Alexander's visit to the Troad and his promise of patronage to New Ilion, the expanding city became the center of a new league celebrating the cult of Athena Ilias. This reinforced the connection of Ilion to the Trojan War stories, and would have brought additional international fame to the geographic region. As a result, new Trojan War visual iconography became much more prevalent in the Troad, helping to continue promoting Trojan War tourism. By the 2nd century BCE, the frieze of the Temple of Apollo Smitheus, a structure referenced in the *Iliad*, even featured a unique scene of Odysseus carrying wood to build the Trojan Horse (Rose, 1998, p. 407).

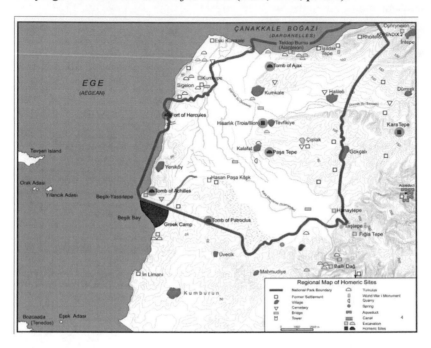

Figure 1 - Map of the Geographical Region around Hişarlik Highlighting Homeric Sites

It is important to note that these architectural references to the Trojan War were not the only visual culture associated with the stories of which ancient people would have been aware. Heroic themes in particular were popular iconography for painted vessels, and after the declaration of Troy as the mother city of Rome in Virgil's *Aeneid*, Trojan War themed paintings became a popular option for the walls of wealthy Roman citizens. These visual reminders helped to reinforce the historic "gaze" that was being formulated thousands of miles from the Troad. They not only promoted the belief in certain stories and elements of the Trojan War, but also provided visual depictions, imagined from literary scenes, and often at off with the actual architectural landscape of the site. Together with the false tumuli, this visual culture was already establishing a tradition of the tourist gaze at Troy, encouraging pilgrims and visitors to visit the site through an imagined landscape based in myth-history.

4. The Modern "Gaze": The Archaeological Site of Troy

Today, visual culture is no less influential for modern tourists than for ancient ones. However, with the development of technology and the evolution of sites as "archaeological Disneylands," (Cleere, 2005, p. 14) places initially focused on education have to constantly combat the gaze created by outside and entertainment influences. Like many, Troy is faced with many of these, particularly through associations that Hişarlik may or may not have to the famous Trojan War and the iconography that accompanies it.

The most prominent influences on the development of a historical tourist gaze are film and other widespread visual media. Movies allow stories to be told to millions of a people, while at the same time providing a visual and sometimes iconic backdrop associated with a historical place. Although many sites have found that historical movies help to draw visitors to struggling places (Edensor, 2005; Rewtrakunphaiboon, 2009; Ritchie & Hudson, 2006), they also provide an interpreted visual landscape, rarely based in reality. As Urry writes, "places are chosen to be gazed upon because there is an anticipation, especially through daydreaming and fantasy… Such anticipation is sustained through a variety of non-tourist practices, such as film…" (1990, p. 3). In the case of the 2004 Wolfgang Peterson film titled *"Troy,"* the architectural and artistic landscape rendered on the screen does not match the archaeological evidence uncovered at Hişarlik, but provides a visual experience that engages the senses. It is an imagined landscape, successfully producing a backdrop for an epic story, but in no way authentic to the history of the Archaeological Site of Ancient Troy. However, after the release of the film, tourism revenue at the site rose 73% (Ritchie & Hudson, 2006, p. 389), showing the impact that the film had on destination tourism to the area.

While increasing revenue is integral to the survival of any archaeological site, the increase in tourists who were inspired by the film means a rise in the number of people arriving at the site with specific visual expectation, hoping to relive the architectural landscapes represented in the movie. Unfortunately for Troy, the archaeological remains and existent visual culture in no way reflect the architectural landscapes or large-scale marble sculpture that the film suggests. As a result, interviews at the site conducted in 2008 and 2011 revealed that visitors were often disappointed in the archaeological remains and expressed that the site was not what they expected it to be (Riorden, 2009).

However, there is one feature of the site that provides visitors with the visual culture that they expect to be presented in relation to the Trojan

War: a large, wooden sculpture, titled *Trojan Horse,* by Turkish architect
Izzet Senemoglu [Figure 2], which was completed in 1975. The 60-foot
installation was suggested by the director of the Çannakale Archaeological
Museum and funded by the Turkish Ministry of Culture and Tourism as a
centerpiece for the 1975 Troia Festivali, or International Troy Festival.
The festival, which celebrates a long history of peaceful resolutions in the
Çannakale region, often includes activities at the archaeological site and is
a large draw for tourism each year. Although the design was conceived
from Senemoglu's imagination as an "homage to the original" ("Wooden
Horse of Troy," 2010), the very presence of the horse seems to confirm to
visitors not educated on the real archaeological record, an association of
the site with the Trojan War, particularly the story of the Trojan Horse.

Figure 2 - Izzet Senemoglu's *Trojan Horse* in Use (Source: photo by Author,
2011).

The sculpture serves a similar purpose to the Hellenistic tombs, by providing visitors with a reference to the Trojan War, where none existed previously. But recently the horse has become more recognizable to an international audience than the archaeological remains, tilting the balance at the site between education and entertainment. Beyond its very presence, a number of factors accentuate its visual impact and growing infamy. Its placement at the entrance to the site in the center of a cleared area makes it the first and largest piece of visual culture experienced by entering visitors, helping to further impact the tourist gaze and create a preconceived visual notion of what the archaeological site will present. The horse is the first encounter that visitors have at the site, creating a dishonest and inauthentic discourse between the archaeological remains and the potential myth-history. However, it must be acknowledged that Senemoglu's sculpture was always intended to be an innocent a photo opportunity or interactive experience for visitors. Created at a time when personal photography was a growing trend, the horse provided a way for visitors to interact physically with part of the archaeological site, which is often not permitted in an effort to preserve world heritage. The sculpture allows people to not only touch and experience a feature at the site, but climb into it, and in a way, become a part of history.

But it is not just experiencing Senemoglu's *Trojan Horse* that has led to both its notoriety and its influence on the gaze. Photography has also played a large role in helping to establish the sculpture as an icon directly related to the site and its myth-historical associations. As Susan Sontag begins her iconic *On Photography*, "To collect photographs is to collect the world" (1977, p. 3), a statement that is certainly valid in historical tourism. Although for Sontag, the ability to share pictures was dependent on having them printed, the development in digital technology has helped photo-sharing reach an all-time high. When Senemoglu's horse was constructed, photos would have to be published in popular periodicals to be shared worldwide. Now, internet search engines, such as Google Images, Flickr and even social networking sites, allow interested people to have hundreds of thousands of photos at their fingertips instantly, without having any physical connection to the photographer.

For archaeological sites with little publicity, this availability of images is a way to promote awareness of what the site has to offer. In the case of Troy, however, the most available photo opportunity is the *Trojan Horse* sculpture, making it one of the most commonly distributed images related to the site. In a reworking of Stuart Hall's "Circle of Representation" (1997, p. 1) Olivia Jenkins approaches the subject, though imagery, illustrating how tourist destination images are often seen and then the subject matter sought specifically to repeat the image (2003, p. 308). For Senemoglu's sculpture, the standard image is constantly repeated, helping to reinforce its iconographic status as one of the main pieces of visual culture available at Troy [Figure 3]. Unlike other visual media intended for tourism, the popularity of the horse is perpetuated mainly by other tourists. In a series of image searches through the Google Images search engine, the term "Trojan Horse" provided an average of more pictures of Senemoglu's horse than any other single representation of a Trojan Horse.[3] Before the 2004 *Troy* film produced another iconographic horse, Senemoglu's sculpture would have been by far the most recognizable and represented Trojan Horse. Generally, the photos taken and shared are of people climbing on the sculpture and having their picture taken, however, the horse is also used in some promotional brochures for traveling in Çanakkale and is mentioned in a number of tour books as a "don't miss" monument.

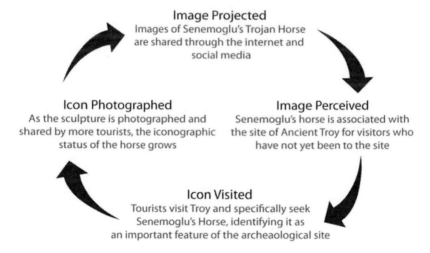

Image Projected
Images of Senemoglu's Trojan Horse
are shared through the internet and
social media

Icon Photographed
As the sculpture is photographed and
shared by more tourists, the iconographic
status of the horse grows

Image Perceived
Senemoglu's horse is associated with
the site of Ancient Troy for visitors who
have not yet been to the site

Icon Visited
Tourists visit Troy and specifically seek
Senemoglu's Horse, identifying it as
an important feature of the archeaological site

Figure 3: 'Circle of Representation' for Ancient Troy (Source: Jenkins, 2003, p. 308; Hall, 1997, 1).

The shear number of photographs shared publically is representative of a growing trend in tourism, known to researchers as "'I was here' tourism." As digital cameras have seen a price drop in the last 10 years making them available to the general public, there has been a significant rise in this type of tourism, where photographs themselves have become one of the most common souvenirs of travelers. These souvenirs also help to spread the knowledge of what exists at the site with the immediacy of which they can be shared with others (Bell & Lyall, 2005). Digital photographs taken on cell phones can be texted or emailed to friends a world away, or even posted directly to Facebook pages and other types of social media. As Urry writes, "to photograph is in some way to appropriate the object being photographed" (1990, p. 138). Senemoglu's horse allows the visitor to photograph and therefore appropriate the visual culture, but also become a part of the visual culture itself by climbing inside the horse and being part of the photograph. Not only does it result in the distribution of the photograph raising the feature's iconic status, but is letting visitors inhabit "history," however false that history really is, consequently enhancing the tourist gaze. With the growing need to keep things fun and exciting for a more modern audience, the horse provides a way for archaeological visitors, especially children, to interact with history in a way that the ancient walls and adult-oriented signage do not. Additionally, Senemoglu's *Trojan Horse* is the representation often used in inexpensive souvenirs available for purchase outside the Troy gates. Through the souvenirs, this particular sculptural representation becomes portable, allowing people to physically appropriate that particular horse interpretation as a reminder of the site.

The impact of the sculpture on the gaze is further exacerbated by the lack of visible signage properly identifying its provenance. Subsequently, several tourists interviewed in a 2008 study expressed their belief that the sculpture was in fact the ancient horse from that stories and that it had been excavated at the site. The same study revealed that over the course of observation in the summer of 2008, multiple tour buses arrived with patrons who disembarked, photographed the horse, and left without viewing the archaeological material at all. For groups that did experience the archaeology, many ranked Senemoglu's horse as one of the elements that they were most impressed with, above "authenticity" and "archaeology" (Riorden, 2009). To these groups, the horse was evidently the most important piece of visual culture related to the archaeological site, and likely what they *expected* to see as opposed to the archaeological remains, demonstrating how the preconceived tourist gaze can overshadow the presentation of the archaeology.

Similarly, Senemoglu's sculpture can be thought of as the most visually relatable and understandable structure for a wide audience at the site. With less-specialized audiences visiting archaeological sites, ancient architecture can be difficult to present to the public in an easily understandable way. Compared with other popular archaeological sites in Turkey, Ancient Troy lacks the gleaming marble reconstructions and recognizable architectural forms, and instead has numerous confused conservation attempts and unidentifiable defensive walls, many of which only retain their foundations. Senemoglu's horse provides an easily recognizable architectural representation, making it easy to understand by itself. The sculpture also provides tourists with a piece of history of which most have heard. Simply, the average visitor would not recognize the significance of a Troy II mudbrick walls, but most have heard the story of the Trojan Horse.

It may also be this association of Senemoglu's Horse to the Trojan War that people tend to relate the most. The famous stories focus on the ideas of heroism, triumph, and the overcoming of adversity, and have become one of the strongest historical sources of a tourist gaze surrounding Ancient Troy. As one of the most iconic symbols for a modern audience associated with the war, the Trojan Horse could be thought of as an iconic *idea* has come to embody the concept of heroism, and is therefore represented in Senemoglu's sculpture. People can identify with the horse as a story that they have heard, but have a harder time identifying with the archaeological remains because the crumbling foundations are not visual identifiers of these memorable concepts. The archaeological remains are not as much part of the gaze as the visual culture or stories and are therefore often forgotten when reliving it, as similarly, the Hellenistic hero tombs provided a piece of three-dimensional visual culture for ancient visitors to relate to the story concepts.

5. Conclusion

Having addressed the historical impact of visual cultural on the perception of Ancient Troy, it seems that presentation through visual cultural often leads to an increase in tourism, but by sacrificing authenticity. Unfortunately, there is a difficult balance between the intentions of archaeologists, often focused on presenting the educational aspects of a site, and the national government, often dependent on tourism income, something that is evident with the modern presentation of the site through installation sculpture and feature films. However, the conclusions of this chapter introduce a new and more difficult issue to overcome for archaeological tourism, namely, how the discourse will proceed.

As a result of its influence on visitors to Troy, Senemoglu's horse has become an integral part of the history of the site, despite the fact that it was constructed almost 2000 years after most other major building projects ended. Modern archaeological interpretation practices would dictate that the horse remain and be itself interpreted to the public, especially because of the history of tourism at Hişarlik, as represented through this type of created visual culture. Senemoglu's Horse has lived at the site for almost 40 years, becoming *itself* a piece of the area's historical past. As one of the most influential pieces of the modern gaze, it has changed the way that the site is perceived, perhaps permanently. Whether the site can be archaeologically proven as Ancient Troy or not, for tourists, it already *is* the site of the famous war, as perceived through the gaze. Although compared to the ancient ruins, as a piece of art it does not have the age value that the ramparts have, it represents an association with one of the most famous events in ancient history, and the bringing together of people from east and west under a shared heritage. As one of the site's most identifiable images, the horse exemplifies the importance of a collective memory and association when dealing with archaeological remains, and will most likely remain with the tombs at the site as a testament to the power that a piece of art can have to create or change history.

Notes

[1] English translation by Godley, A, D. (1920). Cambridge, MA: Harvard University Press.
[2] English Translation by Perrin, B. (1919). Cambridge, MA: Harvard University Press.
[3] Searches were done once a week during the months of December 2011 and January 2012. On average, the search engine provided a total of 234 images over 8 pages. Senemoglu's sculpture averaged 52 photos of the 234. Following Senemoglu's *Trojan Horse*, the sculpture used in the Wolfgang Peterson 2004 Movie *Troy* that is now in the Çanakkale harbor, had an average or 42 images out of 234.

References

Bell, C., & Lyall, J. (2005). "I was Here": pixilated evidence. In D. Crouch, R. Jackson, & F. Thompson (Eds.), *The Media and the Tourist Imagination* (pp. 135-142). NY: Routledge.

Cleere, H. (2005). *Archaeological Heritage Management*. NY: Routledge.

Edensor, T. (2005). Mediating William Wallace: Audio-visual technologies in tourism. In D. Crouch, R. Jackson, & F. Thompson (Eds.), *The Media and the Tourist Imagination* (pp. 105-118). NY: Routledge.

Hall, S. (Ed.). (1997). *Representation: Cultural Representations and Signifying Practices*. London: Sage.

Jenkins, O.H. (2003). Photography and travel brochures: The circle of representation. *Tourism Geographies*, 5(3), 305-328.

Larsen, J. (2006). Geographies of tourist photography: Choreographies and performances. In J. Falkheimer, & A. Jansson (Eds.) *Geographies of Communication: The Spatial Turn in Media Studies* (pp. 243–60). Göteborg: Nordicom.

Luce, J.V. (1998). *Celebrating Homer's Landscapes: Troy and Ithaca Revisited.* New Haven, CT: Yale University Press.

Rewtrakunphaiboon, W. (2009) Film-induced tourism: Inventing a vacation to a location. *BU Academic Review*, 8(1), 33-42.

Riorden, E. (2009). *Troy: An Archaeological Site Management Masterplan.* Cincinnati, OH: Riorden.

Ritchie, J.R., & Hudson, S. (2006). Promoting destinations via film tourism: An empirical identification of supporting marketing initiatives. *Journal of Travel Research*, 44, 387-396.

Sontag, S. (1990). *On Photography.* NY: Anchor Books.

Urry, J. (1990). The Tourist Gaze: Leisure and Travel in Contemporary Societies. London: Sage.

Wood, M. (1996). *In Search of the Trojan War.* Berkeley, CA: University of California Press.

Wooden Horse of Troy. (2010). Retrieved January 23, 2012, from http://www.grandanzachotel.com/wooden-horse-of-troy.htm

CHAPTER FIVE

TOURISTS OF NATURAL AREAS: PLACE-ATTACHMENT AND INVOLVEMENT

CLÁUDIA SEABRA, CARLA SILVA, JOSÉ LUÍS ABRANTES AND MARGARIDA VICENTE

Abstract

This chapter intends to contribute to a more depth study of the relationship between those two constructs, specifically in the natural areas' context. The main objective is to create a scale to measure involvement of tourists with destinations both as products (involvement) and as places (place-attachment). Insights from an empirical study of 615 natural areas' tourists indicate that this multi-dimensional scale incorporates constructs from involvement and place-attachment. Discussion centers on the implications of this scale for theory development and management decisions. Tourism firms may better understand the involvement of tourists with the buying decisions and also how they connect with the destinations they visit. Also, managers can understand the impact of these two types of linkages can have on tourists' decision making, namely in what regards to natural areas. Directions for future research are also presented. **Keywords**: Nature tourism, place-attachment, involvement.

1. Introduction

Tourism studies have experienced significant advances through the intersection of theories developed in several disciplines: Psychology, Sociology, Anthropology, Geography, Marketing, among others. This interconnection is visible in two concepts that have received increasing attention from researchers. They measure how tourists relate with tourism products and with the destinations visited. Involvement from Marketing reflects the perceived importance and/or personal interest that consumers link to the purchase, consumption of goods, services or ideas (Mowen & Mirror, 1998). Place Attachment from Environmental Psychology and Geography represents the effective linkage between people and specific places (Hidalgo & Hernández, 2001). Recent studies have tested the linkage between those two concepts (Gross & Brown, 2008).

The new paradigm in tourism research emphasizes the understanding of emotional and symbolic subjective meanings associated with nature places and also the connection of people to those places (Williams & Vaske, 2003). Moreover it stresses that natural areas are more than geographical environments with physical characteristics. They are fluid, convertible, dynamic contexts of interaction and memory, and therefore susceptible to different links / relationships (Stokowski, 2002). People's place attachment, refers to the involvement of tourists with the places and destinations visited. Is a complex phenomenon that involves social, psychological and cultural interpretations, as well as meanings built on the interaction between individuals and places (Brandenburg & Carroll, 1995; Relph, 1976; Stedman, 2003). In the contemporary era, the connection to places by individuals must be understood from a multidimensional analysis (Appadurai, 1996), by understanding the ties that connect communities to environments (Feld & Basso, 1996).

There are differences among individuals, which depending on the product or the situation, make some consumers more interested, concerned or involved in the purchase decisions. Consumers' involvement influences their buying decisions (Kassarjian, 1981) it influences the proximity relationship of individuals with products from pre-purchase up to post-purchase (Slama & Tashchian, 1985). Tourist products usually are high involving since they represent high monetary and non-monetary costs and are based on extensive problem solving processes (Sirakaya & Woodside, 2005).

The combined use of place attachment and involvement concepts occurred only recently in tourism study. The pioneer researchers were Kyle and his colleagues that studied Involvement (Kerstetter, Confer & Graefe, 2001; Kyle & Chick, 2002; Kyle, Kerstetter & Guadagnolo, 1999, 2002; Scott & Shafer, 2001) and place attachment (Kyle, Absher & Graefe, 2003; Moore & Graefe, 1994; Moore & Scott, 2003) as separate constructs. The same authors combined those two concepts on a study in 2003 where they were successful in measuring the relationship between involvement in leisure activities and place attachment among hikers (Kyle, Absher & Graefe, 2003). This chapter intends to contribute to a more in depth study of the relationship between those two constructs, specifically in natural areas' context. The main objective is to create a scale to measure involvement of tourists with destinations both as products (involvement) and as places (place-attachment).

2. Literature Review

In recent decades, social scientists in Geography, Psychology and Tourism developed a set of concepts to describe the relationship between people and places (Budruk *et al.*, 2008; Kianicka *et al.*, 2006), being "place-attachment" one of the most consensual ones. This concept, whose application in the area of tourism began in the '80s (Hwang, Lee & Chen, 2005), refers to the process by which individuals form emotional bonds with places (Sime, 1995). In other words, the "sense of belonging", the "feel of place" or "being home" is considered a sign that an individual has created an emotional connection with a certain place (Yuksel, Yuksel, & Bilim, 2010).

2.1. Place attachment

Some authors conceptualize place-attachment as an emotional connection to a particular environment (Hidalgo & Hernández, 2001; Low & Altman, 1992), others define it as an emotional investment to a place (Hummon, 1992), and also as a way in which individuals value and identify themselves with a particular place (Moore & Graefe, 1994). But generally, place-attachment is defined as an emotional bond between people and certain places where they live or visit (Mazumdar & Mazumdar, 1999), which makes them want to stay in those places or nearby feeling comfortable and safe (Hidalgo & Hernández, 2001). Implicitly, the place-attachment's concept is defined as a positive concept (Manzo, 2003; Moore, 2000), assuming that one can be connected to a place is something good and that this psychological condition brings benefits to people and communities (Lewicka, 2005, 2008).

Place-attachment influences what individuals see, think and feel about the place (Yuksel, Yuksel, & Bilim, 2010) and therefore includes emotional and symbolic expressions (Hwang, Lee & Chen, 2005). People develop a sense of belonging, identity, and dependence on certain places to the point they consider them "their place", their "favorite place" or "the only place" (Korpela *et al.*, 2001). In fact, some sites are of particular interest and exert fascination to people, creating a strong linkage (Stedman, 2003; Tuan, 1980; Williams & Stewart, 1998). This connection can be with real spaces, but also with mythical places, hypothetical or imaginary (Low & Altman, 1992). A tourist can develop a connection to a destination due to activities that he develops or to what the place symbolizes itself (Yuksel, Yuksel, & Bilim, 2010).

Place-attachment results from the specific place and the individual's characteristics (Hammitt, Backlund & Bixler, 2006). Attractions offer individuals the opportunity to (re)affirm the sense of belonging and attachment to a place (Palmer, 1999). Research shows that for many reasons, people are attracted to natural environments (see Kaplan & Kaplan, 1989; Knopf, 1983, 1987) and that, over time, they create and strengthen links with these natural spaces (Kyle, Mowen & Tarrant, 2004). In fact, natural environments, such as mountains, offer a range of physical, psychological and social benefits that make them attractive areas from the tourist point of view (Kaplan & Kaplan, 1989; Ulrich, 1979; Ulrich *et al.*, 1991). Moreover, these natural environments are often described as the favorite places (Korpela *et al.*, 2001). And the more familiar these nature spaces are, more preferred they become (Sonnenfeld, 1968; Wohlwill, 1983).

Place-attachment is a multidimensional construct that incorporates two dimensions (Brown & Raymond, 2007) that have recently been applied to the tourism area. Place-identity represents the functional dimension and Place-dependence the emotional or symbolic one (Kyle *et al.*, 2003, 2004; Moore & Scott, 2003; Williams, Patterson, & Roggenbuk,, 1992; Yuksel, Yuksel, & Bilim, 2010).

Common questions like "who we are and where do we belong" (Harvey, 1996, p. 246) are also reflected in tourism (Williams & Kaltenborn, 1999). The concept of place-identity, being a construct used by environmental psychology, has also been used to study leisure and tourism (Williams, Patterson, & Roggenbuck, 1992). This dimension of place-attachment is used to characterize the role of places as identification's sources and individuals' affiliation to certain places (Proshansky 1978; Williams & Kaltenborn, 1999). Proshansky (1978) refers to the place identity as the unique relationship between the person and the physical environment, suggesting that environment helps to create and maintain the self (Lee, 2001; Low & Altman, 1992). Place-identity is thus a relationship between the self and the place, based on a set of memories, interpretations, ideas and feelings about this place (Proshansky, Fabian, & Kaminoff, 1983).

In sum, place-identity is an important symbolic link between individual and places (Proshansky, Fabian, & Kaminoff, 1983; Stedman, 2003). A destination is a place with a number of appealing features to the tourist

(Hu & Ritchie, 1993). However, the connection to a destination needs to be expanded beyond the attributes of place, considering that it is also an entity that tourists experience and with which they identify themselves (Lee, 2001).

The concept of place-dependence stems from a transactional perspective that suggests that people evaluate places through alternatives (Brocato, 2006). It refers to the way that a place can reach the goals of an individual (Jorgensen & Stedman, 2001). Individuals evaluate places according to the ability that those places have to meet their functional needs (Brocato, 2006). Place-dependence occurs when individuals demonstrate a functional need for the place which cannot be transferred to another place (Stokols & Schumaker, 1981). Place-dependence refers also to the set of social and physical resources that meet the individual's specific and desired activities and that represent what is unique in the place, differentiating it from other alternative or similar ones (Bricker & Kerstetter, 2000; Kyle *et al.*, 2004). Also, is strongly correlated with the perception that the place has unique qualities and characteristics (Jacob & Schreyer, 1980).

2.2. Involvement

Research on the involvement concept began in 1947 (Sheriff & Cantril, 1947), however the term was popularized in 1965 (Krugman, 1965). Many definitions have been advanced over the past decades. Despite numerous proposals for conceptualization, there are some commonalities that allow the construction of a synthetic definition of the concept. Thus, involvement is a state of mind of the individual interest, excitement and importance in relation to an internal stimulus (idea, motivation, desire or need) or external (product, location, purchase decision) (Muehling, Laczniak, & Andrews, 1993).

Involvement in tourism has been defined as "a psychological state of motivation, arousal and interest between an individual and a recreational activity, tourist destination, or related equipment at any given time, characterized by the perception of the following elements: importance, pleasure value, value symbolic, risk probability and consequences of risk "(Havitz & Dimanche, 1990, p.180). Or in a simpler way is the unobserved state of motivation, interest and excitement for a recreational activity or associated product. Involvement refers, in short, to what tourists think about the leisure and recreation, which affect their behaviors (Havitz & Dimanche, 1997).

Involvement influences the degree of commitment in which consumers are committed in different aspects of the process of consumption: product, demand for information, decision making and the purchase (Broderic & Mueller, 1999; Zaichkowsky, 1985). It is the basis of the decision to purchase (Zaichkowsky, 1986) and affects profoundly the perceived value of products and its evaluation (Bolton & Drew, 1991).

Tourist products are by nature highly engaging, especially in what regards to the destination choice since high-involvement processes are required, due to its intangibility and inseparability (Swarbrooke & Horner, 1999). The decision structure is cognitive and sequential (Stewart & Stynes, 1994). When consumers are involved, they give attention, perceive the importance and behave in a different way than when they are not (Zaichkowsky, 1986)

Several scales were used to operationalize the concept of involvement in the tourism context. Most of them were developed in research on consumer behavior and then adapted and modified by researchers to tourism research (Havitz & Dimanche, 1999; Havitz, Dimanche, & Howard, 1993; Jain & Srinivasan, 1990; Jamrozy, Backman, & Backman, 1996; Josiam, Smeaton, & Clements, 1999; Kim, Scott, & Crompton, 1997). Examples of these generic scales are the Personal Involvement Inventory (PII) from Zaichkowsky (1985) and the Consumer Involvement Profile (CIP) of Laurent and Kapferer (1985).

The PII instrument (Zaichkowsky, 1985) was widely used in general consumer behavior and in the tourism context. With a dimensional structure, the PII measures the involvement concept with a 20 items' inventory grouped into four constructs - importance, relevance, attitude and hedonism. Up to the 80's most researchers used it to measure involvement in tourism (Havitz & Dimanche, 1997).

The study by Laurent and Kapferer (1985) opened the debate on the involvement dimensionality. The CIP had quite an acceptance among tourism researchers (Havitz & Dimanche, 1997). This scale has a multidimensional structure and makes the profile analysis of consumer involvement from five dimensions: relevance / product interest, symbolic value, pleasure or hedonic value of the product, risk probability and consequences of risk.

CIP and PII instruments show advantages (see Mittal, 1995) in tourism involvement analysis. The multidimensional scales provide a greater content validity and application in the contexts of leisure, recreation and tourism experiences (Havitz, Dimanche, & Howard, 1993). The components of symbolic value, risk and centrality provide important information about involvement (Havitz & Dimanche, 1997). However, other researchers tried improve involvement scales, namely in tourism. The McQuarrie and Munson (1986) instrument proposes an intermediate scale between CIP and PII. With a multifaceted aspect the Revised Personal Involvement Inventory (RPII) was also applied by researchers in the leisure and recreation context.

The Enduring Involvement Index (EII) has a one-dimensional aspect and uses, as main factors, the interest and importance to measure involvement (Bloch, Sherrell, & Ridgeway, 1986). The first scale worthy of reference (Havitz & Dimanche, 1997) specifically built for the tourism context is the Leisure Recreation Involvement (LRI) of Ragheb (1996). It is a 24 items structure grouped into six dimensions: importance, interest, pleasure, centrality, meaning and intensity. The first four dimensions are derived from scales already defined.

In sum, in the leisure and tourism area, authors used one of the six scales: PII, CIP, CIPM, RPII, EII and LRI (Havitz & Dimanche, 1997). In this study the scale used to measure involvement was based on those scales and in previous studies (Gursoy & Gavcar, 2003) and has six dimensions: Pleasure / Interest Probability Risk, Importance of Risk, Signs of Prestige / Self-Expression, Attraction and Centrality.

3. Methodology

The research setting refers to a survey approach, applied to tourists in mountain natural spaces in Portugal: Serra da Estrela, Serra do Gerês, Serra da Arrábida, Serra do Caramulo. We obtained a final sample of 615 valid questionnaires. We developed a scale to measure two different concepts: place-attachment and involvement. An initial version of the instrument was developed using scales previously established in the literature to measure place attachment (Brown & Raymond, 2007) and involvement (Gursoy & Gavcar, 2003). These scales were then discussed with people capable of understanding the nature of the concept being measured. We then translated the initial scales into four languages: Portuguese, French, German and Spanish and then the instrument was back-translated to English. After revisions, we used a pre-test sample of 30 tourists in natural areas in order to test the reliability of the scales (through Cronbach alpha). The pre-test results were used to further refine the questionnaire.

In total, 16 items were used for place-attachment measured trough a five points Likert scale, between 1 - Strongly disagree and 5 - Strongly agree. A 28 items scale was used to the Involvement concept measured trough a five points Likert scale, between 1 - Strongly disagree and 5 -

Strongly agree. We collected the final data from September to November 2009. Tourists were randomly selected in loco across four mountain natural areas in Portugal, from those agreeing to participate in the study. The questionnaires were self-administrated, which allowed us to ensure that the data was not biased. We obtained a final sample of 615 valid responses. Tourists in this study sample were mainly from urban areas (56,3%), single (47%) and married (42%), under 26 years old (35,3%), between 26 and 35 (22,8%) and 36-45 years old (22,6%). Mainly they have higher education (36,3%), with a high percentage of students (24%), commercial and administrative workers (13,2%) and civil servants (12,2%), with incomes of 1000 euro/month (67,0%).

4. Results

In order to assess the validity of the measures, the items were subjected to a confirmatory factor analysis (CFA), using full-information maximum likelihood (FIML) estimation procedures in LISREL 8.3 (Jöreskog & Sörbom, 1996). In this model, each item is restricted to load on its pre-specified factor, with the three first-order factors allowed to correlate freely. A scale with 19 items grouped in three dimensions was obtained (see Figure 1).

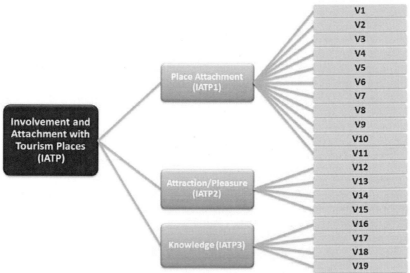

Figure 1 – The Involvement and Attachment with Tourism Places (IATP) Scale

Table 1 - Constructs, Scale Items, Reliabilities and T-Values

Constructs, Scale Items and Reliabilities	Std.Val ues
IATP1 – Place-Attachment (α=.921; $\rho_{vc(n)}$ =.52; ρ=.92)	
V1 This place means a lot to me	.720
V2 This place says a lot about who I am	.775
V3 I miss this place when I am not here	.737
V4 I strongly identify myself with this place	.723
V5 This place is the best that I know	.713
V6 I am very attached to this place and to the people who live here	.683
V7 This place is very special to me	.760
V8 I would not substitute this mountain place for another place	.696
V9 Doing what I do at this place is very important to me	.671
V10 I prefer being in this place than in any other place	.693
V11 I feel that this place is part of me	.681
IATP2 – Attraction/Pleasure (α=.808; $\rho_{vc(n)}$ =.51; ρ=.89)	
V12 Tourism experiences are really important to me	.720
V13 It gives me pleasure to purchase a vacation	.703
V14 I really like to participate in tourism experiences	.725
V15 I can say that travel destinations are a matter of interest for me	.718
IATP3 - Knowledge (α=.810; $\rho_{vc(n)}$ =.52; ρ=.81)	
V16 Compared to people who travel a lot, I am very familiar with a wide variety of vacation destinations	.757
V17 Compared to average person, I am very familiar with a wide variety of vacation destinations	.746
V18 Compared to people who travel a lot, I am very familiar with a wide variety of vacation destinations	.719
V19 I consider myself as a knowledgeable person about tourism experiences	.662

Notes: α = Internal reliability (Cronbach, 1951); $\rho_{vc(n)}$ = Variance extracted (Fornell & Larcker, 1981); ρ= Composite reliability (Bagozzi, 1980)
The IATP1, IATP2 and IATP3 scales were assessed with a scale ranging between "1 - Strongly disagree" and "5 - Strongly agree".

The chi-square for this model is significant (χ^2=592.386, 149 df, p<.00). Since the chi-square statistic is sensitive to sample size, we also assessed additional fit indices that reveal an acceptable fit: the comparative fit index (CFI) is .921, the incremental fit index (IFI) is .921, the Tucker-Lewis fit index (TLI) is .909. Since fit indices can be improved by allowing more terms to be freely estimated, we also assessed the Root

Mean Square Error of Approximation (RMSEA), which assesses fit and incorporates a penalty for lack of parsimony (Holbert & Stephenson, 2002). An RMSEA of .05 or less indicates a close fit to the population, while .08 to .10 indicates a satisfactory fit, with any score over .10 indicating an unacceptable fit (Steiger, 1980). The RMSEA of this measurement model is .070. We also assessed RSMR Standardized Root Mean Square Residual, which is .053 less than .08 considered a good fit.

Table 1 provides an overview of the standardized values of each item on its intended construct. As shown in this table, all the three dimensions present the desirable levels of composite reliability i.e. .8 or higher (Bagozzi, 1980). Convergent validity is evidenced by the large and significant standardized loadings of each item on its intended construct (the average loading size was of .715). Discriminant validity among the constructs is stringently assessed using the Fornell and Larcker (1981) test; all possible pairs of constructs passed this test. Evidence of discriminant validity was also revealed by the fact that all the constructs' inter-correlations were significantly different from 1 – the highest is for IATP2 and IATP3, 0.572 – and the shared variance between any two constructs (i.e. the square of their inter-correlations) was less than the average variance extracted for each construct. Hence, none of the correlations in the final model was sufficiently high to jeopardize the constructs' discriminant validity (Anderson & Gerbing, 1988).

5. Conclusion

Tourism research has evolved with the linkage between different disciplines. The complexity of tourism phenomenon itself demands the contribution of many study fields. In this chapter, we undertook a literature revision of two important concepts in tourism study: place-attachment and involvement, namely in natural areas study. An exploratory analysis was made in order to build a measure instrument and explore the connections between the two constructs.

In this chapter, we develop a scale that measures the various types of connections that tourists establish not only with the tourism product (involvement) but also with the visited destinations (place-attachment): the Involvement and Attachment with Tourist Places Scale. Results indicate that place-attachment is a one-dimensional construct differing from literature that categorizes the concept in two dimensions: place-identity and place-dependence (Brown & Raymond, 2007). In what regards to involvement, results indicate that this concept has two dimensions: Attraction/Pleasure and Knowledge.

Place-attachment and involvement's dimensions emerge as key to understanding the connection of individuals with tourism in two ways: the product (involvement) and the destination (place-attachment). In this study, the instrument is applied particularly to natural areas.

The selection of a strategy for tourism depends on how tourists connect with products and destinations. It is expected that through the application of the Involvement and Attachment with tourist places, together with other variables, in the context of market studies, tourism organizations may better understand the type of connection that tourists establish with tourism and what its impact on tourists' decision making. They may, as a consequence, use a framework to develop and implement strategies to increase the value associated with destinations and their services. These scale dimensions might provide some guidance on how to better pursue an information-oriented business strategy. By identifying tourists' levels of connection with tourism it becomes possible to make choices regarding the best marketing strategies to address, such as identifying different market segments and corresponding differentiated strategies, or improving the destination's positioning. Finally, the scale developed here can be an important basis for the segmentation of a tourist market.

From a theoretical perspective, to our knowledge, a measurement scale to assess contact with dimensions of involvement and place-attachment has never been operationalized in a tourism context. Although we cannot claim to have definitively captured all dimensions of tourists' connections with the tourist product and destination, we believe that we come closer to capturing these overall evaluations by extracting the underlying commonality among dimensions. Towards this fact, we expect that the Involvement and Attachment with Tourist Places Scales presented here contributes to both the tourism and the service marketing literature. In sum, at a time when marketing researchers are challenged to provide research with practical implications, it is believed that this theoretical framework may be used as a basis to pursue service-oriented destination and business strategies while taking into consideration the contact that tourists have with terrorism.

There are some limitations of the presented research approach to be considered. The first limitation is that the final instrument (i.e. the questionnaire) may have created common method variance that could have inflated construct relationships. This could be particularly threatening, if the respondents were aware of the conceptual framework of interest. However, they were not told the specific purpose of the study, and all of the construct items were separated and mixed so that no respondent should have been able to detect which items were affecting which factors.

The second limitation has to do with the study setting; the data was gathered in four nature places only in Portugal, which may limit the generalizability of the results. However, the empirical results presented in this study can be applied to other destinations and natural areas. Thus, in order to establish the data generalizability, it is suggested to gather data in other destinations.

Future research is encouraged to test our instrument across other tourism settings. To do so, we encourage researchers to add new items and factors applicable to the research setting. Continued refinement of the Involvement and Attachment with Tourist Places Scale proposed and supported in this study is certainly possible, based on further qualitative research. Finally, further research is required when analyzing the antecedents and consequences of Involvement and Attachment with Tourist Places Scale.

References

Anderson, J., & Gerbing, D. (1988). Structural equation modeling in practice: A review and recommended two-step approach. *Psychological Bulletin, 103*(3), 411-423.

Appadurai, A. (1996). The production of locality. In A. Appadurai, *Modernity at Large: Cultural Dimensions of Globalization* (pp. 178-200). Minneapolis: University of Minnesota Press.

Bagozzi, R. (1980). *Causal models in marketing.* NY: John Wiley.

Bloch, P., Sherrel, D., & Ridgeway, N. (1986). Consumer search: An extended framework. *Journal of Consumer Research, 13*(June), 119-126.

Bolton, R., & Drew, J. (1991). A multistage model of customers' assessments of service quality and value. *Journal of Consumer Research, 17*, 375-384.

Brandenburg, A., & Carroll, M. (1995). Your place or mine? The effect of place creation on environmental values and landscape meanings. *Society and Natural Resources Management, 8*, 381-398.

Bricker, K., & Kerstetter, D. (2000). Level of specialization and place attachment: An exploratory study of Whitewater recreacionists. *Leisure Sciences, 22*, 233-257.

Brocato, E. (2006). Place attachment: An investigation of environments and outcomes in services context. *PhD Thesis.* University of Texas at Arlington.

Broderick, A., & Mueller, R. (1999). Theorectical and empirical exegesis of the consumer involvement construct: The psychology of the food shoper. *Journal of Marketing Theory and Practice, 7,* 97-108.

Brown, G., & Raymond, C. (2007). The relationship between place attachment and landscape values: Toward mapping place attachment. *Applied Geography, 27,* 89-111.

Budruk, M., White, D., Wodrich, J., & van Riper, C. (2008). Connecting visitors to people and place: Visitors' perceptions of authenticity at Canyon de Chelly National Monument, Arizona. *Journal of Heritage Tourism, 3(3),* 185-203.

Cronbach, L. (1951). Coefficient alpha and the internal structure of tests. *Psychometrika, 16,* 297-334.

Feld, S., & Basso, K. (1996). *Senses of Places.* Santa Fe, Mexico: School of American Research Press.

Fornell, C., & Larcker, D. (1981). Evaluating structural equation models with unobservable variables and measurement error. *Journal of Marketing Research, 18*(February), 39-50.

Gross, M., & Brown, G. (2008). An empirical structural model of tourists and places: Progressing involvement and place attachment into tourism. *Tourism Management,* 1141-1151.

Gursoy, D., & Gavcar, E. (2003). International leisure tourists' involvement profile. *Annals of Tourism Research, 30,* 906-926.

Hammitt, W., Backlund, E., & Bixler, R. (2006). Place bonding for recreation places: Conceptual and empirical development. *Leisure Studies, 25(1),* 17-41.

Harvey, D. (1996). *Justice, nature and the geography of difference.* London: Blackwell.

Havitz, M., & Dimanche, F. (1990). Propositions for testing the involvement construct in recreation and tourism contexts. *Leisure Science, 12,* 179-197.

—. (1997). Leisure involvement revisited: Conceptual conundrums and measurement advances. *Journal of Leisure Research, 29,* 245-278.

—. (1999). Leisure involvement revisited: Drive properties and paradoxes. *Journal of Leisure Research, 31,* 122-149.

Havitz, M., Dimanche, F., & Howard, D. (1993). A two sample comparison of the personal involvement inventory (PII) and involvement profile (IP) scales using selected recreations activities. *Journal of Applied Recreation Research, 17,* 331-364.

Hidalgo, M., & Hernández, B. (2001). Place attachment: Conceptual and empirical questions. *Journal of Environmental Psychology, 21,* 273-281.

Holbert, R., & Stephenson, M. (2002). Structural equation modelling in in the human communication sciences, 1995-2000. *Human Communication Research, 28*, 531-551.

Hu, Y., & Ritchie, B. (1993). Measuring destination attractiveness: A contextual approach. *Journal of Travel Research, 32(2)*, 25-34.

Hummon, D. (1992). Community attachment. Local sentiment and sense of place. In I. Altman, & S. Low, *Place Attachment* (pp. 253–277). NY: Plenum Press.

Hwang, S.-N., Lee, C., & Chen, H.-J. (2005). The relationship among tourists' involvement, place attachment and interpretation satisfaction in Taiwan's national parks. *Tourism Management, 26*, 143-156.

Jacob, G., & Schreyer, R. (1980). Conflict in outdoor recreation: A theorical perspective. *Journal of Leisure Research, 12*, 368-380.

Jain, K., & Srinivasan, N. (1990). An empirical assessment of multiple operationalizations of involvement. *Advances in Consumer Research, 17*, 594-602.

Jamrozy, U., Backman, S., & Backman, K. (1996). Involvement and leadership in tourism. *Annals of Tourism Research, 23*, 908-924.

Jöreskog, K., & Sorbom, D. (1996). *LISREL 8: User's reference guide.* Chicago: Scientific Software International.

Jorgensen, B., & Stedman, R. (2001). Sense of place as an attitude: Lakeshore property owners' attitudes toward their properties. *Journal of Environmental Psychology, 21*, 233-248.

Josiam, B., Smeaton, G., & Clements, C. (1999). Involvement: Travel motivation and destination selection. *Journal of Vacation Marketing, 5*, 167-175.

Kaplan, R., & Kaplan, S. (1989). *The Experience of Nature: A Psychological Perspective.* NY: Cambridge University Press.

Kassarjian, H. (1981). Low involvement: A second look. In K. Monroe (Ed.), *Advances in Consumer Research* (Vol. 8, pp. 31-34). Ann Arbor, MI: Association for Consumer Research.

Kerstetter, D., Confer, J., & Graefe, A. (2001). An exploration of the specialization concept within the context of heritage tourism. *Journal of Travel Research, 39(3)*, 267-274.

Kianicka, S., Buchecker, M., Hunziker, M., & Müller-Böker, U. (2006). Locals' and tourists' sense of place: A Case study in a swiss alpine village. *Mountain Research and Development, 26(1)*, 55-63.

Kim, S., Scott, L., & Crompton, J. (1997). An exploration of the relationships among social psychological involvement, behavioral involvement, comitment and future intensions in the context of bird watching. *Journal of Leisure Research, 29*, 320-341.

Knopf, R. (1983). Recreational needs and behavior in natural settings. In I. Altman, & J. Wohlwill, *Human Behavior and Environment: Behavior and Natural Environment* (Vol. 6, pp. 205-240). NY: Plenum Press.

—. (1987). Human behavior, cognition, and affect in the natural environment. In D. Stokols, & I. Altman, *Handbook of Environmental Psychology* (Vol. 1, pp. 783-825). NY: John Wiley.

Korpela, K., Harting, T., Kaiser, F., & Fuhrer, U. (2001). Restorative experience and self-regulation in favorite places. *Environmental and Behavior, 33*, 572-589.

Krugman, H. (1965). The impact of television advertising: Learning without involvement. *Public Opinion Quarterly, 29*, 349-356.

Kyle, G., & Chick, G. (2002). The social nature of leisure involvement. *Journal of Leisure Research, 34*(4), 426-448.

Kyle, G., Absher, J., & Graefe, A. (2003). The moderating role of place attachment on the relationship between attitudes toward fees and spending preferences. *Leisure Sciences, 25*(1), 33-50.

Kyle, G., Graefe, A., Manning, R., & Bacon, J. (2003). An examination of the relationships between leisure activity involvement and place attachment among hikers along the appalachian trail. *Journal of Leisure Studies, 35*, 249-273.

—. (2004). Effect of activity involvement and place attachment on recreationists' perceptions of setting density. *Journal of Leisure Research, 36(2)*, 209-231.

Kyle, G., Kerstetter, D., & Guadagnolo, F. (1999). The influence of outcome messages and involvement on participant reference price. *Journal of Park and Recreation Administration, 17*(3), 53-75.

—. (2002). Market segmentation using participant involvement profiles. *Journal of Park and Recreation Administration, 20*, 1-21.

Kyle, G., Mowen, A., & Tarrant, M. (2004). Linking place preferences with place meaning: An examination of the relationship between place motivation and place attachment. *Journal of Environmental Psychology, 24*, 439-454.

Laurent, G., & Kapferer, J. (1985). Measuring consumer involvement profiles. *Journal of Marketing Research, 22*(2), 41-53.

Lee, C. (2001). Predicting tourist attachment to destinations. *Annals of Tourism Research, 28(1)*, 229-232.

Lewicka, M. (2005). Ways to make people active: The role of place attachment, cultural capital and neighborhood. *Journal of Environmental Psychology, 25*, 381-395.

—. (2008). Place attachment, place identity, and place memory: Restoring the forgotten city past. *Journal of Environmental Psychology, 28*, 209-231.

Low, S., & Altman, I. (1992). Place attachment: A conceptual inquiry. In I. Altman, & S. Low, *Place Attachment* (pp. 1-12). New York and London: Plenum Press.

Manzo, L. (2003). Relationships to non-residential places: Towards a reconceptualization of attachment to place. *Journal of Environmental Psychology, 23(1)*, 47-61.

Mazumdar, S., & Mazumdar, S. (1999). Women's significant spaces: Religion space and community. *Journal of Environmental Psychology, 19(2)*, 159-170.

McQuarrie, E., & Munson, M. (1987). A modification of PII and consumer involvement profiles. *Advances in Consumer Research, 14*, 35-40.

Mittal, B. (1995). A comparative analysis of four scales of consumer involvement. *Psychology & Marketing, 12*, 663-682.

Moore, J. (2000). Placing home in context. *Journal of Environmental Psychology, 20(3)*, 207-218.

Moore, R., & Graefe, A. (1994). Attachment to recreation settings: The case of rail-trail users. *Leisure Sciences, 16*, 17–31.

Moore, R., & Scott, D. (2003). Place attachment and context: Comparing a park and a trail within. *Forest Science, 49(6)*, 1-8.

Mowen, J., & Minor, M. (1998). *Consumer Behavior.* New Jersey: Prentice-Hall.

Muehling, D., Laczniak, R., & Andrews, J. (1993). Defining, operationalizing, and using involvement in advertising research: A review. *Journal of Current Issues and Research in Advertising, 15*(Spring), 21-58.

Palmer, C. (1999). Tourism and the symbols of identity. *Tourism Management, 20(3)*, 313-321.

Proshansky, H. (1978). The city and self identity. *Environment and Behavior, 10*, 147-169.

Ragheb, M. (1996). Measuring leisure and recreation involvement. In P. Stokowski, & J. Hulstman (Edits.), *Abstracts from the 1996 symposium on leisure research* (pp. 82-94). Arlington: National Recreation and Park Association.

Relph, E. (1976). *Place and Placelessness.* London: Pion Limited.

Scott, D., & Shafer, C. (2001). Recreation specialization: A critical look at the construct. *Journal of Leisure Research, 33*(3), 319-343.

Sherif, M., & Cantril, H. (1947). *The Psychology of Ego-involvement.* NY: John Wiley.

Sime, J. (1995). Creating places or designing spaces? In L. Groat, *Giving Place Meaning: Readings in Environmental Psychology* (Vol. 4, pp. 55-63). San Diego: Academic Press.

Sirakaya, E., & Woodside, A. (2005). Building and testing theories of decision making by travellers. *Tourism Management, 26*(6), 815-832.

Slama, M., & Taschian, A. (1985). Selected socioeconomic and demographic characteristics associated with purchasing involvement. *Journal of Marketing, 49*, 77-82.

Sonnenfeld, J. (1968). Variables values in space and landscape. *Journal of Social Issues, 22*, 71-82.

Stedman, R. (2003). Is it really just a social construction? The contribution of the physical environment to sense of place. *Society and Natural Resources, 16(8)*, 671–685.

Steiger, J. (1980). Tests for comparing elements of a correlation matrix. *Psychological Bulletin, 87*(2), 245-251.

Stewart, S., & Stynes, D. (1994). Toward a dynamic model of complex tourism choices: The seasonal home location decision. *Journal of Travel & Tourism Marketing, 3*(8), 69-88.

Stokols, D., & Shumaker, S. (1981). People in places: A transactional view of settings. In J. Harvey, *Cognition, Social Behavior and the Environment.* New Jersey: Erlibaum.

Stokowski, P. (2002). Languages of place and discourses of power: Constructing new senses of place. *Journal of Leisure Research, 34*(4), 368-382.

Swarbrooke, J., & Horner, S. (1999). *Consumer Behavior in Tourism.* Oxford: Butterworth-Heinemann.

Tuan, Y. (1980). Rootedness versus sense of place. *Landscape, 24(1)*, 3–8.

Ulrich, R., Simons, R., Losito, B., Fiorito, E., Miles, M., & Zelson, M. (1991). Stress recovery during the exposure to natural and urban environments. *Journal of Environmental Psychology, 11*, 201-230.

Williams, D., & Kaltenborn, B. (1999). Leisure places and modernity: The use and meaning of recreational cottages in Norway and the USA. In D. Crouch, *Leisure Tourism Geographies: Practices and Geographical Knowledge* (pp. 214-230). London & NY: Routledge.

Williams, D., & Stewart, S. I. (1998). Sense of place: An elusive concept that is finding a home in ecosystem management. *Journal of Forestry, 96(5)* , 18–23.

Williams, D., & Vaske, J. (2003). The measurement of place attachment: Validity and generalizability of a psychometric approach. *Forest Science, 49(6)*, 830-840.

Williams, D., Patterson, M., & Roggenbuck, J. (1992). Understanding antecedents of repeat visitation and tourists' loyalty to a resort destination. *Proceedings of the 1997 Travel and Tourism Research Association Annual Conference.* Boulder, C.O.: TTRA.

Wohlwill, J. (1983). The concept of nature, a psychologist's view. In I. Altman, & J. Wohlwill, *Human Behavior and Environment: Behavior and Natural Environment* (Vol. 6, pp. 1-34). NY: Plenum Press.

Yuksel, A., Yuksel, F., & Bilim, Y. (2010). Destination attachment: Effects on consumer satisfaction and cognitive, affective and conative loyalty. *Tourism Management, 31*, 274-284.

Zaichkowsky, J. (1985). Measuring the involvement concept. *Journal of Consumer Research, 12*(December), 341-352.

—. (1986a). Conceptualizing involvement. *Journal of Advertising, 15*(3), 4-34.

CHAPTER SIX

THE CONTRIBUTION OF GEOGRAPHY AND ECONOMICS TO TOURISM DOCTORAL RESEARCH IN THE US, CANADA, AUSTRALIA AND NEW ZEALAND

BRENT MOYLE, BETTY WEILER AND CHAR-LEE MCLENNAN

Abstract

Tourism doctoral research has grown exponentially in recent years. However there is little research which investigates the disciplinary orientation of tourism doctoral theses. This chapter examines the contribution of the two disciplines of geography and economics to tourism doctoral research. Drawing on a database of 1,888 tourism doctoral theses completed in the United States, Canada, Australia and New Zealand this research uncovered that 211 theses were influenced by economics and 206 were influenced by geography. While geography and economics were two of the earliest disciplines to influence doctoral tourism research, they are also the disciplines to have declined the most in their influence. Future research is needed to explore the consequences of such trends for tourism research, scholarship and practice. **Keywords:** Doctoral research, disciplines, multidisciplinary.

1. Introduction

Scholars assessing and reporting on the growth, breadth and maturity of tourism research have drawn on a variety of information sources, including the number of tourism academics working in universities, of peer-reviewed journal publications and authors, and of educational programs producing tourism graduates (Downward & Mearman, 2004;

Faulkner, Pearce, Shaw, & Weiler, 2003; Goeldner, 1999; Sheldon, 1990, 1991; Weiler, 2001). Nonetheless, assessing a field of research by the quantity of input (number of programs, researchers, research funding) or output (number of journal papers, graduates, dissertations) presents an incomplete and, arguably, a superficial perspective. The challenge is to find appropriate indicators of research quality, as many measures such as journal rankings, citations and impact factors are highly contested (McKercher, Law, & Lamb, 2006).

Another measure of 'the level of sophistication of research' (Faulkner *et al.,* 2003, p. 304) has been to look at the growth in postgraduate research, including the disciplinary context and contribution of this research. Given that the application of theory to make a substantial and original contribution to knowledge is a common criterion upon which doctoral theses are examined, doctoral dissertation research provides a useful measure for gauging the intellectual health of a body of research (Das & Handfield, 1997). Moreover, while the extent to which a particular field has established a distinct body of theory is sometimes seen as a measure of its maturity (Jafari, 1990; Spear, 2007), in an area of study such as tourism that is inherently interdisciplinary, Spear (2007) and others argue that the application of theory and methods from other disciplines including multidisciplinary research, is the best indication of research maturity. For Adams and White (1994, p. 573), the worst-case scenario is a field of study that promotes 'mindless empiricism' that is devoid of theory and fails to develop on the theorising of established disciplines.

Geography and economics are two disciplines which have contributed extensively to the evolution of the tourism field (Gray, 1982; Hall & Page, 2006). Recognition of this contribution by tourism scholars came early in the form of overviews published in the *Annals of Tourism Research's* special issue on Tourism Social Science in 1991. The literature suggests that geography and economics have contributed to the development and evolution of tourism research in a number of different ways (Butler, 2004). Geography is linked to tourism research through its connection to the inquiry of matters associated with place, space and environment (Hall & Page, 2009; Pearce, 1979). Geography has some well-established conceptual and applied research interests that have helped develop and establish the tourism field (Lew, 2001). Tourism geography studies emerged in the 1920s and 1930s in the US and rapidly increased correlating with growth in mass tourism during the twentieth century (Mitchell & Murphy, 1991). However in recent years there have been a number of developments shifting the direction of the contribution of geography to tourism research, resulting in an area known as tourism geographies (Lew, Hall, & Timothy, 2008). The key areas that geography has contributed to the tourism field include, though are not limited to: explaining spatialities, human and environment interactions, tourism planning, tourism development and its associated impacts on places (Hall & Page, 2009). Interestingly, geography has been identified as essential in the tourism field, yet paradoxically tourism is often missing from the geographic literature (Hall & Page, 2006).

The application of economic concepts, theories and methods is prevalent within the tourism literature and dates back to the middle of the twentieth century when the tourism industry was rapidly emerging and seeking to justify its existence through economic studies advocating its importance to the national economy. Towards the end of the 1970s a more critical viewpoint emerged with a number of studies published in the tourism field that disproved earlier conclusions of the importance of tourism and, instead, had a focus on the negatives of tourism (Moyle, Croy, & Weiler, 2010). This cautionary platform led to the emergence of new concepts such as ecotourism, cultural tourism, green tourism and sustainable tourism, and there was subsequent criticising of pure economic methodologies. This preceded the adaptancy phase, which saw the development of tourism economics slow from its earlier rapid development phase (Gartner, 2004).

Today, tourism economics continues to take methodologies and theories from economics to develop tourism theory. In more recent years the field has adopted advanced econometric techniques, tourism satellite accounts, general equilibrium models, cost-benefit analysis and scenario planning to answer a number of theoretical questions in a variety of tourism contexts (Dwyer, Forsyth, & Spurr, 2004). Moreover, tourism economics has also been concerned with issues encompassing both the demand and supply side of tourism, such as international demand, wages, income and employment generation, competition, prices, characteristics of tourism products, the use of scarce resources, labour, capital, land and environmental resources (Lim, 1997). Most recently, institutional and evolutionary economics has been emerging within the tourism economics field seeking to explain some fundamental tourism problems, such as the dynamics of destination evolution (McLennan, Ruhanen, Ritchie & Pham, 2012).

Although evidence of the contribution of geography and economics to tourism exists in many forms, the present chapter adds an important layer to this story by analysing the contribution of geography and economics to tourism doctoral research in the United States (US), Canada, Australia and New Zealand (NZ).

2. Literature Review

Tourism research has increased dramatically at tertiary educational institutions, as evidenced in part by the spike in doctoral qualifications around the world (Ruhanen & McLennan, 2010). This chapter leverages off similar studies on the disciplinary orientation of the tourism field which first emerged over 20 years ago (Jafari & Aaser, 1998). The methods and findings of these previous studies are discussed in detail in Weiler, Moyle and McLennan (2012) and highlight important conceptual and methodological improvements made for the current study, which were primarily focused on identifying the disciplines that inform doctoral research in tourism as opposed to identifying the disciplinary context of the research (i.e. the school, department or administrative unit in which the research was housed). While determining disciplinary influence by analysing abstracts has not been undertaken in tourism research to date, this approach has been used in studies in other fields and is considered to be an established and rigorous method of assessing the interdisciplinary nature of a particular field of research (Adams & White, 1994).

In tourism studies, assessing doctoral research has been conducted using departments or schools to classify theses into particular disciplines. The first of these studies was conducted by Jafari and Aaser (1988) who assembled a dataset of 149 American doctoral dissertations relating to tourism over the period 1951 to 1987. Jafari and Aaser (1988) found growth in doctoral research from the early 1970s–1987, with the key disciplines producing tourism dissertations including economics (26%), anthropology (16%), geography (15%) and recreation (15%).

To determine how patterns had changed since Jafari and Aaser (1988), Meyer-Arendt and Justice (2002) conducted a similar study of American and Canadian doctoral dissertations from 1987–2000. Meyer-Arendt and Justice (2002) concluded that recreation (97) had surpassed economics as the discipline granting the greatest number of tourism-focused doctoral degrees, followed by anthropology (50), geography (50), education (29), business administration (29), history (28) and economics (26). Disciplines such as environmental studies and psychology were identified to be emerging during this time period (Meyer-Arendt & Justice, 2002).

Also following the lead of Jafari and Aaser (1988), other parts of the world have begun to assess tourism dissertations. Unlike the North American studies, Hall and Pedrazzini (1989) assessed all dissertations at the postgraduate level in Australia. The majority of the 28 dissertations identified were Masters Degrees (86%), with only three PhDs completed prior to 1988. Drawing from the work of Hall and Pedrazini (1989), Weiler and Laing (2008) explored trends in postgraduate tourism research in Australia from 1969–2005. They found an uneven distribution of postgraduate tourism research, both geographically and with respect to discipline, with business, management and marketing dominating.

In addition to studies undertaken on North American and Australian doctoral research, Botterill, Haven and Gale (2002) undertook an analysis of doctoral dissertations in the United Kingdom (UK) and Ireland. The data collected in their study identified 149 theses completed between 1990 and 1999 at 51 universities. In this study, rather than looking at the disciplinary context, the authors analysed the subject matter studied. More recently Huang (2011) found economics (47) to be the discipline engaged in the largest number of doctoral tourism theses in China, followed by geography (41), management (33), tourism management (17), forestry (17), history (13), and ecology (11). These findings reveal that the disciplinary context of doctoral-level tourism research in China is similar to what was in the US and Canada in the earlier period of the 1970s and 1980s.

The findings from these previous studies provide some indication of the disciplines that most often provide the study context for doctoral-level tourism research. However, these disciplines have been determined largely by identifying the departments or schools in which the research was undertaken. While Hall (1991) argued that this would give the best possible indication of the discipline of research, this approach has two important limitations. Firstly, it does not account for the fact that research undertaken in schools such as business that are inherently interdisciplinary often draws on theory and methods from a range of other disciplines. Secondly, the approach forces allocation of each thesis to a single discipline, thus eliminating the potential to assess the extent to which an individual thesis is informed by multiple disciplines.

As stated at the outset, genuine evidence of disciplinary breadth and multidisciplinarity are seen as indicative of a field's level of research maturity and point to where theoretical development may be present or absent. Thus, in view of the limitations of previous studies and the aim of the present study, this study applies the method of Adams and White (1994) who determined the disciplines that influenced dissertations in public administration and five other fields by analysing the abstracts of the theses rather than the departments or schools within which the research was undertaken.

The focus of these previous studies on postgraduate tourism research was to assess the multitude of disciplines that have contributed to the evolution of the tourism field from around the world. These studies, although comprehensive, have not explicitly considered in depth the contribution of specific disciplines to tourism doctoral research. With this in mind, the authors (Weiler et al., 2012) undertook a comprehensive study of doctoral-level tourism research, highlighting that some disciplines were more prominent than others in informing tourism research, that these changed over time, and that these differed between countries. Leveraging off this research, the aim of the present chapter is to investigate the contribution of two key disciplines—geography and economics—to doctoral tourism research in the US, Canada, Australia and NZ. These two disciplines were selected for this chapter primarily because not only were they prominent in contributing to early doctoral-level research in tourism, but also because they were the two disciplines that were found to have declined the most in influencing tourism doctoral research. This chapter examines both the changes over time and the differences between countries in the contribution of economics and geography to doctoral-level tourism research.

3. Methodology

Using several electronic databases, Weiler *et al.* (in press) developed a comprehensive database of all tourism-focused theses that have been completed in the US, Canada, Australia and NZ. Search terms identified from previous studies (Hall & Pedrazzini, 1989; Meyer-Arndt & Justice, 2002; Weiler & Laing, 2008) were used and included hotel, hospitality, leisure, tourism, tourist, travel, tour, recreation, holiday, vacation, guide, trip and heritage. This resulted in a total of over 20,000 dissertations being assessed for inclusion in the study, of which 18,000 were excluded based on analysis of the abstracts, researcher judgement and cross-checking by two other researchers.

The new customised database comprises the author, year of completion, title, academic department, faculty, university, country, subject area, abstract, keywords and number of pages for 1,888 valid doctoral dissertations. To achieve the aim of the present study, one of the authors analysed the thesis title, full abstract, list of subject areas and keywords of every thesis in the database in order to extract information about the disciplines which informed each thesis and to discern whether the thesis was multidisciplinary (Adams & White, 1994). As already noted, this contrasts with previous research which relied on the disciplinary context (i.e. the academic department or faculty in which the thesis was completed), providing a more refined measure of disciplinary influence. To assemble a list of the disciplines that influence tourism doctoral research in the US, Canada, Australia and NZ this study leveraged off Jafari and Ritchie's (1981) list, which was subsequently updated by Goeldner and Ritchie (2006).

The list by Goeldner and Ritchie (2006) had 21 disciplines ranging from some of the more common such as geography, economics and psychology, to the newly-added disciplines such as entrepreneurship and architecture which are more contested. It is acknowledged that the labelling of many of these fields of study as disciplines is contentious, particular the newly-added ones. Indeed, there has been much debate in the literature surrounding the disciplinary status of tourism (Leiper, 2000; Tribe, 1997, 2000). Nonetheless, the works of Jafari and Ritchie (1981), and Goeldner and Ritchie (2006) provide a useful point of departure for a disciplinary list with which to code the abstracts; a list which was later reduced to 14 key disciplines. More detail about the methods and limitations are included in Weiler et al. (2012).

4. Results

A total of 1,888 tourism-focused doctoral dissertations were completed in the US, Canada, Australia and NZ between 1951 and 2010. As with tourism research generally (Amoah & Baum, 1997), growth over time in doctoral-level tourism research in these four countries has been exponential, with more than 100 doctoral theses completed each year for most of the past decade.

The US produced the most tourism doctoral graduates (63%), followed by Australia (24%), Canada (7%) and NZ (6%). Given that the population of the US is more than five times that of the other three countries combined and has far more universities it is not surprising that the majority of dissertations were produced in the US. What is somewhat surprising is Australia's contribution to doctoral-level tourism research. While only eight tourism-focused theses had been completed in Australia prior to 1990, nearly a quarter of all doctoral theses in tourism over the 60-year period in the four countries included in this study were from Australian universities. A total of 230 universities across the four countries were found to have generated tourism-focused doctoral theses. Ten universities in the US, Canada, Australia and NZ produced 26% of all tourism-focused doctoral theses. At the lower end of the scale, 38 universities recorded only a single tourism-focused doctoral thesis over the

60-year data collection period. This indicates that in all four countries some universities have focused on tourism while others have not. More detail about the contribution of individual universities to doctoral tourism research is reported in Weiler et al. (2012).

Many more disciplines are influencing doctoral-level research in tourism than has been acknowledged in previously published studies. Each of the disciplines of psychology, environmental studies, anthropology, history, economics, geography, sociology, marketing, business, political science, parks and recreation, urban and regional planning, hotel and restaurant administration, and education have contributed to at least 70 dissertations. The first three disciplines—psychology, environmental studies and anthropology—have been particularly notable in informing tourism theses: 813 (43%) of all tourism-focused dissertations have drawn on at least one of these. While some of these theses have been informed by a second discipline, this still suggests some imbalance in which disciplines inform tourism research. It is unclear why this imbalance occurs, but may be a result of the growth of these disciplines generally and the fostering of research by academic staff in some of these disciplines (Tribe & Airey, 2007). The remainder of this chapter focuses on the results relating to the aim of the present study; that is, the contribution of economics and geography to tourism doctoral research, how this has changed over time, and the differences between countries.

4.1 The Influence of Economics and Geography on Tourism Doctoral Theses

Geography and economics were two of the earliest disciplines in doctoral tourism research. Indeed, geography was the discipline that informed the very first tourism doctoral thesis recorded in the four countries of interest. This thesis was produced by H.H. Caldwell in 1951 at Clark University and its focus was on resource development for tourism in Idaho. Almost two decades later, the first tourism thesis informed by economics emerged. This thesis was produced by W.W. Goldsmith in 1968 at Cornell University and it investigated the impact of tourism on the Puerto Rican economy. In the intervening two decades, the only other disciplines to inform tourism doctoral research were urban and regional planning and parks and recreation.

Since these pioneering theses, a total of 206 and 211 tourism theses have been informed by geography and economics respectively, of which 12 were informed by both disciplines. Overall, geography ranks sixth and economics ranks seventh as disciplines influencing doctoral tourism research over the 60-year period in these four countries. This is somewhat different to previous findings, where geography and economics are prominent as disciplinary contexts for tourism doctoral research. As would be expected, tourism theses influenced by economics tended to be undertaken in Economics and Econometric Schools or Departments (41%). This was followed by Geography and Geosciences (12%); Business (9%); Marine and Environmental Studies (9%); Information Management and Marketing (6%); and Tourism, Hospitality, Parks and Recreation (6%) Schools or Departments. Similarly, theses influenced by geography were most commonly found in Geography and Geosciences Schools or Departments (58%). This was followed by Marine and Environmental Studies (12%); Tourism, Hospitality, Parks and Recreation (11%); American Studies (6%); and Business (6%).

Eighty-five per cent of the tourism theses informed by economics and geography were single-location focused. That said, there was considerable diversity in study locations, with 195 different locations being cited in the abstracts. The economic-informed theses were most likely to focus on Australia (10), China (6), Fiji (5) and Thailand (5), while the geography-informed theses focused on China (9), British Columbia (5) and NZ (5). Finally, economics-informed theses are significantly shorter than geography-informed theses (economics mean = 239 pages and median = 202 pages compared to geography mean = 286 pages and median = 269 pages).

Of the 16 disciplines analysed in the initial study (Weiler *et al.,* 2012), geography and economics have declined the most in their influence, with the drop in economics being particularly dramatic. While both economics and geography have had absolute growth since tourism theses commenced, economics significantly ($p<.001$) declined proportionately as a discipline used in tourism theses after 2000 (see Figure 1). The figures post-2000 (see Table 1) are particularly telling, indicating a levelling-off of economically-informed theses. This decline was prominent in the US and Australia, where economics had originally been a founding discipline.

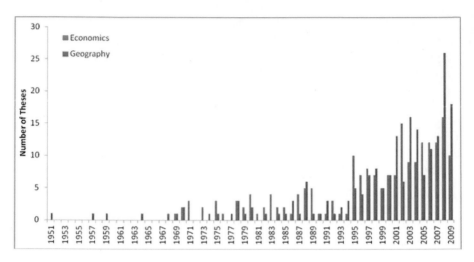

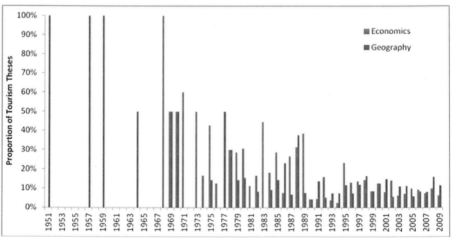

Figure 1 - Number and Proportion of Tourism Doctoral Dissertations Informed by Economics and Geography

The Contribution of Geography and Economics

Table 1- Changes over Time in the Influence of Economics and Geography on Tourism Doctoral Research

All Tourism Theses	Before 2000			2000 Onwards			Total theses	
	No.	Percentage of tourism theses	Percentage before 2000	No.	Percentage of tourism theses	Percentage after 2000	No.	Percentage of tourism theses
Tourism economic theses	93	16%	44%	118	9%	56%	211	16%
Tourism geography theses	68	12%	33%	138	11%	67%	206	16%
Tourism theses	577		31%	1,311		69%	1888	

Multidisciplinary tourism theses	No.	Percentage of multidisciplinary tourism theses	Percentage of multidisciplinary theses before 2000	No.	Percentage of multidisciplinary tourism theses	Percentage of multidisciplinary theses after 2000	No.	Percentage of multidisciplinary tourism theses
Tourism economic theses	36	24%	32%	76	13%	68%	112	15%
Tourism geography theses	29	19%	22%	100	17%	78%	129	17%
Tourism theses	152		20%	599		80%	751	

Over the 60-year period of tourism doctoral research in the four countries, 129 (63%) of the geography-informed theses were multidisciplinary, as compared to 112 (53%) multidisciplinary economics-informed theses. As shown in Table 1, both economics (p<.001) and geography (p<.001) were found to have become significantly more multidisciplinary since 2000. The multidisciplinary tourism economic theses were found to be also informed mainly by environmental studies (31), political science (23), geography (12), sociology (12), and parks and recreation (10). The multidisciplinary geography tourism theses, on the other hand, were mainly informed by environmental studies (28), sociology (17), urban and regional planning (17), history (15), economics (12), anthropology (11), and psychology (10). It is notable that the multidisciplinary theses influenced by both economics and geography were found to be more likely to be influenced by environmental studies than any other discipline, with environmental studies composing 22% of the multidisciplinary tourism economic studies and 18% of the multidisciplinary tourism geography studies. This is perhaps not surprising in the case of geography-informed theses, given the gain in prominence of environmental studies as a discipline in recent years, which has been due in part to the phenomenon of many geography departments adding environmental studies to their name (Harvey, Forster & Bourman 2002), or even replacing the name geography with environmental studies.

4.3 Cross-country Analysis

Both economics and geography are among the top ten disciplines of influence in all four countries; however, in Canada geography is notable as the leading discipline to inform tourism research. Not surprisingly, given that the US produced nearly two-thirds of all doctoral-level tourism theses in the four countries as noted earlier, the US leads in producing doctoral-level research informed by economics and geography. Around 68% of tourism economic theses were produced in the US (143), followed by 23% being produced in Australia (48), 5% in Canada (11) and 4% in NZ (9). Similarly, most of the tourism geography theses were produced in the US (58% or 120 theses), followed by 21% being produced in Canada (44), 15% in Australia (31) and 5% in NZ (11). Tourism economic theses represented the larger proportion of all tourism theses in the US (12%), followed by Australia (11%), NZ (8%) and Canada (8%). Tourism geography theses, on the other hand, represented the larger proportion of all tourism theses in Canada (33%), compared with only 10% in the US, 9% in NZ and just 7% in Australia.

5. Conclusion

Overall, while past studies identified economics and geography as the key disciplinary context for tourism-focused doctoral research, particularly in research conducted prior to 2000, the present study indicates that their relative influence is declining. The lower ranking of economics and geography as disciplines informing tourism doctoral-level research in this chapter is a result of both actual changes over the past 10 to 20 years as well as greater sophistication in both the data sources and the methods used in the present study. In the case of geography, it is clear that some of this decline is due to the growth of environmental studies, which ranks second overall in disciplinary influence on doctoral-level tourism research.

In addition, the growth in multidisciplinary research may have allowed the influence of other disciplines to grow proportionately. While some such as Tribe and Airey (2007) may see this disciplinary breadth as a positive thing, others might well argue that, in the case of economics in particular, the levelling off of the absolute (as well as relative) numbers of economically-informed theses could lead to an under-supply of graduates with the capacity to undertake tourism research underpinned by economic theory in coming years. This deficiency may be acutely noticed within the government sector, where economics and econometrics are desirable qualities, resulting in increased employment of economists and researchers with little to no tourism background.

Further research is needed to explore both the antecedent factors and the consequences of these trends for doctoral tourism research and tourism research generally. There is also scope for analysing the trends in other disciplines where the pre- and post-2000 data show large differences, such as environmental studies, business and marketing—all of which had considerable growth in the past decade. The reasons for and the impacts of the differences between the top disciplines that inform doctoral research in each country also merit further investigation; that is, anthropology in the US, geography in Canada, environmental studies in Australia and psychology in NZ. Given that doctoral graduates represent the next generation of tourism researchers, these trends and differences could well have implications for the capacity of tourism researchers and therefore the future of tourism research, scholarship and practice in each country.

References

Adams, G.B., & White, J.D. (1994). Dissertation research in public administration and cognate fields: An assessment of methods and quality. *Public Administration Review*, *54*(6), 565–576.

Amoah, V.A., & Baum, T. (1997). Tourism education: Policy versus practice. *International Journal of Contemporary Hospitality Management*, 9(1), 5–12.

Botterill, D., Haven, C., & Gale, T. (2002). A survey of doctoral theses accepted by universities in the UK and Ireland for studies related to tourism, 1990–1999. *Tourist Studies*, *2*(3), 283–311.

Butler, R.W. (2004) Geographical research on tourism, recreation and leisure: Origins, eras and directions. *Tourism Geographies*, 6(2), 143-162.

Das, A., & Handfield, R.B. (1997). A meta-analysis of doctoral dissertations in purchasing. *Journal of Operations Management*, *15*(2), 101–121.

Downward, P., & Mearman, A. (2004). On tourism and hospitality management research: A critical realist proposal. *Tourism and Hospitality Planning and Development*, *1*(2), 107–122.

Dwyer, L., Forsyth, P., & Spurr, R. (2004). Evaluating tourism's economic effects: New and old approaches. *Tourism Economics*, 25, 307-317

Faulkner, B., Pearce, P., Shaw, R., & Weiler, B. (2003). Tourism research in Australia: Confronting the challenges of the 1990s and beyond. In B. Faulkner, L. Jago & L. Fredline (Eds.), *Progressing Tourism Research* (pp. 303–340). Clevedon: Multilingual Matters.

Gartner, W. (2004). Rural tourism development in the USA. *International Journal of Tourism Research*, 6, 151-164.

Goeldner, C.R. (1999). Directions and trends in tourism research: Past, present and future. In V.C.S. Heung, J. Ap, & K.F. Wong (Eds.), *Proceedings of Asia Pacific Tourism Association Fifth Annual Conference* (pp. 33–43). Hong Kong: APTA.

Goeldner, C.R., & Ritchie, J.R.B. (2006). *Tourism, Principles, Practices and Philosophies* (10th ed.). NJ: John Wiley.

Gray, P.H. (1982) The contributions of economics to tourism. *Annals of Tourism Research*, *9*(1), 105-125.

Hall, C.M. (1991). Tourism as the subject of post-graduate dissertations in Australia. *Annals of Tourism Research*, *18*(3), 520–523.

Hall, C.M., & Page, S.J. (2006). *The Geography of Tourism and Recreation: Environment, Place and Space* (3rd ed.). NY: Routledge.

—. (2009) Progress in tourism management: From the geography of tourism to geographies of tourism – A review. *Tourism Management,* 30(1), 3-16.

Hall, C.M., & Pedrazzini, T. (1989). *Australian higher degree theses in tourism, recreation and related subjects.* Occasional Paper No. 2. Lismore: Australian Institute of Tourism Industry Management, University of New England, Northern Rivers.

Harvey, N., Forster, C., & Bourman, R.P. (2002). Geography and environmental studies in Australia: Symbiosis for survival in the 21st Century. *Australian Geographical Studies,* 40(1), 21-32.

Huang, S. (2011). Tourism as the subject of China's doctoral dissertations. *Annals of Tourism Research,* 38(1), 316-319.

Jafari, J. (1990). Research and scholarship: The basis of tourism education. *Journal of Tourism Studies, 1*(1), 33–41.

Jafari, J., & Aaser, D. (1988). Tourism as the subject of doctoral dissertations. *Annals of Tourism Research, 15*(3), 407–429.

Jafari, J., & Ritchie, J.R.B. (1981). Towards a framework for tourism education: Problems and prospects. *Annals of Tourism Research, 8,* 13–34.

Leiper, N. (2000). An emerging discipline. *Annals of Tourism Research, 27*(3), 805–809.

Lew, A.A. (2001) Defining a geography of tourism. *Tourism Geographies,* 3(1), 105-144.

Lew, A., Hall, C.M., & Timothy, D. (2008) *World Geography of Travel and Tourism: A Regional Approach.* Oxford: Elsevier.

Lim, C. (1997). Review of international tourism demand models. *Annals of Tourism Research,* 24(4), 835-849.

McKercher, B., Law, R., & Lamb, T. (2006). Rating tourism and hospitality journals. *Tourism Management, 27,* 1235–1252.

McLennan, C., Ruhanen, L., Ritchie, B.W., & Pham, T. (2012). Dynamics of destination development: Investigating the application of transformation theory. *Journal of Hospitality & Tourism Research, 36*(2), 164-190.

Mitchell, L.S., & Murphy, P.E. (1991) Geography and tourism. *Annals of Tourism Research, 18*(1), 57-70.

Meyer-Arendt, K., & Justice, C. (2002). Tourism as the subject of North American doctoral dissertations, 1987–2000. *Annals of Tourism Research, 29*(4), 1171–1174.

Moyle, B.D., Croy W.G., & Weiler, B. (2010). Community Perceptions of Tourism Impacts on Bruny and Magnetic Islands, *Asia Pacific Journal of Tourism Research, 15*(3), 353-366.

Pearce, D.G. (1979). Towards a geography of tourism, *Annals of Tourism Research 6*, 245-272.

Ruhanen, L., & McLennan, C.J. (2010). "Location, location, location"— The relative importance of country, institution and program: A study of tourism postgraduate students. *Journal of Hospitality and Tourism Management, 17*(1), 44–52.

Sheldon, P. (1990). Journal usage in tourism: Perceptions of publishing faculty. *Journal of Tourism Studies, 1*(1), 42–48.

—. (1991). An authorship analysis of tourism research. *Annals of Tourism Research, 18*, 473–484.

Spear, H.J. (2007). Nursing theory and knowledge development: A descriptive review of doctoral dissertations, 2000–2004. *Advances in Nursing Science, 30*(1): E1–E14.

Tribe, J. (1997). The indiscipline of tourism. *Annals of Tourism Research, 24*(3), 638–657.

—. (2000). Indisciplined and unsubstantiated. *Annals of Tourism Research, 27*(3), 809–813.

Tribe, J., & Airey, D. (2007) A review of tourism research. In J. Tribe & D. Airey (Eds.), *Developments in Tourism Research* (pp. 3–14). Oxford: Elsevier.

Weiler, B. (2001). Tourism research and theories: A review. In A. Lockwood, & S. Medlik (Eds.), *Tourism and hospitality in the 21st Century* (pp. 82–93). Oxford: Butterworth-Heinemann.

Weiler, B., & Laing, J. (2008). *Postgraduate tourism research in Australia: A trend analysis of 1965–2005*. Paper Presented at CAUTHE, Gold Coast, Australia, 2008.

Weiler, B., Moyle, B., & McLennan, C. (2012). Disciplines that influence tourism doctoral research: The United States, Canada, Australia and New Zealand. *Annals of Tourism Research, 39*(3), 1425-1445.

CHAPTER SEVEN

LANDSCAPE PERCEPTION AND ITS IMPLICATIONS IN TOURISM

ANITA BERNATEK AND MICHAŁ JAKIEL

Abstract

Landscape is one of the most important reasons for choosing a tourist destination. Therefore, research on landscape perception may have implications for the tourist industry. This chapter is a comparative study on landscape perception in Poland and Turkey. The landscape photographs used in the study are from Poland and Turkey and focus on ten major types of landscape - five in each country. The photographs were classified using the European Landscape Classification (LANMAP). The analysis is based on interviews with Polish and Turkish citizens who rated natural landscapes on the Likert scale. In general, the perception of the landscape is similar in Poland and Turkey. However, certain differences were identified. Poles prefer mountain landscapes, whereas Turks prefer forest landscapes. This can be explained by various factors, mainly in terms of landscape familiarity. **Key words:** Landscape, cross-cultural comparison, photo-based assessing procedures.

1. Introduction

The term *landscape* is used very often in daily life and in different scientific disciplines. All human activities are settled in the landscape. Even though it is something common, the landscape is a basic component of the world's natural and cultural heritage. The landscape can exert an influence on human sentiments and human behavior (Paraskevopoulos & Papadopoulos, 2009). Accordingly, different landscape perceptions may imply a variety of behaviors. Thus, the selection of a tourist destination also depends on one's perception of the landscape. Therefore, research on landscape perception possesses significant value in the marketing of tourist services and attractions. Given the increasing competition between tourist destinations, it is crucial to understand how individuals perceive certain landscapes.

Photographic images of landscapes used in surveys are perceived differently by different cultural groups (Dewar *et al.*, 2007), which is why this research study is concentrated on the perception of landscape by two culturally different groups. Moreover, most research on landscape perception and assessment is undertaken with respect to only one national culture and one language, thus avoiding the challenges that might come with multi-cultural and polyglot samples (Jacobsen, 2001, 2007).

The aim of this chapter is to compare visual preferences for various landscape types between respondents from Poland and Turkey. The landscapes selected for analysis are from Poland and Turkey, which also makes it necessary to analyze for landscape familiarity. Furthermore, the relationship between landscape perception and sports was investigated. In addition, an analysis of holiday destinations was performed. Landscapes are an extremely important resource for the tourist industry. Hence, the research findings may be used in the management of the tourist industry.

2. Literature Review

The definition of the landscape is different in landscape ecology and in visual landscape studies (Brabyn, 2009). The landscape as an ecosystem underscores aesthetic (scenery) and biodiversity values but misses the visual phenomena. In this chapter, on human visual perception, the landscape is understood as a "portion of the world visible to an observer from a specific position" (Conzen, 1990). This definition combines the physical and human aspects of the landscape.

The landscape has been a special area of interest and innovation in spatial policy in the international community (Brunetta & Voghera, 2008). International interest in the study of the landscape began in the 1970s. The Convention Concerning the Protection of the World's Cultural and Natural Heritage was adopted by UNESCO in 1972. In 1979, the Council of Europe adopted the Convention on the Conservation of European Wildlife and Natural Habitats – and in 1985 – the Convention for the Protection of the Architectural Heritage of Europe. However, landscape was treated in an indirect manner by each convention. In recent years, the significance of the landscape was noted by the Council of Europe, which adopted the European Landscape Convention (ELC, 2000) in 2000. The ELC is the first international legal instrument, which is exclusively focused on the landscape. It contains definitions and basic information about the protection, management and planning of all landscapes in Europe (ELC, 2000). The immense significance of this document is highlighted in its preamble: "Aware that the landscape contributes to the formation of local cultures and that it is a basic component of European natural and cultural heritage, contributing to human well-being and consolidation of European identity" (ELC, 2000). Each document discussed above shows the increasing role of the landscape in the life of modern society.

It is said that the twenty first century will be an age of tourism (Alsayyad, 2001). This is why one cannot forget that the landscape is among the most important features of contemporary tourism, being a typical choice for many tourists (Jacobsen, 1997). Landscape perception has been studied for some time now, but there are few empirical studies on tourists' perceptions of the landscape and preferences, and even fewer studies that employ photographic visualizations of the landscape (Fyhri *et al.*, 2009; Jacobsen, 2007).

Some cross-cultural comparisons of landscape perception are available in the research literature: Western Australian (Kaplan & Herbert, 1987), Korean (Yang & Kaplan, 1990, Yang & Brown, 1992), Greek (Eleftheriadis *et al.*, 1990, Paraskevopoulos & Papadopoulos, 2009), New Zealander (Fairweather & Swaffield, 2001), Scandinavian (Fyhri *et al.*, 2009). All of these studies concentrated on landscapes in one country, which were assessed by different cultural groups, primarily by tourists and residents of those countries.

Other researchers have suggested the role of personality as well as gender and cultural differences in landscape perception (Macia, 1979). Moreover, some studies showed similarities (e.g. Eysenck & Iwawaki, 1971), while other studies presented differences in landscape preferences between various nationalities (Buhyoff *et al.*, 1983).

According to many landscape research studies, perception depends on the components of the physical landscape and on the values, past experiences and socio-cultural conditioning of the observer (Brabyn, 1996). Therefore, responses to the landscape can be treated as a result of the interaction of individuals with the physical and cultural environments at particular times (Emmelin, 1996; Muir, 1999; Scott, 2002). It is suggested that a positive assessment of a landscape is derived from the totality of the landscape, not only from the particular elements of its features (Appleton, 1994). Therefore, it is important to treat the landscape as unity.

3. Methodology

In this research study, photo-based interviews were conducted in Poland and Turkey. Ten color photographs showing different landscape types were included in a questionnaire. The scenes were projected simultaneously in order from 1 to 10. The respondents were asked to rate how much they like each slide using the five-point Likert scale (5=strongly like, 1=strongly dislike). Moreover, all the respondents had to choose one or two places (as shown) where she/he would like to spend a holiday. This method, which is based on human observers' expressions of preference (choice, like/dislike), is used in most types of research on landscape perception (Daniel & Meitner, 2001). Accompanying the photo-questionnaire was a set of verbal questions designed to investigate the respondents' sports interests, holiday destination preferences and basic information such as age, gender, level of education, childhood environment and present living environment.

Respondents in Poland (Cracow) and Turkey (Istanbul) were surveyed in December of 2011 and January of 2012. The survey was made available in both Polish and Turkish. It was designed to cater to cultural differences among the respondents, as it was acknowledged that multicultural research requires special considerations (Becker & Murrman, 2000).

The study involved 140 individuals from Poland and Turkey who volunteered to provide their landscape perception. The Polish and Turkish samples consisted of 70 individuals each. Individuals who participated in the study varied in terms of age, level of education, personal interests and hometown. Both groups consisted of predominantly young people (more than 90%) under the age of 35. In the Polish group, 62.9% of the respondents were between 18 and 24, whereas in the Turkish group, it was 64.3%. Respondents 25 to 35 years of age constituted 27.1% of the Polish group and 28.6% of the Turkish group. Almost two thirds of the Polish and Turkish respondents practice sports. It was established that 48.6% of the Polish respondents and 40.0% of the Turkish respondents practice sports that require some contact with the mountain landscape – hiking, skiing, and climbing.

The survey sample consisted of two different groups: 1) individuals who grew up in an urban area, and 2) individuals who grew up in a rural area. Seventy percent of the Polish respondents had grown up in an urban area, whereas 91.4% of the Turkish respondents had grown up in an urban area. However, the distribution for the present living environment was not varied – most of the respondents now live in urban areas (Polish – 92.9%, Turkish – 100%).

Ten color photographs (15 cm × 21 cm) were employed as a basis for the questionnaire in this research study – five from Poland and five from Turkey. Only ten types were selected in order to reduce the number of images. Too many images might cause difficulties in the assessment procedure.

One of the challenges in this research project was related to the selection of the photographs. Previous studies have found a preference for water as scenery (Zube *et al.*, 1982; Kent & Elliot, 1995). Therefore, in this chapter, in order to avoid choosing a landscape because of water features (coast, lakes, rivers), the landscapes selected did not contain such features. All the photographs were taken from a broad perspective, which treats the landscape as a whole. Hence, the most significant elements in the field of view, primarily relief and vegetation, were shown in each photograph. The amount of light in each photograph was also similar. The images show scenes in the summer on sunny days – an important characteristic of photographs used for comparative purposes (Brown & Daniel, 1991). Furthermore, the landscapes were either natural or semi-natural. This is also important in the context of the tourist industry. Landscape is one of the most important reasons for choosing a tourist destination (Jacobsen, 2007). It has been shown that tourists will often not return to areas that fail to offer environmental attractions (Middleton & Hawkins, 1998).

The objective of the research was to choose five dominant landscape types for Poland and Turkey. The landscapes shown in the survey represent different types thought to be representative of Poland and Turkey (Table 1). Landscapes were classified using the European Landscape Classification (LANMAP) (Mücher *et al.*, 2010). Photographs numbered 4, 5, 8, 9 and 10 show what are presumed to be mountainous landscapes.

Table 1 – Photographs of Landscapes Used in the Research

POLAND		
Photograph 1	Photograph 2	Photograph 3
Continental lowland (*Western Pomerania*)	**Boreal hills** (*Podlasie lowland*)	**Continental hills** (*Jurassic Highland*)
Photograph 4		Photograph 5
Continental Mts (*Gorce Mountains*)		**Alpine Mts** (*Tatra Mountains*)
TURKEY		
Photograph 6	Photograph 7	Photograph 8
Anatolian Mts (*Cappadocia, inner Anatolia*)	**Mediterranean hills** (*Southern Marmara region*)	**Mediterranean Mts** (*Taurus Mountains*)
Photograph 9		Photograph 10
Mediterranean high Mts (*Pontic Mountains*)		**Anatolian high Mts** (*Erciyes – Inner Anatolia*)

4. Results

Average preferences for different types of landscape were measured separately in each cultural group using the five-point Likert scale (5=strongly like, 1=strongly dislike). Both Poles and Turks showed a high preference for continental mountains represented in Photo 4 (Poles – 4.46; Turks 4.51). Also, the same type of landscape – Mediterranean hills (photograph 7) – has the lowest rate given by Poles and Turks (3.39, 3.09, respectively (Figure 1). It is interesting that, on average, Poles rated Turkish landscapes higher than Turks did. Likewise, Turks rated Polish landscapes higher than Poles did (Figure 1). In addition, landscapes with forests or trees in general were rated higher by Turks than Poles (Photos 1 to 4). Each type of landscape scored at least 3 points, which means that respondents generally liked the presented photographs. A few respondents "strongly liked" all the photographs, which had a substantial effect on the mean rating for each landscape.

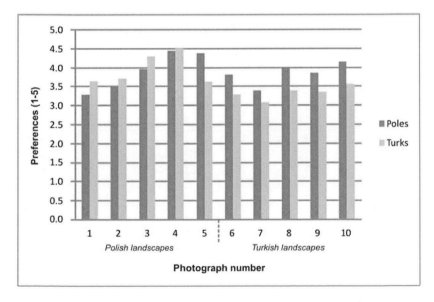

Figure 1– Mean Ratings for Images of Landscapes

There were fewer strongly negative responses than strongly positive responses in both cultural groups (Figure 2). More than half of Polish respondents provided a strongly positive opinion of Alpine mountains (Photo 5 – 62.9%), Anatolian high mountains (Photo 10 – 54.3%) and continental mountains (Photo 4 – 54.3%). Turkish respondents provided a strongly positive opinion of continental mountains (Photo 4 – 61.4%) and continental hills (Photo 3 – 52.9%).

No more than 15% of Polish and Turkish respondents provided a strongly negative opinion of any of the landscapes selected. The most negative Turkish opinion concerned Anatolian mountains (Photo 6 – 14.3%) and Anatolian high mountains (Photo 10 – 12.9%). On the other hand, no more than 10% of Polish respondents strongly disliked Anatolian high mountains (Photo 10) (Figure 2).

In summary, the majority of Polish respondents strongly liked Alpine mountains (Photo 5), while Turkish respondents strongly liked continental mountains (Photo 4). Both landscapes are from Poland. Two types of landscape – boreal hills (Photo 2) and continental hills (Photo 3) were not strongly disliked by either group, whereas other types of landscape aroused strong feelings, both positive and negative (Figure 2).

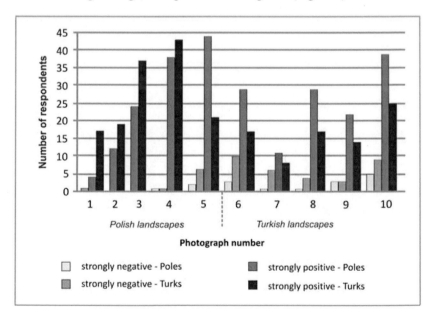

Figure 2 – Positive and Negative Ratings among Cultural Groups

Both Polish and Turkish respondents were asked to choose one or two hypothetical holiday destinations from among the landscapes shown. More than one third of respondents chose continental mountains (Photo 4) as a hypothetical holiday destination. However, each cultural group responded to this request somewhat differently. The most popular hypothetical holiday destinations among Polish respondents were Alpine mountains (Photo 5) and Anatolian high mountains (Photo 10), whereas among Turkish respondents, continental hills (Photo 3) and continental mountains (Photo 4). None of the Polish respondents chose continental lowlands (Photo 1) as a hypothetical holiday destination, while none of the Turkish respondents chose Mediterranean hills (Photo 7). In summary, Poles preferred high mountains, while Turks preferred continental mountains and forested hills.

As mentioned previously, 48.6% of Polish and 40.0% of Turkish respondents practice sports that require contact with mountain landscapes. Poles who practice mountain sports prefer more types of mountain landscapes. This is not true of Turks who practice mountain sports. Furthermore, there is no clear relationship between practicing mountain sports and rating other types of landscape.

5. Conclusion

The Poles and Turks surveyed rated landscapes similarly. Both groups preferred continental mountains and tended not to prefer Mediterranean hills. In addition, the majority of the respondents liked the landscapes shown and none were rated as poor.

The differences found between the two groups were mostly in the area of strong opinions and the selection of holiday destinations. The most attractive landscape for Poles was high mountains, while for Turks it was continental mountains and hills with forests. In Turkey, there are not many forests, which makes forested areas a somewhat "exotic" landscape and perhaps more attractive for that reason. On the other hand, Poles are accustomed to forest landscapes and generally tend to prefer different landscapes. On average, Poles rated Turkish landscapes higher than Turks did. Conversely, Turks rated Polish landscapes higher than Poles did. Therefore, landscape familiarity affects personal landscape preferences. Many individuals tend to like places, which are new and different from those known to them.

The relationship between landscape perception and practicing sports was not readily observable. Research has shown that Poles who practice mountain sports tend to prefer mountain landscapes. However, the same is not true of Turks who practice mountain sports.

While the research study has shown that both Poles and Turks rate landscapes similarly, some differences can be elucidated. This confirms earlier studies, which suggested both similarities (e.g. Eysenck & Iwawaki,

1971) and differences (Macia, 1979, Buhyoff *et al.*, 1983) in landscape assessment among different cultures. Furthermore, vegetation is an important feature in landscape perception (Yang & Brown, 1992, Fyhri *et al.*, 2009). For instance, forests have also been found to be a favorite type of landscape for a holiday in Greece (Eleftheriadis *et al.*, 1990). This can be explained by an appreciation for atypical surroundings.

Certain limitations arise when using a landscape assessment method based on photographic images. The selection of photographs was one of the key challenges in this research study. The research conclusions can substantially depend on the appropriateness of the photographs selected. The selection of landscape types, photographic representations of each landscape, and the quality of the photographs can affect the study. Nevertheless, the photographs selected were deemed to be representative of certain landscapes and high quality from a technical perspective. Another problem is differences in the criteria adopted by the individuals rating the landscapes. Respondents were expected to rate the landscapes and not the technical quality of the photographs. However, respondents could still choose to rate the technical quality of each photograph without mentioning it explicitly. Furthermore, the information collected in this research study is just a small contribution to the analysis of cross-cultural landscape perception. The subject seems to be very interesting and needs to be explored in further studies. This paper presents preliminary results and provides some thoughts for future research.

A basic implication of this type of research concerns the choice of marketing strategy for the tourist industry. A good understanding of landscape preferences helps in the preparation of an effective tourist offering for different cultural groups. In order to advertise Poland in Turkey, forest landscapes in Poland need to be emphasized in tourist brochures. On the other hand, the advertising of Turkey in Poland should concentrate on high mountain landscapes. This assumes that water-based attractions such as rivers and lakes do not need any special advertising in light of previous research results (Zube *et al.*, 1982; Kent & Elliot, 1995). Finally, the use of photographs in this type of research is consistent with the way most advertising agencies promote tourists attractions.

Acknowledgement

The authors wish to thank Mr. Marcin Cekiera (Pedagogical University of Cracow, Poland) for his help in conducting interviews with respondents in Turkey and Dr. Suleyman Incekara (Fatih University, Istanbul, Turkey) for his helpful review of the questionnaire used in the research study.

References

Alsayyad, N. (2001). *Consuming Tradition, Manufacturing Heritage: Global Norms and Urban Forms in the Age of Tourism.* London: Routledge.

Appleton, J. (1994). Running before we can walk: Are we ready to map "beauty"? *Landscape Research*, 19(3), 112-119.

Becker, C., & Murrman, S.K. (2000). Methodological considerations in multicultural research. *Tourism Analysis*, 5, 29-36.

Brabyn, L. (1996). Landscape classification using GIS and national digital databases, *Landscape Research*, 21(3), 277-299.

—. (2009). Classifying landscape character. *Landscape Research*, 34(3), 299-321.

Brown, T.C., & Daniel, T.C. (1991). Landscape aesthetics of riparian environments: relationship of flow quantity to scenic quality along a wild and scenic river. *Water Resources Research*, 27, 1787-1795.

Brunetta, G., & Voghera, A. (2008). Evaluating landscape for shared values: Tools, principles, and methods. *Landscape Research*, 33(1), 71-87.

Buhyoff, G.J., Wellman, D.J., Koch, J.E., Gauthier, L., & Hultman, S. (1983). Landscape preference metrics: An international comparison. *Journal of Environmental Management*, 16, 181-190.

Conzen, M.P. (1990). *The Making of the American landscape*, London: Routledge.

Daniel, T.C., & Meitner, M.M. (2001). Representational validity of landscape visualizations: the effects of graphical realism on perceived scenic beauty of forest vistas. *Journal of Environmental Psychology*, 21, 61-72.

Dewar, K., Mei Li, W., & Davis, C.H. (2007). Photographic images, culture, and perception in tourism advertising: A Q methodology study of Canadian and Chinese university students. *Journal of Travel & Tourism Marketing*, 22(2), 35-44.

Eleftheriadis, N., Tsalikidis, I., & Manos, B. (1990). Coastal preference evaluation: Comparison among tourists in Greece. *Environmental Management*, 14(4), 475-487.

Emmelin, L. (1996). Landscape impact analysis: A systematic approach to landscape impacts policy. *Landscape Research*, 21(1), 13-35.

EU (2000). *The European Landscape Convention.* The European Union, Council of Europe Treaty Series no. 176.

Eysenck, H.J., & Iwawaki, S. (1971). Cultural relativity in aesthetic judgement: An empirical study. *Perceptual and Motors Skill,* 32, 817-818.

Fairweather, J.R., & Swaffield, S.R. (2001). Visitor experiences of Kaikoura, New Zealand: An interpretative study using photographs of landscapes and Q method. *Tourism Management,* 22, 219-228.

Fyhri, A., Jacobsen, J.K.S., & Tømmervik, H. (2009). Tourists' landscape perceptions and preferences in a Scandinavian coastal region. *Landscape and Urban Planning,* 91, 202-211.

Jacobsen, J.K.S. (1997). Transience and place: exploring tourists' experience of place. *Nordlit,* 1, 23-45.

—. (2001). Nomadic tourism and fleeting place encounters: Exploring different aspects of sightseeing. *Scandinavian Journal of Hospitality and Tourism,* 1, 99-112.

—. (2007). Use of landscape perception methods in tourism studies: A review of photo-based research approaches. *Tourism Geographies,* 9(3), 234-253.

Kaplan, R., & Herbert, E.J. (1987). Cultural and sub-cultural comparisons in preferences for natural settings. *Landscape and Urban Planning,* 14, 281-293.

Kent, R.L., & Elliot, C.L. (1995). Scenic routes linking and protecting natural and cultural landscape features: A greenway skeleton. *Landscape and Urban Planning,* 33, 341-355.

Macia, A. (1979). Visual perception of landscape: Sex and personality differences. Proceedings of "Our National Landscape". *USDA Forest Service GNR,* PSW-35, 279-286.

Middleton, V.T.C., & Hawkins, R. (1998). *Sustainable Tourism: A Marketing Perspective.* Oxford: Butterworth-Heinemann.

Muir, R. (1999). *Approaches to Landscape.* London: Macmillan.

Mücher, C.A., Klijn, J.A., Wascher, D.M., & Schaminée, J.H.J. (2010). A new European Landscape Classification (LANMAP): A transparent, flexible and user-oriented methodology to distinguish landscapes. *Ecological Indicators,* 10, 87-103.

Paraskevopoulos, S., & Papadopoulos, I. (2009). Exploring students' perceptions about landscapes. *The International Journal of Learning,* 16(5), 561-575.

Scott, A. (2002). Assessing public perception of landscape: The LANDMAP experience. *Landscape Research,* 27(3), 271-295.

Yang, B-E., & Brown, T.J. (1992). A cross-cultural comparison of preferences for landscape styles and landscape elements. *Environment and Behavior,* 24(4), 471-507.

Yang, B-E., & Kaplan, R. (1990). The perception of landscape style: A cross-cultural comparison. *Landscape and Urban Planning*, 19, 251-262.

Zube, E.H., Sell, J.L., & Taylor, J.G. (1982). Landscape perception: Research, application and theory. *Landscape Research*, 9, 1-33.

CHAPTER EIGHT

CRUISE TOURISM DEVELOPMENT: A COMMUNITY PERSPECTIVE

GIACOMO DEL CHIAPPA, MARTA MELEDDU AND MANUELA PULINA

Abstract

This chapter analyses residents' perceptions toward the impacts produced by the cruise activity in Olbia, a port of call on the island of Sardinia (Italy). The study uses a sample of 947 residents living at different distances from the port and in different areas of the city. By applying a correspondence analysis and an analysis of variance/ multivariate analysis of variance, findings reveal that residents are concerned about the negative social and environmental impacts produced by cruise activity. Furthermore, they highlight that significant differences based on socio-demographic characteristics exist in residents' perceptions and attitudes towards cruise tourism development. Implications for policymakers are discussed and suggestions for further research are given.
Keywords: Cruise tourism, community-based tourism, tourism development.

1. Introduction

In the last two decades the cruise industry has been experiencing significant expansion (Chin, 2008). It constitutes a significant part of international worldwide tourism, corresponding to 1.6% of total tourists and 1.9% of the total number of nights (Brida & Zapata-Aguirre, 2010). This growth is expected to continue into the future. In the period 2010–2014, 29 new cruise vessels are predicted, providing 850,900 new beds, with a total investment of €13,800,000,000 (Wild, 2010). Based on data of members of Cruise Lines International Association (hereafter CLIA) cruise tourism in the Mediterranean area represents 12% of the overall cruise market (CLIA, 2008) with Italy the second top destination in this market, after Spain (Risposte Turismo, 2010). According to Risposte Turismo (2012), in 2011 the number of cruise passengers in Italy was 11,463 million, with a growth of 18.9% with respect to the previous year.

So far, several papers have discussed costs and benefits of this economic activity on destinations, categorizing its impacts in three main areas: economic, environmental and socio-cultural effects (Brida, Del Chiappa, Meleddu, & Pulina, 2012a, 2012b; Brida & Zapata, 2010; Dwyer & Forsyth, 1998; Klein, 2010). There are also some published papers that aim to analyze residents' perceptions of cruise tourism development (Brida et al., 2012a, 2012b; Brida, Riaño, & Zapata-Aguirre, 2011; Del Chiappa & Abbate, 2012; Diedrich, 2010; Gatewood & Cameron, 2009; Hritz & Cecil, 2008; Hull & Milne, 2010; Marušić, Horak, & Tomljenović, 2008). However, it could be argued that knowledge on this topic for the Mediterranean area still needs to be further expanded.

This chapter aims to explore more deeply this area of research by discussing findings of an empirical investigation on a sample of 947 residents living in Olbia, a port of call and cruise tourism destination on the island of Sardinia, Italy. In particular, to establish residents' perceptions and attitudes towards cruise activity, a statistical investigation is run, via a correspondence analysis and a MANOVA exercise.

This chapter is structured as follows. In the next section, a literature review is provided. In the third section, the methodology and research design that is used is highlighted. The fourth section presents the main findings from the statistical investigation. Concluding remarks are given in the last section, where directions for future research and managerial implications for destination marketers and policymakers are outlined.

2. Literature Review

Host communities' perceptions of the impact of tourism have been the object of research in the past three decades, and several models have been developed to understand residents' perceptions and attitudes towards tourism development.

In sustainable tourism, local communities play an important dual role. Residents are expected to be an integral part of the tourism product (Simmons, 1994): "the industry uses the community as a resource, sells it as a product, and in the process affects the lives of everyone" (Murphy, 1985, p. 165). The local community is one of the principle stakeholders as it is the one most closely affected by the positive and negative impacts that tourism development can produce economically, environmentally and socio-culturally (Madrigal, 1995; Perdue, Long, & Allen, 1990).

This means that the perceptions of the local community and its attitude towards the impact of any proposed tourism development model should be taken into account when planning the future of any tourism destination (Del Chiappa, 2012; Mowforth & Munt, 2003). This is something that should be done over time. According to Doxey's index of irritation, as tourist development proceeds, the relationship between the local community and tourists goes from euphoria to apathy, annoyance and, finally, antagonism (Doxey, 1976). Similarly, according to the tourist area life cycle, a correlation between residents' perceptions/attitudes and the tourism life cycle phase does exist. Initially, residents may have a positive attitude towards their guests, but as their number increases, the local community starts to be concerned about the impacts of tourism.

In proposing a further, complementary model to that of the life cycle (Butler, 1980), Weaver (2000) highlights the need to regulate the use of tourism resources to modify tourist flows and defined four types of tourism destinations; that is, circumstantial alternative tourism, deliberate alternative tourism, unsustainable mass tourism, and sustainable mass tourism (SMT) destinations are distinguished by a high intensity of tourism development that does not exceed the local carrying capacity. Setting sustainable mass tourism as the desired outcome for most destinations, Weaver (2012) defines three convergent developmental trajectories which can be initially dominated by considerations of growth (organic), regulation (incremental), or both (induced), and discussed the dynamics of the local community for each of them. In the induced path, the local community is displaced and has to be reinvented with a new and larger population. In the organic path, the integrity of the community is eroded, thus requiring a reinvigoration in the rejuvenation stage. Finally, in the incremental path local residents are empowered and then reinforced through continual adaptation for additional growth.

However, it should be highlighted that, when planning the future development of tourism, policymakers should not act only on the basis of residents' perceptions. On the contrary, they should also closely evaluate the overall and objective costs and benefits that cruise activity generates, such as the number of residents who are involved in the cruise sector, the many economic impacts (direct, indirect and induced) associated with different types of cruise-related expenditures (passengers and crew-related expenditure, vessel-related and supporting expenditure) and the amount of financial resources that were and still need to be invested in developing infrastructures supporting the cruise development.

Factors affecting residents' attitude towards tourism can be categorized into extrinsic and intrinsic factors, where the former refers to the characteristics of the destination, while the latter refers to characteristics of the host community (Faulkner & Tideswell, 1997).

Researchers commonly consider the following main extrinsic factors, among others: the degree or stage of tourism development (Doxey, 1976; Gursoy & Rutherford, 2004), the level of economic activity in the host area (Johnson, Snepenger, & Akis, 1994) and the degree of tourism seasonality (Fredline & Faulkner, 2000).

Among the intrinsic factors, the following are commonly considered: the perceived balance between positive and negative impacts (Dyer, Gursoy, Sharma, & Carter, 2007), geographical proximity to concentrations of activity (Fredline & Faulkner, 2000), their rural, urban or coastal area of residence (Nunkoo & Ramkissoon, 2010), length of residency (Gu & Ryan, 2008), degree of tourism concentration (Pizam, 1978), level of contact with tourists, economic reliance and dependence on tourism (Ap, 1992) and socio-demographic characteristics of residents (Belisle & Hoy, 1980).

In the literature, only a few contributions aim to study residents' attitudes and perceptions towards cruise tourism (Brida et al., 2011; Diedrich, 2010; Hritz & Cecil, 2008; Marušić et al., 2008).

Prior research shows that not all communities tend to welcome cruise ships, as in the case of Victoria, British Columbia (Scarfe, 2011). Hritz and Cecil (2008), in their exploratory qualitative analysis in Key West (Florida), reported local stakeholders being concerned about the threat that cruise tourism can produce for the island's calmness and preservation. Brida et al. (2011) report how residents in Cartagena de Indias (Colombia) thought that the positive effects of cruise tourism development outweighed the negative impacts. Marušić et al. (2008) in their study on Dubrovnik (Croatia) show residents feeling the adverse impact of cruisers because of the almost immediate congestion their land visits created. Brida et al. (2012a) report residents in the city of Messina feeling moderately concerned about the negative impact that cruise tourism may exert on their wellbeing, increased congestion, crime and the environment in terms of pollution, waste and congestion in recreational areas. At the same time, further developments of the cruise tourism market in Messina appeared to be most wanted by residents whose income depended on the cruise sector, middle-aged people, highly educated, living close to the tourism area, residing in Messina for less than five years and interacting intensively with tourists (Del Chiappa & Abbate, 2012).

Recently, studies on residents' perceptions and attitudes started to compare cruise tourism with other types of tourism. For example, Del Chiappa and Abbate (2012) show that the local community in Messina would rather favour the development of historic/cultural tourism, followed by "sea, sun and sand" tourism, cruise tourism and sport tourism. Employing probabilistic modeling, Pulina, Meleddu and Del Chiappa (2013), show that the local community in Olbia preferred to invest at a high/very high level in the well-established "sea and sun" tourism activity. Finally, Brida *et al.* (2012a) show that no significant differences exist in terms of residents' perceptions of externalities in Messina (Sicily island, Italy) and Olbia despite the fact that these destinations are experiencing a different stage of their life cycle, thus providing some evidence of a lack of correlation between residents' perceptions and the tourism life cycle phases as suggested by prior theory.

3. Methodology

The site researched for this study is Olbia, a port of call cruise destination in the north-east of Sardinia, Italy. According to Risposte Turismo (2012), the number of cruise passengers calling at Olbia increased from 42,437 in 2001 to 141,632 in 2011, thus making Olbia the fourteenth cruise tourism destination in Italy. Based on these figures, we can state that Olbia is still in its early stage of cruise tourism development. Hence it seems of interest to analyse how residents perceive this economic activity.

To this aim, a questionnaire was constructed that included items selected on the basis of some pillar research in the field of community-based tourism (e.g. Dyer *et al.*, 2007; Gursoy & Rutherford, 2004; Perdue *et al.*, 1990) and also on research that investigated residents' perceptions and attitudes towards cruise tourism development (Brida *et al.*, 2011, 2012a, 2012b; Del Chiappa & Abbate, 2012).

The questionnaire was divided into two sections. While the first section focused on socio-demographic information, the second section listed 27 items related to residents' perceptions towards the economic, environmental and socio-cultural impact generated by cruise tourism development. Following several previous papers (e.g. Andereck, Valentine, Knopf, & Vogt, 2005; Brida *et al.,* 2011; Kibicho, 2008), a five-point Likert scale was used (1 = *completely disagree*; 5 = *completely agree*) to evaluate residents' responses.

An initial pilot test was conducted on a sample of 30 residents. This exercise was done to verify the validity of the questionnaire's content, to test respondents' understanding of the questions and the usefulness of the scale used to make the assessments. No relevant concerns were reported in the pilot tests.

Hence, the research involved data collection in Olbia during the summer peak of the cruise season in 2011. Based on the official data published by the Italian National Institute of Statistics (ISTAT) about the socio-demographic characteristics of Olbia's residents, respondents were selected with a quota random sampling procedure. The quotas were set on age (specifically, three classes were considered: 16–40, 41–65 and over 65) and gender, and covered cases characterized by heterogeneous demographics features.

The final sample size was determined according to a 95% confidence level with a 3% error. Therefore, to have a representative sample at a 2% level, 916 completed questionnaires were needed.

Data were collected through face-to-face interviews conducted by 10 trained interviewers directly supervised by the authors. Interviewers were also instructed on the streets and areas where to administrate the questionnaire. Only individuals older than 16 years old were allowed to take part in the survey. A total of 947 complete questionnaires were obtained, thus yielding a sample that is representative of the resident population in Olbia at a 2% level.

4. Results

Table 1 provides descriptive statistics, means and standard deviations of all the items used to assess the residents' perceptions.

Through a factor analysis run with categorical variables – that is, a correspondence analysis – the initial set of items was reduced to a more manageable group. The objective was to eliminate redundancy in the original data and reduce the attributes to a set of factors which combine the original attributes. The attributes with a loading score (i.e. variable contribution) lower than a set critical value (in this case 0.40) were excluded from the analysis (e.g. Hatcher, 1994).

Hence the initial 27 attributes were reduced to 18. The procedure eventually led to $n = 5$ factors, since factors with eingenvalues greater than one were retained, as the Kaiser criterion suggests. We calculated the relative weight of each factor in the total variance – that is, how much each factor explains of the total variance – while cumulative inertia shows the amount of variance explained by $n + (n + 1)$ factors (Escofier & Pages, 1988).

Table 1 – Descriptive Statistics

Cruise tourism impacts: items	Mean	Std
Increases public investment and infrastructure	3.13	1.221
Increases private investment and infrastructure	3.26	1.123
Increases job opportunities	3.33	1.234
Forces change in actual standard of life	2.23	1.249
Increases disposable income	2.95	1.150
Increases quality of life	2.97	1.113
Enhances cultural exchange	3.56	1.137
Increases the number of cultural/recreational activities	3.22	1.080
Values local tradition and authenticity	3.48	1.127
Enhances the quality of commercial facilities	3.40	1.143
Enhances safety standard in the destination	2.88	1.083
Enhances socio-cultural life for residents	3.12	1.110
Enhances environmental protection	2.88	1.168
Leads to infrastructure improvement	2.75	1.241
Leads to public services improvements	2.84	1.196
Leads to valorization of the historic patrimony	3.29	1.153
Leads to urban and rural gentrification	3.03	1.166
Increases costs of living for the local community	2.66	1.225
Produces benefits only for external entrepreneurs	3.27	1.198
Has a crowding-out effect on other relevant projects	2.63	1.151
Increases traffic and road accidents	2.44	1.185
Increases micro-crime	2.52	1.238
Tourists influence daily life	2.02	1.172
Deteriorates the eco-system	2.56	1.227
Increases environmental and marine pollution	2.86	1.261
Increases congestion in public and recreational areas	2.63	1.212
Increases waste	2.79	1.328

Table 2 shows that our five factors explain more than half (60.1%) of the total data variance). Cronbach's alpha was then applied as the most commonly used measure to test the reliability of the extracted factors. Values higher than 0.7 suggest reliability of the factors. However, the last two factors present a value of 0.65 and 0.52, respectively, indicating that their reliability is at least questionable and possibly poor. Yet since they are meaningful, these factors are retained in order to avoid the loss of the exploratory power of the identified factors (see also Kibicho, 2008).

To establish the adequacy of the correspondence analysis, two tests were conducted. Specifically, the Kaiser-Meyer-Olkin Measure of Sampling

Adequacy with values between 0.70 and 0.83 indicated the analysis was satisfactory (Kaiser, 1974); in this case the value is 0.90.

Table 2 – Items with the Highest Contribution to Each Factor

	Var. cont.	Explained inertia %	Accumulated inertia %	Cronbach's Alpha
Factor 1: Social positive impact		27.7	27.7	0.73
Valorization of local tradition and authenticity	0.70			
Enhancement cultural exchange	0.69			
Increase quality of life	0.65			
Factor 2: Socio-environmental negative impact		17.7	45.4	0.88
More inland and marine pollution	0.82			
Deterioration of the eco-system	0.80			
More waste	0.80			
More congestion in public and recreational areas	0.79			
More traffic and road accidents	0.75			
More micro-crime	0.71			
Factor 3: Welfare positive impact		5.5	50.9	0.85
Infrastructure improvement	0.79			
Public services improvements	0.78			
Rural and urban gentrification	0.74			
Conservation and valorization of the historical assets	0.66			
Factor 4: Economic negative impact		5.7	55.6	0.65
The benefits from cruise activity accrue to external entrepreneurs	0.75			
Higher cost of living for the local community	0.78			
Cruise development has a crowding-out effect on other relevant projects	0.42			
Factor 5: Economic positive impact		4.5	60.1	0.52
Cruise activity forces a change in actual standard of life	0.76			
Increase in disposable income	0.46			

In addition, Bartlett's Test of Sphericity (= 12,132.824; significance = 0.000) indicated that the null hypothesis (i.e. correlation matrix is an identity matrix) is rejected.

Looking first at the positive impacts of cruise tourism from a socio-cultural, economic and environmental perspective, three factors are obtained. The first factor (factor 1: social positive impact) includes items related to residents' positive perceptions of their heritage asset and the interaction with other cultures (i.e. valorization of local tradition and authenticity; enhancement of other cultural and communities knowledge; increase in residents' quality of life). The total data variance explained by this factor (27.7%) indicates that this is the predominant one. The second factor (factor 3: welfare positive impact) relates to items that are perceived as having the potential to improve services and infrastructure, leading to an overall increase in the welfare of the local community (i.e. infrastructure improvement [roads, communication, water pipes, etc.]; public services improvements; rural and urban gentrification; conservation and valorisation of the historical asset). The third factor (factor 5: economic positive impact) includes attributes related to economic effects (i.e. cruise activity forces a change in actual standard of life; increase in disposable income).

On the other hand, two factors relate to residents' negative perceptions on cruise activity. The first factor (factor 2: social and environment negative impact) contains items related to both social and environmental negative effects produced by cruise activity (i.e. more inland and marine pollution; deterioration of the eco-system [sand erosion, damages to flora and fauna]; more waste; more congestion in public and recreational areas; more traffic and road accidents; micro-crime increases). Overall, this factor presents attributes with the highest loadings within the range of 0.71 and 0.82. The second factor (factor 4: economic negative impact) consists of items related to perceived economic negative effects. Residents perceive that the benefits produced by cruise activity go to outsider firms and overall cruise development has crowding-out effects on other relevant projects with a consequent increase in their cost of living (i.e. the benefits from cruise activity go to external entrepreneurs; increased costs of living for the local community; cruise development has a crowding-out effect on other relevant projects).

After having established the main factors, the next step of the investigation consists of running a one-way univariate and multivariate analysis of variance (ANOVA/MANOVA) to evaluate the differences in respondents' perceptions of specific variables. MANOVA is used when there are two or more dependent variables under investigation and problems of autocorrelation may arise. In Tables 3–5, the ANOVA and MANOVA show that significant differences exist in respondents' perception and attitude towards cruise tourism based on residents' economic sector of activity/occupation, the distance of their home from the port and whether they had a cruise experience in the past. Considering Table 3, on the whole, respondents seem to believe that cruise tourism exerts relatively balanced positive and negative impacts, and for social impacts, in particular, we note that the mean is above three in all the cases.

Table 3 – ANOVA/MANOVA for Occupation Status

Factors ^	Means								ANOVA	
	O1	O2	O3	O4	O5	O6	O7	O8	F-stat	Prob.
Factor 1	3.31 [a]	3.25 [b]	3.38 [b]	3.40 [b]	3.18 [b]	3.38 [b]	3.14 [b]	3.39 [b]	238.58 [b]	0.00
Factor 2	2.63	2.60 [b]	2.73 [b]	2.79 [b]	2.83 [b]	3.14 [b]	2.76 [b]	2.76 [b]	94.45 [b]	0.00
Factor 3	2.70 [a]	3.10 [a]	3.10 [b]	3.07	2.90 [b]	3.08 [b]	2.95	3.13 [b]	63.28 [b]	0.00
Factor 4	2.87 [a]	3.27 [b]	3.14 [b]	2.88 [a]	3.02 [b]	3.18	3.38 [b]	3.14 [b]	113.49 [b]	0.00
Factor 5	2.36 [b]	2.30 [a]	2.52 [b]	2.67 [b]	2.99 [b]	2.52 [a]	2.45 [a]	2.47 [b]	283.22 [b]	0.00

Notes: ^ The MANOVA is run on attributes for all factors; MANOVA TESTS: Pillai's' Trace = 0.223, F-stat = 1.398 prob. = (0.001); Wilks' Lambda = 0.796, F-stat = 1.406 prob. = (0.001); Hotelling's Trace = 0.234, F-stat = 1.413 prob. = (0.001); Roy's Largest Root = 0.084, F-stat = 4.077 prob. = (0.000); ANOVA on items of each factor of relevance: [a] and [b] 5% and 1% level of significance.

Notes: O1 = primary sector; O2 = secondary sector; O3 = Tertiary sector; O4 = tourism sector; O5 = students; O6 = retired; O7 = Unemployed; O8 = Other (e.g. housekeeper).

Specifically, respondents belonging to the tourism sector (O = 4) believe that cruise activity can enhance improvement in social interactions and in their overall quality of life (i.e. valorization of local tradition and authenticity; enhancement of other cultures and communities knowledge; increase resident's quality of life).

Overall, residents who are retired (O = 6) view the cruise activity as having a negative impact from a social and environmental perspective (with the highest mean 3.14). However, on balance, they perceive cruise activity as exerting positive effects more than negative ones. From an economic perspective, unemployed (O = 7) residents believe that cruise activity does not have a positive outcome on the local economy; nevertheless, they also think that this activity yields a social positive impact.

Table 4 presents residents' perspectives related to how far they live from the port. Overall, respondents who are further away from the port think that the cruise activity is able to exert higher positive impacts in terms of welfare and economics. Also, these residents are more aware of the negative social and environmental impact on the territory (mean 3.20).

Table 4 – ANOVA/MANOVA for Distance of Residence from the Port

| Factors^ | Mean | | | | | | | ANOVA | |
	Km_0–1	Km_2	Km_3	Km_4	Km_5	Km_6_10	Km>10	F-stat	Prob.
Factor 1	3.17[b]	3.33[b]	3.30[b]	3.35[b]	3.24[b]	2.96[b]	3.17[b]	244.90[b]	0.00
Factor 2	2.68[b]	2.72[b]	2.72[b]	2.74[b]	2.67[b]	2.97[b]	3.20[a]	98.24[b]	0.00
Factor 3	2.95[b]	3.00[b]	3.14[b]	3.03[b]	3.08[b]	3.10[b]	3.96[a]	70.61[b]	0.00
Factor 4	3.67[b]	3.12[b]	3.11[b]	3.07[a]	3.12[b]	3.06[b]	3.14	109.92[b]	0.00
Factor 5	2.44[b]	2.53[b]	2.50[b]	2.40[b]	2.43v	2.56[b]	3.46	294.19[b]	0.00

Notes: ^ The MANOVA is run on attributes for all factors, for each variable of interest; MANOVA TESTS: Pillai's' Trace = 0.492, F-stat = 1.231 prob. = (0.002) Wilks' Lambda = 0.604, F-stat = 1.234 prob. = (0.002); Hotelling's Trace = 0.518, F-stat = 1.234 prob. = (0.002); Roy's Largest Root = 0.097, F-stat = 4.240 prob. = (0.000); ANOVA on items of each factor of relevance: [a] and [b] significant at 5% and 1% level

Notes: KM_0–1 = between 0 and 1km from the port; KM_2 = 2km from the port; KM_3 = 3km; KM_4 = 4km; KM_5 = 5km; KM_6 = between 6 and 10km; KM_>10 = higher than 10km.

Interestingly, residents who live nearer to the harbour perceive less economic benefit from cruise activity, since they believe that profits are more likely to stay with external firms and they have to face a higher cost of life.

Finally, it may be interesting to understand whether residents who have taken a cruise trip in the past have a different perception than those who never have (see Table 5). Except for the social and environmental effects, respondents who took a cruise trip have a higher perception of the positive impacts produced within the local community.

Besides, they are relatively more aware of the negative impacts from an economic perspective (mean 3.23).

Table 5 – ANOVA/MANOVA for Cruise Esperience

FACTORS ^	Means		ANOVA (for croc)	
	Croc = 0	Croc = 1	F-stat	Prob.
Factor 1	2.88 [b]	3.29 [b]	244.90 [b]	0.00
Factor 2	3.34 [b]	2.77 [b]	98.24 [b]	0.00
Factor 3	2.77 [b]	3.10 [b]	70.61 [b]	0.00
Factor 4	3.10 [b]	3.23 [b]	109.92 [b]	0.00
Factor 5	2.43 [b]	2.70 [b]	294.19 [b]	0.00

Notes: ^ The MANOVA is run on attributes for all factors; MANOVA TESTS: Pillai's' Trace = 0.051, F-stat = 2.557 prob. = (0.000); Wilks' Lambda = 0.9349, F-stat = 2.557 prob. = (0.000); Hotelling's Trace = 0.053, F-stat = 2.557 prob. = (0.000); Roy's Largest Root = 0.053, F-stat = 2.557 prob. = (0.000); ANOVA on items of each factor of relevance: [b] 1% level of significance.

Notes: Croc = 0 residents who did not go on a cruise; Croc = 1 residents who went on a cruise.

5. Conclusion

The aim of this chapter was to investigate residents' perceptions towards the development of cruise tourism within the city of Olbia, a cruise port of call on the island of Sardinia (Italy). The findings reveal that residents in Olbia are particularly concerned by the negative impact produced by cruise activity both in terms of social and environmental impacts. However, they also feel that this economic activity is able to exert positive effects, especially in terms of social interactions and the overall welfare of the local community. Furthermore, they highlight that residents' perceptions towards the impacts of cruise tourism do change based on sector of activity/employment, geographical proximity to port area, and prior experience in cruising when having holiday.

These empirical findings are relevant for researchers, destination managers, policymakers and cruise operators/companies. From a theoretical perspective, the study adds to the growing literature in the field of residents' perceptions towards cruise tourism development. In an effort to increase the favourableness of residents' attitudes towards tourism, findings make policymakers, destination managers and cruise companies aware of the necessity to analyze the different expectations/perceptions of local stakeholders and then run internal marketing/communication activities delivering messages which focus on the positive balance between the potential positive and negative impacts of cruise tourism (Perdue et al., 1990). This is needed because residents cannot be expected to be fully cognizant of the impacts arising from cruise tourism development and/or they could evaluate these impacts more negatively. Accordingly, with social exchange theory (Ap, 1992), if residents perceive that cruise tourism is bringing more benefits than costs they would support its development. Further, the findings underline the importance of involving the local community in tourism planning and monitoring how residents' perceptions of cruise tourism change over time as tourism develops.

Although these findings contribute to investigate a somewhat neglected area in tourism research, the study does have some limitations. In particular, although interviewers were instructed to administrate interviews in the different areas/neighbourhoods of the city, a convenience sample was employed instead of an "area sample" that is considered as more advisable. Further research is still needed first to verify if findings can be generalized and/or if they change according to the extrinsic factors of the tourism destination chosen as the research site (e.g. the degree or stage of tourism development, the level of economic activity in the host area, the seasonality of tourism). Second, further research is needed to investigate the role that other intrinsic variables (e.g. community involvement, community attachment) can exert in discriminating residents' perceptions and attitudes towards cruise tourism development. Finally, future research should aim to monitor whether and how residents' preferences and perceptions change over time along with each stage of the cruise tourism life cycle, as well as after particular critical events. In addition, policy decisions concerning a further cruise tourism development in the area should be carefully analyzed in a community perspective.

References

Andereck, K.L., Valentine, K.M., Knopf, R.C., & Vogt, C.A. (2005). Residents' perceptions of community tourism impacts. *Annals of Tourism Research*, *32*(4), 1056–1076.

Ap, J. (1992). Residents' perceptions on tourism impacts. *Annals of Tourism Research*, *19*(4), 665–690.

Belisle, F.J., & Hoy, D.R. (1980). The perceived impact of tourism by residents: A case study in Santa Maria, Columbia. *Annals of Tourism Research*, *12*(1), 83–101.

Brida, J.G, Del Chiappa, G., Meleddu, M., & Pulina, M. (2012b). A comparison of residents' perceptions in two cruise ports in the Mediterranean. *International Journal of Tourism Research*, DOI: 10.1002/jtr.1915.

—. (2012a). The perceptions of an island community towards cruise tourism: A factor analysis. *Tourism: An International Inderdisciplinary Journal*, *60*(1) 29–42.

Brida, J.G., Riaño, E., & Zapata-Aguirre, S. (2011). Resident's attitudes and perceptions towards cruise tourism development: A case study of Cartage de Indias (Colombia). *Tourism and Hospitality Research* *11*(3), 187–202.

Brida, J.G., & Zapata-Aguirre, S. (2010). Cruise tourism: Economic, socio-cultural and environmental impacts. *International Journal of Leisure and Tourism Marketing*, *1*(3), 205–226.

Butler, R.W. (1980). The concept of a tourism area cycle of evolution: Implications for management resources. *The Canadian Geographer*, *24*(1), 5–16.

Chin, C.B.N. (2008). *Cruising in the Global Economy: Profits, Pleasure and Work at Sea*. Aldershot: Ashgate.

Cruise Lines International Association (CLIA). (2008). *Cruise market overview: Statistical cruise industry data through 2007*. Retrieved September 20, 2012, from http://www.cruising.org/press/overview2008/printPDF.cfm.

Del Chiappa, G. (2012). *Community integration: A case study of Costa Smeralda, Italy*. In E. Fayos-solà (Eds), *Knowledgment Management in Tourism: Policyy and Governance Applications* (Bridging Tourism Theory and Practice, Volume 4, pp. 243-263). Bingley: Emerald.

Del Chiappa, G., & Abbate, T. (2012). Residents' perceptions and attitudes toward the cruise tourism development: Insights from an Italian tourism destination. In J.C. Andreani and U. Collesei (Eds.), *Proceedings of the XXII international conference marketing trends*. Paris, France, and Venice, Italy: Marketing Trends Association.

Diedrich, A. (2010). Cruise ship tourism in Belize: The implications of developing cruise ship tourism in an ecotourism destination. *Ocean & Coastal Management*, *53*, 234–244.

Doxey, G. (1976). When enough's enough: The natives are restless in old Niagara. *Heritage Canada*, *2*, 26–27.

Dwyer, L., & Forsyth, P. (1998). Economic significance of cruise tourism. *Annals of Tourism Research*, *25*(2), 393–415.

Dyer, P., Gursoy, D., Sharma, B., & Carter, J. (2007). Structural modelling of resident perceptions of tourism and associated development on the Sunshine Coast, Australia. *Tourism Management*, *28*(2), 409–422.

Escofier, B., & Pages, J. (1988). *Analyses factorielles simples et multiples* [Single and multiple factor analysis]. Paris: Dunod.

Faulkner, B., & Tideswell, C. (1997). A framework for monitoring community impacts of tourism. *Journal of Sustainable Tourism, 5*(1), 3–28.

Fredline, E., & Faulkner, B. (2000). Host community reactions: A cluster analysis. *Annals of Tourism Research, 27*(3), 763–784.

Gatewood, J.B., & Cameron, C.M. (2009). *Belonger perceptions of tourism and its impacts in the Turks and Calcos Islands. Research project report.* Retrieved September 16, 2012, from http://www.lehigh.edu/~jbg1/Perceptions-of-Tourism.pdf

Gu, H., & Ryan, C. (2008). Place attachment, identity and community impacts of tourism – the case of Beijing Hutong. *Tourism Management, 29*(4), 637–647.

Gursoy, D., & Rutherford, D. (2004). Host attitudes toward tourism. An improved structural model. *Annals of Tourism Research, 31*(3), 495–516.

Hatcher, L. (1994). *A Step-by-Step Approach to Using the SAS System for Factor Analysis and Structural Equation Modelling.* Cary, NC: SAS Institute.

Hritz, N., & Cecil, A. (2008). Investigating the sustainability of cruise tourism: A case study of Key West. *Journal of Sustainable Tourism, 16*(2), 168–181.

Hull, J.S., & Milne, S. (2010). Readiness planning in the arctic: Building community support. In M. Luck, P.T. Maher, & E. Steward (Eds.), *Cruise Tourism in Polar Regions: Promoting Environmental and Social Sustainability* (pp. 180-204). London: Earthscan.

Johnson, J.D., Snepenger, D.J., & Akis, S. (1994). Residents' perceptions of tourism development. *Annals of Tourism Research, 21*(3), 629–642.

Kaiser, H.F. (1974) An index of factorial simplicity. *Psychometrika, 39*, 31–36.

Kibicho, W. (2008). Community-based tourism: A factor-cluster segmentation approach. *Journal of Sustainable Tourism, 16*(2), 211–221.

Klein, R.A. (2010). Cruises and bruises: Safety, security and social issues on polar cruises. In M. Luck, P.T. Maher, & E. Steward (Eds.), *Cruise Tourism in Polar Regions: Promoting Environmental and Social Sustainability* (pp. 57-74). London: Earthscan.

Madrigal, R. (1995). Resident's perceptions and the role of government. *Annals of Tourism Research, 22*(1), 86–102.

Marušić, Z., Horak, S., & Tomljenović, R. (2008). The socio-economic impacts of cruise tourism: A case study of Croatian destinations. *Tourism in Marine Environments, 5*(2–3), 131–144.

Mowforth, M., & Munt, I. (2003). *Tourism and sustainability: Development and new tourism in the third world* (2nd ed.). London: Routledge.

Murphy, P.E. (1985). *Tourism: A community Approach.* NY: Methuen.

Nunkoo, R., & Ramkissoon, H. (2010). Sall island urban tourism: A residents' perspective. *Current Issues in Tourism, 13*(1), 37–60.

Perdue, R.R., Long, P.T., & Allen L. (1990). Resident support for tourism development. *Annals of Tourism Research, 17*(4), 586–599.

Pizam, A. (1978). Tourism's impacts: The social costs to the destination community as perceived by its residents. *Journal of Travel Research, 16*(4), 8–12.

Pulina, M., Meleddu, M., & Del Chiappa, G. (2013). Residents' choice probability and tourism development. *Tourism Management Perspectives, 5,* 57-67.

Risposte Turismo. (2010). *Il traffico crocieristico in Italia nel 2010.* Retrieved May 20, 2012, from http://www.risposteturismo.it/riviste.php?pag=4#

—. (2012). *Il traffico crocieristico in Italia nel 2011.* Osservatorio Nazionale del Turismo. Retrieved September 20, 2012 from http://www.risposteturismo.it/.

Scarfe, B. (2011). *Costs and benefits of cruise ship tourism in Victoria.* James Bay Neighbourhood Association. Retrieved September 20, 2012, from http://www.jbna.org.

Simmons, D.G. (1994). Community participation in tourism planning. *Tourism Management, 15*(2), 98–108.

Weaver, D. (2000). A broad context model of destination development scenarios. *Tourism Management, 21*(3), 217–224.

—. (2012). Organic, incremental and induced paths to sustainable mass tourism convergence. *Tourism Management, 33*(5), 1030–1037.

Wild, D. (2010). *Cruise Statistics.* G.P. Wild (International) Limited/BREA.

CHAPTER NINE

JEWELRY RETAIL AND TOURISM: A RELATION OF UNRELATED VARIETY

HILAL ERKUS-OZTURK AND PIETER TERHORST

Abstract

In this paper, we examine how tourism in Amsterdam and Antalya has become intertwined with two specific cultural-product industries, namely diamond retail in the former and golden jewelry retail in the latter. For a long time, the development trajectories of jewelry trade and tourism had nothing to do with each other but over the last forty years or so they have become ever more interwoven. The theoretical point we want to make in this paper is that tourism in both cities has become more diversified through unrelated variety. Tourism and jewelry trade that were formerly disconnected have come to generate to generate spill-overs to each other. As a result, due to tourism both cities have grown out to important trading centres of jewelry that, in their turn, have made both cities more attractive to tourists. Although the mechanism of diversification is the same, the trajectories of both trading centres, including their locational development, have been quite different. Due to its tour-operator dominated tourism, Antalya's jewelry trade has been decentralised while Amsterdam's diamond trade has remained concentrated in the historic core. **Key words:** Jewelry trade, diversification, unrelated variety.

1. Introduction

There is no doubt that tourism is a driver of urban economic growth. The more tourists visit a city and the more money they spend, the more goods and services are produced and the more investments in buildings, infrastructure and many other things are made. What extra goods and services precisely are produced due to the extra expenditures of tourists?

Tourism researchers often stress that tourism does not fit the usual profile describing an industry or recognizable industrial sector such as steel, automobiles or insurance. In tourism no single product is produced but rather a wide range of products and services that interact to provide an opportunity to fulfil a tourist experience that comprises both tangible parts (e.g. hotel, restaurant, or air carrier) and intangible parts (e.g. sunset, scenery, mood). It is precisely because tourism is a multi-product and multi-services industry that the sector is difficult to define. No wonder that there is a lot of debate on how to define tourism, i.e. what industries should be included (Debbage & Ioannides, 1997; Judd, 2006; Shaw & Williams, 2004). But in these debates, it is almost always forgotten that tourism should not be defined in static but in dynamic terms. The growth of tourism generates a diversification of the economy as a result of which more industries that were originally disconnected from tourism have become interwoven with and, therefore, have become part of the tourism industry.

In this chapter, we examine how tourism has become intertwined with two specific cultural-product industries in two cities, namely diamond retail in Amsterdam and golden jewelry retail in Antalya. Up to now both industries have hardly been subjected to any detailed analysis (Da Silva, 2007). For a long time, the development trajectories of jewelry trade and tourism were fully disconnected from each other but over the last decades they have become ever more interwoven. Due to tourism, both cities have grown out to important trading centres of jewelry that, in their turn, have made both cities a more attractive tourist destination. Formulated in somewhat more theoretical terms, the development paths of both industries in both cities that originally had nothing to do with each other, have become intertwined by generating spill-overs to each other. As a result, tourism in both cities has become more diversified through unrelated variety (on which more later).

Although the mechanism of diversification is the same, the trajectories of both trading centres, including their locational development, have been quite different. In the late 19th and early 20th century, Amsterdam was one of the leading centres of diamond cutting, polishing and trade in the world but has ever since then been in decline until the growth of tourism has revitalized diamond trade. The buildings of the former diamond-cutting firms in and near the historic core have been transformed into exposition- and retail centres that attract a lot of tourists. Due to tourism, Antalya has grown out to the second largest jewelry centre of Turkey but because of its specific form of (mass) tourism, jewelry retail has become ever more decentralized to peripheral locations. By comparing the different trajectories of jewelry trade of Amsterdam and Antalya we will have a better grip on the mechanisms of how jewelry retail has become intertwined with tourism. Our cases are mainly based on secondary data. To get additional information, primary data were also collected by doing some interviews with representatives of the Jewelry Associations and some Tourism Area Investor's Associations in Antalya.

2. Economic Specialisation and Diversification, Related and Unrelated Variety

In economic geography there is on-going debate whether, in the long run, cities are better off with economic specialisation or diversification (Van der Panne, 2006). Cities are better off with economic specialisation, it is argued, because they can take advantage of internal economies of scale and localisation economies. By the latter is meant that firms in the *same* and related industries profit from spatial clustering due to a specialised local labour market, the local availability of suppliers of specialised inputs and (semi-) public goods that can only be used by the same and related industries, bonding social capital (strong ties between actors in the same industry) and local circulation of tacit knowledge. However, specialisation makes cities vulnerable to maturing industrial life cycles, external shocks, and processes of lock-in resulting in declining innovation and economic stagnation.

By contrast, Jane Jacobs (1967) and her followers have argued that cities are better off with economic diversification because they are better proof to industry-specific shocks. And, more importantly in the context of this paper, firms in *different* industries take advantage of so-called urbanization economies, i.e. a variety of positive externalities, the availability of (semi-) public goods that can be used by different industries, a pool of specialised workers whose skills can be used in different industries, knowledge spill-overs between firms in different industries and bridging social capital (weak ties between actors in different industries) that all stimulate innovation, economic diversification and prevent processes of lock-in. But do *all* spatially clustered firms belonging to different industries benefit from knowledge spill-overs and generate more economic diversification? Frenken *et al.* (2007) and Boschma & Iammarino (2009) argue that it happens more likely between firms in different industries with a low cognitive distance. For instance, Max Factor began to make hot-proof make-up in the 1920s after having seen that the make-up of actresses in the Hollywood film industry dripped of their faces due to heat of the lamps in the studios. The film industry and the make-up industry were in a relation of *related variety*. If knowledge spill-overs and economic diversification are generated between firms in different industries that do *not* share complementary competences (their cognitive distance is high) they speak of a relation of *unrelated variety*. As will be argued below, tourism and jewelry retail in Amsterdam and Antalya are in a relation of unrelated variety.

3. Tourism, Cultural Industries and Conspicuous Consumption

Over the last three decades, capitalism has taken the form of *cognitive-cultural* capitalism (Scott, 2007) that has radically changed the form of urbanization. Cognitive-cultural capitalism is, among many other things, characterised by new leading sectors such as business services, cultural industries and neo-artisanal production, and the current form of urbanization is featured by gentrification, a growing importance of clusters of cultural industries, an upgrading of inner cities, and a rise of new spaces of consumption, boosted up by the growth of urban tourism. In the literature there is some discussion to what extent these processes are predominantly limited to inner cities or that they simultaneously taking place in more peripheral locations. Newman & Smith (2000) and Hutton (2004) stress the importance of cultural production and creative industries in inner cities. Scott (2000b), Nachum & Keeble (2003), and Gornostaeva (2008), on the other hand, pay more attention to the benefits of moving towards the periphery or to sub-centres because of the problematic nature of city centres or the attractiveness of peripheral locations.

Cultural industries are industries that produce goods and services with a high aesthetic and symbolic value (Scott, 2004). It's beyond doubt that the aesthetic and symbolic value of jewels very high. By wearing expensive, high-quality jewels women (and, to a much lesser extent, men) show their class position and, in doing so, distinguish themselves from other classes. Bourdieu (1984) argues, on the basis of empirical research, that classes distinguish themselves not simply by a single item but by a set of items that form a coherent whole. The new riches (nouveaux riches) in the Netherlands, for instance, show their jewels much more conspicuously than the old riches and simultaneously distinguish themselves by their style of clothing, cars, furniture, and body aesthetics too. It is highly likely that the aesthetic and symbolic value consumers give to jewels varies with national consumption cultures. Daloz (2010) has demonstrated that symbols of elite distinction vary greatly between societies. What in one society is a source of symbolic superiority is in another a sign of vulgarity.

Rich Americans are much more likely to make material display of their personal wealth than rich Dutchmen who, probably due to the legacy of a Calvinist culture, show much more modesty in their conspicuous consumption. Roodheuvel (2012) has shown that the consumption behaviour of rich Singaporeans with respect to luxurious Swiss watches differs from that of the Dutch riches. That is why jewelry retailers in Singapore as well as in Amsterdam have adapted themselves to the different consumption cultures of tourists.

It is surprising that in the broad literature on cultural industries tourism is hardly ever mentioned. It seems that most of the researchers of cultural industries hardly realise that many cultural industries are intertwined with tourism. But they clearly are. Aoyama (2009), for instance, shows that tourism has played a very important role in the revival of the flamenco industry in Southern Spain. Scott (2010) shows how important tourism has been in the revitalization of a variety of crafts and cultural products in the English Lake District. Tourism researchers, on the other hand, pay a lot of attention on the interrelation of tourism and cultural industries.

To start with, if we define a tourism industry as all natural resources and all social, economic, political, and cultural activities that produce the 'the tourist's experience' (Judd, 2006), it is clear that many cultural industries such as museums, the reproduction of monuments, music festivals among many others contribute to the latter, and should be seen as part of the tourism industry. In addition, there is a growing literature on cultural tourism, which stresses that tourists are looking for "authentic" cultural products (Dunbar-Hall, 2001; Picard, 1998). Notwithstanding all that, some cultural industries are seldom considered as part of the tourism industry. For instance, the Dutch cut-flower industry clearly is a cultural industry because flowers have only an aesthetic and symbolic value, not a utilitarian one. Although the Dutch cut-flower industry had originally nothing to do with tourism, it has gradually become part of it. The well-organised Dutch growers of cut flowers have laid out the Keukenhof flower garden, south-west of Amsterdam, which attracts around 800.00 visitors each year from all over the world. And the Amsterdam flower market is a great tourist attraction, although tourists hardly buy cut flowers because they are highly perishable (they only buy flower bulbs). Thus the Dutch cut-flower industry and tourism have become intertwined in a relation of unrelated variety. The same applies to the jewelry industry as will be analysed in more detail below.

4. Deconcentration of Jewelry Retail in Cities

Jewelry retail firms are mostly located in or close to the historic cores of cities that simultaneously are the main tourist attraction areas. The same applies to the jewelry manufacturing firms in cities that are leading jewelry production centres, such as Antwerp, Birmingham, New York, Los Angeles, Bangkok and Arezzo (Lazzeretti, 2006; Scott, 2000a; Wicksteed, 2004). However, over the last three decades, there has been a deconcentration of jewelry retailers to more peripheral locations in cities (as well as to other cities) that is above all related to the restructuring of the sector.

Till the 1980s, the jewelry industry was a highly fragmented industry with a very few large manufacturing firms and only a handful of retail chains applying modern marketing techniques ("Management Horizons", 1981). In those days, most of the jewellery stores were small, family-oriented businesses (Da Silva, 2007). The economic crisis of the 1970s and early 1980s, however, led to stagnating jewelry sales that resulted a restructuring of jewelry retail. Many of the small businesses did not survive while selling at a larger scale through chain stores and catalogue showrooms gained importance ("Management Horizons", 1981). In course of time, the jewelry retail has become ever more variegated into individual retail stores, retail chain stores, departmental stores, travelling salespeople and, more recently, media sales outlets (Da Silva, 2007, p. 51). This consolidation process in the jewelry industry started in North America and was soon followed by Europe. In the latter, catalogue showrooms, large jewellery chains, department stores, and mail order companies made inroads into the market at the expense of the traditional retail specialists (Da Silva, 2007, 60). These non-traditional retail outlets had the effect of broadening the consumer base and lowering the price by fashion oriented items ("Management Horizons", 1981). As a result of this restructuring process, jewelry retails chains and jewelry showrooms opened their new businesses in the peripheries of cities, which is most clearly seen in the regional shopping malls in the USA (Du Boulay, 1984), while the traditional retail stores that had survived the crisis of the 1970s and early 1980s continued to be located in the historic cores of cities.

5. Changing Trajectory of Global Jewelry Production

Over the last three decades, a global shift of jewellery production as well as demand has taken place. Countries that played a minor role in the world's jewelry production have begun to challenge the dominant position of the leading countries. The rise of these newcomers is not only based on growing exports but also on increasing domestic demand, due to rising incomes and the important role jewels play in their cultural life (think of jewels as a gift in marriages and births) (Da Silva, 2007, 56). Since mid-1980s India, Thailand, Taiwan and Hong Kong have become important jewellery production centres (Murray *et al.*, 1990). While the jewellery production in the Middle and Far East increased by 120 and 250 percent between 1986 and 1992, it was only by 50 percent in the developed countries (Murray *et al.*, 1993, 1994). One of the most crucial factors of the strong production growth in the developing world was the gradual dismantling of restrictive laws that governed the ownership and trading of gold, most notably in Turkey and India. Liberalisation, combined with rising personal incomes, made gold more accessible to a larger consumer market (Da Silva, 2007, p.74).

Turkey has always played a significant role in jewellery trade. Gold is an integral part of Turkish culture and is highly valued as an investment tool. However, gold imports in Turkey were illegal for many years. In 1982, the government took the initiative to liberalize regulations regarding the import of bullion, and the export of manufactured gold items (Da Silva 2007; Du Boulay, 1992). This trade liberalization has triggered the fabrication of jewelry products for both domestic use and exports (Murray *et al.*, 1991). Formal jewellery exports from Turkey are destined mainly to Germany and the United States which together account for 80 percent of Turkey's formal jewelry exports (Murray *et al.*, 1997, 1998). But a lot of exports are via tourists (particularly the Germans and the Russians) who buy jewels as a souvenir as well as through organised, unofficial channels which can account for as much as 50% of total sales (Murray, *et al.*, 1993). Particularly the so-called "suitcase trade" plays an important role in informal exports. By that is meant trade by Russian and, to a lesser extent, Eastern European tourists who purchase jewels in, mostly, semi-wholesale chains and take them back to their home country for resale.

The diamond trade is traditionally dominated by Jewish communities in different cities of the world. The rise and fall of diamond centres is highly related with the history of Jewish migration. Already in the 15th and most of the 16th century Antwerp was *the* centre of diamond cutting and polishing in the western world. The city's raw diamonds were imported from India (particularly Portugal's colony Goa was the centre of trade of raw diamonds) and Brazil, and later from South Africa, Congo, Russia, Sierra Leone, and Angola. When Antwerp fell into the hands of Spaniards in 1585 (the Low Countries were in a war of independence with Spain), many Jewish traders fled to Amsterdam and joined the already large community of Jewish refugees from Spain and Portugal. The immigrants brought with them their business expertise and trading networks to Amsterdam. In the late 19th century, the diamond industries of both Amsterdam and Antwerp flourished but already in the early 20th century Antwerp surpassed Amsterdam that began to decline (on which more later). In the 20th century, Antwerp has grown out to one of the most famous diamond cities of the world, partly fuelled by immigration of Jews from Poland, Hungary, North Africa, Israel, the US, Russia, and Georgia (Siegel, undated). In course of time, however, the city has felt competition of (the Jewish community of) New York, Tel Aviv, and Bombay.

6. Amsterdam Diamond Trade Intertwined with Tourism

As early as in the sixteenth century, Amsterdam became a world centre of diamond cutting and trade which was fully dominated by the Jews. In those days, Amsterdam was a refugee place for Portuguese Jews who came to Amsterdam for its religious freedom. The diamond industry was one of the few industries not controlled by guilds (from which the Jews were excluded). During the last three decades of the nineteenth century, the Amsterdam's diamond industry prospered by cheap diamonds imported from South Africa. These diamonds were polished and processed in Amsterdam's high-end factories. At that period, Amsterdam grew out to one of the leading diamond cutting and polishing centres of the world. At the beginning of the twentieth century, there were seventy diamond factories in the city that were technologically the most advanced of the time. Over twelve thousand workers were employed in that industry in those days who formed the elite of the working class. They were highly skilled, founded the first labour union in the Netherlands, named Diamond Workers Trade Union, and belonged to the best paid workers of the working class.

In the 1920s the Amsterdam diamond industry began to decline because it began to feel the ever stronger competition of the Antwerp diamond industry, which also is in the hands of Jews. The holocaust of World War II gave the deathblow to the Amsterdam diamond industry, but not to the Antwerp diamond industry. As said before, it was the latter that has become Europe's leading diamond centre. Why precisely Antwerp has taken over the position of Amsterdam is difficult to say. The scarce literature on this topic suggests that Amsterdam lost its position before World War II due to the high wages of the strongly unionized Amsterdam diamond workers while the wages in the Antwerp diamond industry were much lower because entrepreneurs had begun to put out the polishing of diamonds to small, rural home industries around Antwerp (Van Tijn, 1989). Probably more is at stake. And it is highly likely that more Antwerp diamond entrepreneurs survived the holocaust because, for reasons that cannot be dealt with here, significantly more Jews from Holland were deported to the Nazi-camps than from Belgium (Griffioen & Zeller, 2011).

Although it had lost its cutting and polishing industry, Amsterdam continued to exist as a diamond trade centre after World War II, be it a minor one compared to Antwerp. Its institutional infrastructure such as Amsterdam Association of Diamond Trade (founded in 1889) and the Amsterdam Diamond Exchange continued to exist as well. The latter has become the breeding ground of organized diamond trading in the world. It protects the interests of the diamond trade in the Netherlands and, in co-operation with other organisations that regulate the diamond trade, it safeguards the strict rules created by the World Federation of Diamond Bourses.

In the 1960s and 1970s, the Amsterdam diamond trade did not perform well, which forced the Amsterdam traders to exploit the opportunities offered by tourism. Ever since the 1960s, Amsterdam tourism has grown with ups and downs (due to the crisis of the late 1970s and early 1980s, changing exchange rates, September eleven, and the crisis-ridden period after 2008). Amsterdam is, contrary to Antalya, a multi-asset tourism city that offers a mix of attractions in a monumental setting. Tourists and day-trippers visit the historic city centre to enjoy its monuments and canals, make use of a huge variety of cultural and leisure facilities (Amsterdam is the cultural capital of the Netherlands) as well as small specialised shops (the historic built environment can hardly accommodate large-scale shopping centres), and experience its libertarian atmosphere as witnessed by "coffee shops" where one can freely buy hash and marihuana, a red-light district with sex shops and a sex museum, and a well-developed gay scene.

Especially in the 1960s and 1970s, the diamond traders began to realize the importance of tourism for diamond trade and started to sell diamonds via tourism. Today Amsterdam has around twelve diamond factories that have been transformed into selling centres. A few of them have been transformed into exposition centres with free guided tours that attract 750.000 visitors a year. The biggest players are *Coster Diamonds* that, since 1995, also owns *Van Moppes Diamonds* and *the Diamond Museum, Gassan Diamonds* that also owns *the Amsterdam Diamond Centre,* and *Amstel City Diamonds.*

Figure 1 - Coster Diamonds Building

Among those *Coster Diamonds*, established in 1840, is the oldest of them. Although a few diamonds are polished, the firm's core businesses are wholesaling- and retail. And it runs a museum as well, namely the Diamond Museum. The firm was originally located in the former Jewish neighbourhood in Amsterdam but moved in 1970 to the Museumplein (Museum Square), a very attractive tourism place on which are located the Van Gogh Museum, the City Museum (Stedelijk Museum), the National Museum (Rijksmuseum), and the Concert Hall (Concertgebouw. It goes without saying that the Diamond Museum plays an important role in exciting interest in and advertising of diamonds, and is attractive to tourists. Coster Diamonds say that over 300,000 visitors a year come to see Coster Diamonds craftsmen at work.

The Gassan diamonds, founded in 1945, is one of the largest in Amsterdam. It is a family-owned business that is located in a restored factory building (the former Boas Diamond Factory) near Waterlooplein (in the former Jewish area). After the war the firm has grown out to a big multinational wholesale- and retail firm with establishments in Pforzheim, Düsseldorf, Tel Aviv, Zug, New York, and Tokyo. In addition, it has tax free shops at Schiphol Amsterdam Airport, London Heathrow and Changi Singapore Airport. It conducts diamond tours in the restored factory building and it goes without saying that it also sells diamonds to visitors. In addition, the firm also is the owner of the *Amsterdam Diamond Centre,* the biggest jewelry shop of Amsterdam, located at Dam Square (the heart of Amsterdam) where not only diamonds but also jewels and expensive watches are sold. In 1990, it started a joint venture with *Stoeltie Diamonds* that sold diamonds and jewels to American tourists in particular. After September 11, however, the decline of US visitors forced Stoeltie Diamonds to close its doors (Gassan Diamonds, n.d.). Apart from these diamonds, *Amstel City Diamonds* are other important player in the Amsterdam world of diamonds with tours and selling.

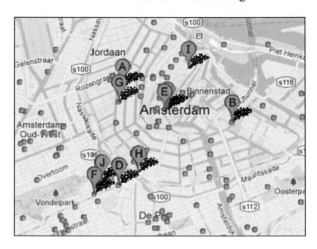

Figure 2(a) - Map of Jewelry Firms in Amsterdam

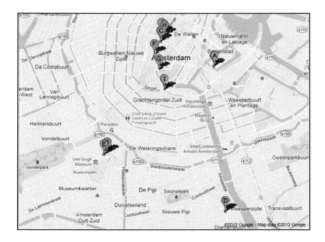

Figure 2(b) - Map of Diamond Firms in Amsterdam

Maps 2a and 2b show the location of jewelry and diamond firms in Amsterdam. They are almost all located in or close to the historic core which is by far the main tourist attraction area. Diamonds and jewels are particularly sold to Asian and Russian tourists who are very much inclined to show their class position with jewels and diamonds.

In sum, the Amsterdam case shows that after World War II the Amsterdam diamond manufacturing industry has evolved towards a diamond wholesale and retail trade sector. It has become a trading node of global production networks of diamonds. This node has become intertwined in a relation of unrelated variety with another node of global production networks, namely that of tourism.

7. Tourism and Jewel Retail in Antalya

Turkey is one of the world leaders of the jewelry industry. It has a long history that dates as long as from the early Bronze Age (Tüzmen, 2006). Especially after the 1980s, Turkey's share in global markets has increased, and the country is now the third largest jewelry exporter in the world, thanks to its heritage, its wide range of product diversity, its flexible production methods, its capacity to adapt quickly to new trends, and its high quality for relatively low prices (Jewelry Exporters' Association [JTR], 2010). Even though the jewelry sector is a leading sector in terms of average capital productivity, its share in total value added in manufacturing is low (Atay *et.al*., 2011).

Jewelry firms, 2872 in total number, are very unequally distributed over the country. Istanbul is the leading city having 1704 firms, followed by Antalya with 415 firms and, at some distance, by Adana with 365 firms (Türk Firma Rehberi, 2012). Antalya has never been a leading centre of jewelry production but has grown out to the second-largest jewelry retail place in Turkey due to its booming tourism. It has now four big jewelry factories and around five hundred small jewelry shops. Jewelry firm formation in Antalya is strongly related with its tourism growth. Over the last twenty years the number of foreign tourists has grown from 810.000's to 10.500.000's (Antalya Governorship Database, 2012). Contrary to expectation, the so-called "suit case trade" does not take place in Antalya. According to jewelry wholesalers, "suit case trade is limited to İstanbul (interview with Jewelry Association of Antalya).

The specific form of Antalya's tourism has led to a spatial deconcentration of jewelry firms. Originally, most of the jewelry firms were concentrated around the Kaleiçi port area, the city's historic centre which attracts many tourists because of its old, restored monuments that are used as hotels, pensions and apartments. There still are lot of jewelry firms located here that exploit this centre of tourist attraction (see point B on maps 3a and 3b. Most of the jewelry shops located here are small and family-owned and sell not only to tourists but also to locals.

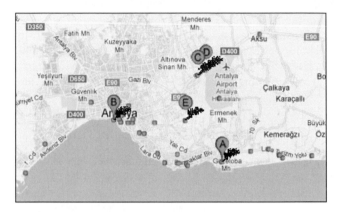

Figure 3a - Map of diamond shops in Antalya

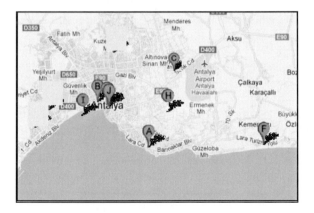

Figure 3b - Map of jewelry shops in Antalya

However, over the last two decades a strong deconcentration process of jewelry shops has taken place. This is, *firstly*, caused by the fact that Antalya's tourism is a   tour-operator dominated mass tourism. Most of the tourists spend their holidays in the peripheral tourism centres of the city as a result of which the historical Kaleiçi area with its small jewelry shops has become less accessible to tourists. In addition, visiting large jewelry shops in the periphery of the city has become part of local tours organized by tour operators. The tour busses make a stop at the large jewelry firms on their way coming back from local tours to nearby provinces, for instance the Pamukkale-Denizli tour. These large jewelry firms are particularly located near the airport road, which is on the entrance of the city from other provinces (see point C and D on map 3(a) and C on map 3(b) and figure 4) and on the Perge road. *Antalya Jewelry Centre, Hadrian Jewelry, Violla Jewelry and Leather, Rom Diamond and Sentalya Tourism Jewelry Centre* are good examples of this type.

Figure 4 - Hadrian Jewelry

The deconcentration of jewelry shops is, *secondly*, related to the development of huge tourism centres in the eastern periphery of the city. Many jewelry shops have been located in shopping malls near big hotels. A good example is the Lara-Kundu Tourism Development Centre Area (see point F on map 3(b) and figure 5), which is famous for big, thematic hotels and shopping malls. The famous Pasha Jewellery is located in such a shopping mall. The tourism zones or, better, tourism enclaves are very much segregated from the city centre because the five-star hotels offer an all-inclusive service. Tourists seldom leave their hotel and, if they do, they go to those nearby malls for shopping. Similar developments are taking place in the touristic sub-provinces of Antalya such as Kemer and Side.

It goes without saying that the deconcentration of jewelry shops is threatening to the small jewelry firms in the Kaleiçi area. No wonder that it is opposed by the Antalya Jewelier Association. Its leader claims that the rise of big jewelry shops in segregated shopping malls has forced many small jewelry shops to close their doors.

In sum, due to its booming tourism Antalya has grown out to an important retail node in a national production network dominated by

İstanbul. The spatial development Antalya's jewelry trade has been strongly shaped by the specific form of its tourism, i.e. tour-operator dominated mass tourism.

Figure 5 - Jewelry Shops in Shopping Malls nearby Lara-Kundu Tourism Zone

8. Conclusion

From our case studies we can conclude that the tourism industry should not be defined in static but in dynamic terms. It does not make sense to define at one moment in time what industries belong to tourism and what not because, in the dynamic process of tourism diversification, industries that have originally nothing to do with tourism may become part of the tourism industry. And tourism, in turn, may become part of other industries. Our case studies show that tourism and jewelry trade that were formerly disconnected to each other have generated spill-overs to each other. In both cities tourism has boosted up jewelry trade and the latter has simultaneously made both cities more attractive to tourists. Tourism in both cities has become more diversified through unrelated variety.

It goes without saying that how precisely the development trajectories of tourism and jewelry trade have become interwoven is context dependent. Amsterdam was once a leading centre of diamond production but began already to decline in the early twentieth century and has, particularly after World War II, been evolved into a trading node in global diamond production networks. Its position as a diamond trade node has been boosted up ever since it has become intertwined with tourism. Diamond traders have followed a deliberate strategy to become part of the tourism industry by transforming the historic buildings of the former diamond factories into a mix of museums and selling places. Partly due to this strategy, Amsterdam has become a more attractive tourism place. Because Amsterdam tourism as well as the former diamond factories are concentrated in the historic core, the spill-overs between tourism and jewelry trade are limited to the latter place.

Jewelry production (and consumption) in Turkey has a long tradition too that dates back from more than a thousand years. Although Istanbul is the main centre of jewelry production and trade, Antalya has grown out to an important node of a national jewerly production network due to its booming tourism. Buying cheap jewels is one of the city's tourist attractions. Although some small-scale jewelry trade is still found around Antalya's historic core (the Kaleiçi area), most of the jewelry trade has been deconcentrated to the periphery of the city. This is the result of Antalya's tour-operator dominated mass tourism. The visiting of large jewelry shops in the periphery of Antalya have become part of local tours organized by tour operators. In addition, the development of huge tourism centres in the eastern periphery of the city has triggered the rise of new shopping malls with a lot of jewelry traders near the big hotels.

References

Antalya Governorship Database (2012). From http://www.antalya.gov.tr/icerik/12/161/rakamlarla-antalya.html

Aoyama, Y. (2009). Artists, tourists, and the state: Cultural tourism and the Flamenco industry in Andalusia, Spain. *International Journal of Urban and Regional Research*, 33(1), 80–104.

Atay, S. (2011). *Kuyumculuk Sektöründe Verimlilik Üzerine bir Araştırma.* From http://www.namardanismanlik.com/dosya/makale/7.pdf

Boschma, R., & Iammarino, S. (2009). Related variety, trade linkages, and regional growth in Italy. *Economic Geography*, 85(3), 289-311.

Bourdieu, P. (1984). *Distinction, a Social Critique of the Judgement of Taste.* London: Routledge.

Coster Diamonds. From http://nl.wikipedia.org/wiki/Coster_Diamonds.

Daloz, J.P. (2010). *The Sociology of Elite Distinction. From Theoretical to Comparative Perspectives.* Basingstoke: Palgrave.

Da Silva, M. (2007). *From Dynamism to Dormancy: the Jewellery Industry in Johannesburg: 1925-2003.* (Ph.D. Dissertation, University of the Witwatersrand), Johannesburg.

Du Boulay, L. (1982). *Gold 1982.* London: Consolidated Gold Fields.

—. (1984). *Gold 1984.* London: Consolidated Gold Fields.

Dunbar-Hall, P. (2001). Culture, tourism and cultural tourism: Boundaries and frontiers in performances of Balinese music and dance. *Journal of Intercultural Studies,* 22(2), 173–87.

Frenken, K., Van Oort, F.G., & Verburg, T. (2007). Related variety, unrelated variety and regional economic growth. *Regional Studies*, 41(5), 685–697.

Gassan Diamonds (2012) In Wikipedia. From http://nl.wikipedia.org/wiki/Gassan_Diamonds.

Gornostaeva, G. (2008). The film and television industry in London's suburbs: lifestyle of the rich or losers' retreat? *Creative Industries Journal*, 1, 47–71.

Griffioen, P., & Zeller, R. (2011). *Jodenvervolging in nederland, Frankrijk en België, 1940-1945.* Amsterdam: Boom.

Hutton, T. (2004). The new economy of inner city. *Cities*, 21(2), 89–108.

Ioannides, D., & Debbage, K. (Eds.) (1997). *The Economic Geography of the Tourist Industry.* London: Routledge.

Jacobs, J. (1967). *The Economy of Cities.* Harmondsworth: Penquin.

Jewelry Exporters' Assoiation [JTR]. (2010). 6 *Golden Standards*, Turkish Jewellery Association. From http://www.jtr.org.tr/En/6golden.aspx.

Judd, D.R. (2006). Commentary: Tracing the commodity chain of global tourism. *Tourism Geographies*, 8(4), 323–336.

Lazzeretti, L. (2006). Density dependent dynamics in the Arezzo Jewellery district (1947-2001): Focus on foundings. *European Planning Studies*, 14(4), 431.

Management Horizons. (1981). *Analysis of alternative marketing channels and channel cost reduction opportunities in the distribution of karat gold jewellery.* (Unpublished report) International Gold Corporation.

Murray, S., Crisp, K., Klapwijk, P., Sutton-Pratt, T., & Green, T. (1990). *Gold 1990.* London: Gold Fields Mineral Services.

—. (1993). *Gold 1993*, London: Gold Fields Mineral Services.

Murray, S., Klapwijk, P., Le Roux, H., & Walker, P. (1997). *Gold 1997*. London: Gold Fields Mineral Services.

—. (1998). *Gold 1998.* London: Gold Fields Mineral Services.

Nachum, L., & Keeble, D. (2003). Neo-Marshallian Clusters and Global Networks - The Linkages of Media Firms in Central London. *Long Range Planning*, 36, 459–480.

Newman, P., & I. Smith. (2000). Cultural Production, Place and Politics on the South Bank of the Thames. *International Journal of Urban and Regional Research*, 24, 9-24.

Picard, M. (1998). *Cultural tourism and touristic culture.* Singapore: Didier Millet.

Roodheuvel, I. (2012). *The Consumption of Time. A Comparative Case Study of Two Local High-End Watch Fields in a Globalizing World.* (Master Thesis Metropolitan Studies), University of Amsterdam.

Scott, A. (1994). Variations on the theme of agglomeration and growth: The gem and jewelry industry in Los Angeles and Bangkok. *Geoforum,* 25, 249-263.

—. (2000a). *The Gem and Jewelry Industry in Los Angles and Bangkok: The Cultural Economy of Cities* (pp. 41-60). London: Sage.

Scott, A. (2000b). The cultural economy of Paris. *International Journal of Urban and Regional Research,* 24, 567–582.

—. (2004). Cultural-products industries and urban economic development: Prospects for growth and market contestation in global context. *Urban Affairs Review,* 39, 461-490.

Scott, A.J. (2007). Capitalism and urbanization in a new key? The cognitive-cultural dimension. *Social Forces,* 85(4), 1465-1485.

—. (2010). The cultural economy of landscape and prospects for peripheral development in the twenty-first century: The case of the English Lake District. *European Planning Studies,* 18(10), 1567-1589.

Shaw, G., & Williams, A.M. (2004). *Tourism and Tourism Spaces.* London: Sage.

Siegel, D. *De Joodse Gemeenschap en de Antwerpse Diamantsector in Historisch Perspectief.* From www.ciroc.nl/papers/Joodsegemeente.pdf

Türk Firma Rehberi. (2012). *Mücevher (Altın ve Kuyumculuk) Perakende Ticareti Firmaları Listesi.* From http://www.turkfirmarehberi.tv.tr/mucevher-altin-kuyumculuk-perakende-ticareti/1/firmalari-listesi.aspx.

Tüzmen, K. (2006). The rising trademark in the world market: Turkish jewelry. *Turk of America.* From http://www.turkofamerica.com/index.php?option=com_content&task=view&id=200&Itemid=70.

Van der Panne, G. (2006). On the Marshall-Jacobs controversy: It takes two to Tango. *Industrial and Corporate Change,* 15(5), 877-890.

Van Tijn, Th. (1989). De Amsterdamse Diamanthandel en –Nijverheid, 1845-1940. *Holland, Regionaal-Historisch Tijdschrift.*

Wicksteed, B. (2004). Clustering, collaboration and competitiveness. Paper presented at *Planted World Conference,* Dublin, October.

CHAPTER TEN

HABITS OF LOCAL RESIDENTS AND TOURISTS VISITING A THEME PARK

MARC LEBLANC

Abstract

There are over a thousand theme parks throughout the world, 20 in Canada. The latter are of average size compared to the largest American and European parks. There are also many smaller parks that play an important role in their region. The *Pays de la Sagouine*, in Canada, is one of these. The purpose of this chapter was to better understand the differences between the local residents and tourist. Its clientele is mostly made up visitors between 46 and 65 years of age. Their main reasons for visiting the park are its theatre performances and monologues. The notoriety is based on three pillars, namely its main character, theatre and music. The local population is more sensitive to increased admission fees.
Keywords: Acadian, cultural tourism, local residents, rural tourism, theme park.

1. Introduction

According to data provided by the International Association of Amusement Parks and Attractions (IAAPA), there are an estimated 700 theme parks worldwide. The 400 American parks attract an average of 300 million visitors per year, while the 300 European parks average 40 million visitors per year. The economic impact of these parks, estimated at over 11 billion dollars in the United States only, is significant.

No official data has been identified for Canada. A web search shows at least 20 large theme parks across the Canadian provinces. They are basically big amusement parks made up of rides, or theme parks portraying a specific theme such as energy, history, etc. What distinguishes the two concepts, among other things, is the fact that amusement parks generally offer a multitude of activities in a concentrated space while theme parks provide a limited number of activities on a much larger territory (Clavé, 2007). There is a series of smaller parks with fewer visitors which, despite their size, can play an important role in their region in terms of tourism development, economic development, and demonstrating regional features.

Such is the case of the *Pays de la Sagouine*, a theme park located in Bouctouche, a small community of about 2,500 people on the east coast of the province of New Brunswick, in Canada. Its concept is inspired by a novel written by Acadian[i] author Antonine Maillet. At the *Pays de la Sagouine*, music meets theatre on a small enchanting island where actors and musicians come together to give live performances.

Despite the importance of theme parks in the tourism industry, Milman (2009) notes that scientific literature on visitor motivations and habits are sparse. Among researchers interested in the theme park phenomenon is Wall (2011), who writes that it is difficult to separate the tourism potential of a cultural product (in her case, Fort Edmonton) and its use by the local population. It is worth noting, incidentally, that tourism development is often based on physical infrastructures, although socio-cultural features can also attract tourists (Lee *et al.*, 2007). Thus, the author states that living history can help preserve the traditions of the local population, but this approach does not always meet tourists' expectations and thus may not produce the revenue boosts which would allow such a park to survive, all the more so because the local population in many cases represents a significant percentage of attendance (Boyd, 2002).

The same author, in citing Inglis & Holmes (2003) and Timothy & Boyd (2006), demonstrates that cultural and historical interpretation in this type of park is faced with a difficult challenge. On the one hand, you want to attract visitors (especially tourists) by offering an accessible and attractive product, and on the other hand, certain stakeholders (especially local residents) want to demonstrate the "true" story and an authentic culture. In most cases, tourists' interests take precedence over historic and cultural integrity, creating a form of historic distortion, to the point of inventing stories and cultural facts! Some authors have thus been prompted to qualify such theme parks as being irrelevant for the local community (Ashworth, 2010; Gordon, 2009). They do however recognize that a misinterpretation of history done in good faith can help create a greater awareness of at least part of a community.

Since the concept of the *Pays de la Sagouine* is based on a work of fiction inspired by true facts, it plays on this ambiguity between history, culture and local traditions. This fits with Cohen's (2007) definition of authenticity, namely the "custom and practice, creativity and dynamic flow of everyday life at a site, as well as the use and perception of the term by various consumers and producers". Local residents seem to be proud of "their" *Pays de la Sagouine* because it brings to life the work of one of their most renowned citizens throughout the international Francophone community. This is a positive perception that creates consensus within the local population and contributes to tourism development (Wall, 2011). The fictional aspect of *Le Pays de la Sagouine* allows the park to rejuvenate itself and create novelty year after year, rather than remaining stuck in a historical straightjacket which allows for only narrow interpretation. In fact, the park's only limitation is the creative potential of its artistic director and managers!

The purpose of this chapter is to better understand the differences between the local population and tourists in terms of socio-demographic variables, habits and reasons for visiting the *Pays de la Sagouine*.

2. What is the Pays de la Sagouine?

As mentioned, the *Pays de la Sagouine* is a theme park where music meets theatre on a small island through the presence of actors and musicians who give live performances on an enchanting site (*Pays de la Sagouine*, 2011). There are in fact a relatively small number of activities on a relatively large territory for this type of concept. The park is located both on the mainland (reception area, restaurant and boutique) and on an island (group of small houses built on piles), linked together by a 400 meter boardwalk.

Established in 1992, the park's mandate is to immerse visitors in the universe of *La Sagouine* (Maillet, 1971), which began as a novel and was then produced as a television series broadcast on Canadian networks.

The park is open from late June to early September and welcomes visitors every day from 10:00 am to 6:00 pm. In the evenings, dinner theatres with the actors from the *Pays de la Sagouine* team are open to visitors. There is normally one dinner theatre every night throughout the summer. Another one is held during the Holiday Season, in November and December, for local residents. Once again, the characters from the *Pays de la Sagouine* are featured in these plays (Economic Planning Group, 2006).

The park opened its doors in 1992. From 1996 to 2005, visitation numbers rose steadily (69,000 to 85,000). During that period, the Province of New Brunswick made significant progress in promoting its tourist destinations, especially beaches (Sawler, 2009). It just so happens that the *Pays de la Sagouine* is located along the Acadian Coast scenic route, whose pull product is mostly its beaches! Furthermore, in 1999, the greater southeastern region of the province of New Brunswick, in which the *Pays de la Sagouine* is located, was host to the International Francophone Summit. Its various events and promotional efforts certainly helped increase visitor numbers at the park.

Generally speaking, the New Brunswick tourism industry has been declining since the mid 2000's (Tourism and Parks, 2010). As one of the pull products of the province, the *Pays de la Sagouine* suffered from the effects of this decline or, at best, stagnation in visitation numbers in the province, its own visitor numbers dropping from 65,700 in 2006 to 56,700 in 2010.

The large majority of *Pays de la Sagouine* visitors are French-speaking tourists. Very few Anglophones or non-Francophone foreigners visit the park (approximately 1 or 2% according to park representatives). Note that the park's programs are almost exclusively offered in French as they intentionally target the Francophone market. In order to attract Anglophone tourists, the park presents its famous dinner theatre, *La Sagouine*, in English one night per week. According to park officials, this event is well attended, but the audience is mostly made up of Francophones who are curious to hear *La Sagouine* speak English or who understand English better than French.

The *Pays de la Sagouine* offers local residents (who live less than 40 km from Bouctouche) the opportunity to buy season passes. On average, approximately 2,000 membership cards are sold each year. These passes allow local residents to visit the park as many times as they wish.

It is estimated that approximately one visitor out of three to five is a local resident. Official data were found for the years 2007 to 2009 (Pays de la Sagouine, 2011).

3. Methodology

The data presented herein are taken from an online survey held during two weeks, from late October to November 10, 2010. The *Pays de la Sagouine* mailing list, containing over 6,000 addresses, was provided by the webmaster and used for the survey.

A first mailing was done in October and November. Two reminder emails were sent out, one seven days after the first mailing and another two days before the final deadline.

In order to encourage people to respond to the survey, the *Pays de la Sagouine* agreed to offer prizes. Despite the fact that respondents identified themselves when they registered their email address for a chance to win a prize, their anonymity was ensured, in particular, by preventing any possible linkage between their answers and their email.

The questionnaire was prepared in consultation with *Pays de la Sagouine* officials. It contains 25 questions on various socio-demographic factors as well as time, frequency and average length of visits. Some of the questions deal with motivations for visiting the park based on what it actually offers or could potentially offer. Respondents also evaluated various themes such as theatre, actors and history. Another series of questions deals with the hospitality aspect of the park's various components (restaurant, reception area and attractions on the island). Finally, respondents were invited to provide suggestions on improving the experience and attracting new visitors.

A pretest was done with 10 visitors in order to determine how well they understood the questions. The Surveymonkey.com site was used as a survey platform and the results were analyzed using SPSS.

A total of 997 French and 157 English questionnaires were received by the end of the survey. After having reviewed those 1,154 questionnaires for duplications and incomplete answers, a total of 1,103 questionnaires were retained, for a proportion of 97,2% Francophone respondents and 2,8% Anglophone respondents.

4. Results

The purpose of this chapter being to compare habits of tourists and local residents who visit the *Pays de la Sagouine*, the following tables provide an overview of their differences.

Respondents were divided into three groups: visitors living less than 40 km from the *Pays de la Sagouine*, alias "locals" (n = 334); visitors living more than 40 km away, mostly in the southern part of the province of New Brunswick (n = 464); and visitors living more than 80 km away, elsewhere in New Brunswick and in neighboring provinces (n = 274).

In Table 1, we can see that more women than men agreed to complete the survey (more than 7 out of 10 respondents). Also, there are very few respondents in the 19-25 age group. This reflects the visitor profile, which is mostly made up of couples with or without young children. Local residents mostly fall in the under-45 age group. Their proportion in the three youngest age groups is higher than that of all the other respondents. Conversely, respondents living over 80 km away from the park are more numerous in the 56-65 age group, where they account for 34.2% of total visitors compared to 26.4% for local residents and 28.4% for visitors living over 40 km away.

Table 1 - Socio-Demographic Data

	Locals (n = 334)	More than 40 km (n = 464)	More than 80 km (n = 274)	Total (%)
Gender				
Female	74.4	72.3	70.4	72.5
Malc	25.6	27.7	29.6	27.5
Age***				
19-25 years	2.4	1.5	1.9	1.8
26-35 years	12.0	10.6	4.1	9.3
36-45 years	24.0	15.1	20.8	19.2
46-55 years	27.0	30.6	26.8	28.4
56-65 years	26.4	28.4	34.2	29.5
66-75 years	8.1	12.3	9.7	10.4
76 years and over	0.0	1.5	2.6	1.3
Education ***				
Elementary School	4.8	1.7	5.5	3.6
Middle School	1.8	2.6	6.6	3.4
High School	24.2	17.3	20.6	20.4
College	40.8	33.0	30.5	34.5
University (bachelor's)	23.9	30.0	27.2	27.5
University (master's)	4.2	14.0	8.8	9.7
University (doctorate)	0.3	0.6	0.7	0.8
Household Revenue***				
Less than $25,000	7.2	2.8	12.2	6.7
$26,000-$40,000	25.4	25.8	23.9	25.3
$41,000-$60,000	25.1	24.3	25.6	24.6
$61,000-$80,000	19.2	15.8	21.0	18.2
$81,000-$100,000	10.7	15.5	8.8	12.3
More than $100,000	12.4	16.0	8.4	12.9

* $p < .05$ ** $p < .01$, *** $p < .001$

With regards to education levels, our data shows that respondents from outside the region (more than 40 km and more than 80 km) are more educated than local residents. One third of the 40 km respondents and 27.2% of the 80 km respondents have a bachelor's degree compared to 23.9% of local residents. Note that the percentage of 40 km respondents with a master's degree (14%) can be explained by the fact that a university town is located within the same distance from the park.

Revenue distribution was similar for all respondents, regardless of region.

Table 2 shows that visitors from more than 80 km away are more likely to spend four (4) hours or more at the park, whereas locals seem to prefer shorter visits, i.e. less than four (4) hours. Overall, most *Pays de la Sagouine* visitors spend one to four hours on site.

Frequency of visits varies from once per week (16.5% for local residents and 12.4% for visitors from more than 40 km away), to once per month (35.4% for local residents; 25.5% for those more than 40 km; and 8.4% for more than 80 km), to once per year (41% for those more than 80 km; 44.6% for more than 40 km; and 34.2% for local residents).

Table 2 – Length of Last Park Visit

	Locals (n = 334)	More than 40 km (n = 464)	More than 80 km (n = 274)	Total (%)
Length of visit*				
Less than one hour	0.3	1.3	1.1	0.9
1-3 hours	37.2	34.4	25.6	33.0
3-4 hours	33.0	34.0	32.6	33.1
4-6 hours	19.5	19.9	23.7	20.8
More than 6 hours	9.9	10.4	17.0	12.2

$p < .05$, ** $p < .01$, *** $p < .001$

Table 3 identifies reasons for visiting the *Pays de la Sagouine*. The park's program is mostly made up of monologues and sketches. *La Sagouine* is the attraction's main character and icon. She is usually on site three or four days per week and gives two or three monologues per day. In addition to this, other actors interpreting various characters entertain the crowds traveling from one small house to another or the audience sitting near the main stage centrally located on the island. Music is also an important part of the entrainment provided throughout the day.

The main statistically significant difference in reasons for visiting the park is to "see the *Sagouine*". Indeed, visitors from more than 80 km and more than 40 km away are more interested by *la Sagouine* than local residents. Curiosity is also more prevalent among visitors living more than 80 km away. Finally, those from more than 80 km and more than 40 km away are more interested in learning more about Acadian history.

Table 3 – Importance of Statements on Reasons for Visiting the *Pays de la Sagouine*

1 = Not important 4 = Very important	Locals (n = 334)	More than 40 km (n = 464)	More than 80 km (n = 274)	Average /4
To watch the monologues and sketches	3.40	3.49	3.50	3.46
To see the stage actors	3.37	3.44	3.38	3.41
To see *la Sagouine****	2.83	2.99	3.20	2.99
To accompany friends or relatives	2.91	2.94	2.85	2.91
To learn more about Acadian history**	2.61	2.70	2.89	2.73
To trace Acadian roots	2.67	2.67	2.73	2.69
Out of curiosity***	2.10	2.12	2.41	2.19

* $p < .05$, ** $p < .01$, *** $p < .001$

With the question asked in Table 4, we wanted to know where the *Pays de la Sagouine*'s notoriety stems from. As indicated, there is a statistically significant difference for the "history of Bouctouche" variable: visitors from more than 80 km away identified this more often than those living more than 40 km away. There is also a difference for theatre between local residents and visitors living more than 80 km away. *La Sagouine* herself is more often cited by tourists than local residents: for both the 40 km and 80 km visitors, she was listed as the first thing that comes to mind.

Table 5 provides insight as to why visitors would return to the *Pays de la Sagouine*. Local residents are more likely than other visitors to hope that admission fees might decrease. This group, along with visitors living more than 40 km away, would also like the sketches to change from year to year. It can also be seen that local residents are more "demanding" in each of the response categories except for dinner theatres. Note that none of the respondent groups were in favor of changing the park's name to make it more attractive for Anglophones. This possibility (i.e. new name) stems from management's desire to find ways of attracting more English-speaking visitors.

Table 4 analyses the differences between the Turkish and Spanish students taking into consideration their membership in the control or experimental group. The findings determine that the change in the Turkish students' evaluation of the destination and their intention to visit the place is greater than that of the Spanish respondents. Nevertheless, the original assessment (prior to the provision of the stimulus) of the Turkish sample is significantly lower than that of the Spanish students. Therefore, the results determine that the initial negative opinion regarding Israel and the lower preference and intention to visit the destination on behalf of Turkish students is somehow offset by the access to additional printed information. However, this change is not enough to reach the results displayed by the Spanish sample.

Table 4 – Answers to the Question "When you think of the *Pays de la Sagouine*, what comes to mind?"

1 = Total disagreement 4 = Total agreement	Locals (n = 334)	More than 40 km (n = 464)	More than 80 km (n = 274)	Average /4
La Sagouine	3.49	3.52	3.61	3.53
Theatre*	3.53	3.51	3.45	3.50
Music	3.49	3.46	3.42	3.46
Dinner theatres	3.40	3.43	3.28	3.39
Acadian culture	3.33	3.20	3.35	3.28
Acadian history	2.98	2.88	3.13	2.97
Antonine Maillet	2.89	2.86	3.21	2.96
Fiction	2.32	2.32	2.45	2.35
History of Bouctouche***	2.34	2.11	2.38	2.25

$* p < .05, ** p < .01, *** p < .001$

Table 5 – Ways of Encouraging Return visits to the *Pays de la Sagouine*.

1 = Total disagreement 4 = Total agreement	Locals (n = 334)	More than 40 km (n = 464)	More than 80 km (n = 274)	Average /4
Change sketches every year*	3.27	3.26	3.08	3.21
Reduce admission fees***	2.98	2.83	2.60	2.81
More activities for children under 12	2.64	2.55	2.45	2.55
More dinner theatres	2.80	2.92	2.88	2.86
Night visits	2.82	2.70	2.80	2.76
Change the name of the park (*Pays de la Sagouine*) to attract more Anglophone visitors	1.26	1.16	1.17	1.20

$* p < .05, ** p < .01, *** p < .001$

5. Conclusion

Comparisons between tourists (more than 40 km and more than 80 km away) and local residents help us to better understand motivations and comprehension of the tourism product called *Le Pays de la Sagouine*. The following observations are drawn from a survey conducted among visitors who accepted to provide park officials with their email addresses. We've assumed that this group represents quite accurately the profile of the park's clientele. Our own observations, feedback from management and limited data available on park visitations all support this theory.

Data provided by the park's management indicate that approximately 20% of visitors are local residents (Pays de la Sagouine, 2010). This percentage may be seen as considerable and as a way to ensure a basic level of income, as mentioned earlier (Leiper, 1997). However, as indicated by the *Pays de la Sagouine*'s chairman, "the difference between a good year and a bad year is not the frequency of visits from local population, but the increase in tourist visits" (Desjardins, 2009).

The *Pays de la Sagouine*'s client base is mostly made up of visitors aged between 46 and 65; they represent over 50% of respondents both among tourists and local residents. The 26-35 age group is smaller among visitors from more than 80 km away compared to local residents. The live performances given by local musicians on the patio during weekends might explain this difference. Park management is satisfied with attendance at these shows, which in fact are intended to attract local residents while exposing tourists to the local culture. Over the years, as one can imagine, the image and significance of *Le Pays de la Sagouine* have changed for local residents. Younger residents probably don't have the same perception as their older counterparts. This difference might explain why the musical evenings on the patio are so popular among the young crowd. The big question now is whether these younger local residents (under 35 years of age) also visit the rest of the attraction as often as the older group. Park officials have also noticed a decline in the number of membership cards sold to local residents. Are younger people buying any?

Cultural tourism is generally associated with a more educated and wealthy population. The survey results tend to confirm this for level of education since more of the tourists are university graduates. They are ready and willing to travel to visit the park. Less effort is required of local residents. Worthy of note, the Bouctouche region population is less educated than the provincial average in New Brunswick (Census, 2006). In terms of revenue, the difference between the three groups of respondents is very small, most having a revenue between $26,000 and $60,000 (CAN dollars).

In addition to wanting to increase the park's visitation numbers, one of the challenges faced by management is to find a way to increase the length of visits. That's what the program is designed to do. Results indicate that nearly 70% of respondents remain on site for one to four hours. Only visitors from more than 80 km away (40%) stay for more than four hours. According to the information provided, park officials would like to prolong visits by at least one hour per person (Doucet, 2009). This increase would probably encourage visitors to consume more products and services on site (i.e. food, beverages, etc.) and could prolong their stay in the region (one more night). To successfully increase sales, officials will have to improve the availability of merchandise throughout the park. There seems to be a willingness to do this, but at the same time a desire to protect the integrity of the site by not making it too commercial. The challenge is to find a happy medium.

Management also indicated that local residents are more sensitive than tourists to retail price hikes within the park. Consequently, a longer visit among local residents may not produce the desired results in terms of revenues. However, the presence of a large number of spectators for the various performances would surely be beneficial because it enhances the quality of the experience for everyone, as indicated by Lovelock & al. (2008) with their expression "People make the place".

The *Pays de la Sagouine* positions itself as being a place where theatre meets music. Reasons for visiting the park, along with its notoriety, are therefore central to its success. According to the survey, respondents come mainly for the theatre: the monologues, the sketches and the actors (other than *la Sagouine*). Even though local residents and tourists do not differ in this respect, it corresponds to Timothy & Boyd's (2003) statement that the link between the product (in this case, the living history) and the community is more important than the authentic replication of details. It is not surprising either that tourists are more interested than others in coming to see *la Sagouine*, which remains the trigger for a park visit. Although the question wasn't expressly asked in the survey, the reason for the first visit may just possibly be to see the park's main character, *la Sagouine*, which has been interpreted by the same actress since the outset in 1972. This actress is now close to 80 years old. In outside circles, no one knows what is being planned for her character. Park officials are no doubt debating the question, but they have given no sign as to what the future holds for *la Sagouine*. It is important that management make its intentions known and take advantage of the situation to "relaunch" the Sagouine "product". It is hard to image that the actress's retirement could toll the end of her character. Why not create a buzz around her replacement?

Still on the topic of reasons for visiting, it is interesting to note that learning about Acadian history is more important for tourists than local residents. The *Pays de la Sagouine* is not a historic site and never promotes itself as such. However, tourists often associate the *Pays de la Sagouine* and the Acadian Historic Village, which is located more than 200 km away and is in fact a living interpretation of Acadian history. Some of the comments made by tourists can be summed up as follows: "We won't be going to the Acadian Historic Village, but we will be visiting the Pays de la Sagouine and will at least learn about part of the Acadians' history" (LeBlanc, 2011).   This is a misguided idea and it demonstrates the limitations of interpreting a fictional work based on local history and culture. Some of the tourists confuse the two. Not so with local residents!

The park's notoriety is based on three pillars, namely its main character (*la Sagouine*), its theatre performances and its live music. These three elements are listed first by respondents. Reasons for visiting the park are slightly different from its notoriety in that Acadian history occupies a different position. It is a reason for visiting, but is not recognized as an important element of the park's notoriety. Having experienced one or several visits to the *Pays de la Sagouine* seems to make this clear to visitors. It is important that management clarify this ambiguity about the product. Since the theatre presentations are based on fiction, park officials would be well advised to promote this in order to show that the plays are constantly renewed and the product is constantly growing (or being relaunched) in its life cycle.

Not surprisingly, local residents and visitors living more than 40 km away are more interested in seeing the program change from year to year. As indicated earlier, this is a relatively large city located some 50 km from *Le Pays de la Sagouine*. Visiting this attraction therefore makes an accessible and interesting day trip. Tourists living 40 or 80 km away probably have some form of attachment to the park, but it likely isn't as strong as local residents'. This represents a significant challenge for management, who are faced with the costs associated with program changes in order to satisfy regular clients and the investment required to attract more tourists (from more than 80 km away). The answer isn't simple since local residents are more sensitive to increases in admission fees, as also noted by Wall (2011) in the case of Fort Edmonton.

Park management wishes to increase the number of Anglophone visitors because they represent an important target audience and are currently not well served (Doucet, 2009). They must however preserve the site's integrity (especially with regards to the use of the French language), or else risk antagonizing its local clientele. They have put forward a few initiatives that show some signs of success, but there remains a lot of work to be done. To get an idea of just how far it could go, management asked respondents about the possibility of changing the park's name in order to attract more Anglophone visitors. Neither local residents nor tourists supported this idea. We can no doubt deduce that respondents want to keep Antonine Maillet's work as authentic as possible. Another explanation would be that the few Anglophones who do visit the park do it with full knowledge of the facts and are interested in being immersed in the Acadian and French culture.

The future development of the *Pays de la Sagouine* rests on a better understanding of its local clientele and tourists. As we have just seen, these two client groups have different perceptions about both the park's programming and marketing (NuFocus, 2009). It is important that the park continue to enjoy the support of local residents, economic and political stakeholders (Clavé, 2010) and tourists. It must therefore avoid disappointing visitors (both local residents and tourists) by offering something that would create false expectations (Beritelli, 2005).

The *Pays de la Sagouine* must rejuvenate itself to become more of a leisure and business complex (Beritelli, 2005) capable of attracting tourists while providing a better quality of life for local residents through the expression of its local culture and pride (Lee et al., 2007), also with live exhibitions (entertainment) allowing for interaction with visitors (Nowacki, 2009). As these lines are being written, officials have begun rethinking the park's future. They want to know where it stands in its life cycle and take measures to ensure its development. The challenge is significant, but exciting!

Note that the results presented herein are from a Web survey of individuals who could be qualified as being "sympathetic" to the *Pays de la Sagouine*, which would constitute the study's main limitation.

Notes

[i] In New Brunswick, approximately 31% of the population (234,000 out of 750,000 people) is of French descent (Census, 2011). Francophones are mostly concentrated on the east coast of the province, a symbolic territory known as Acadie. After the Natives, the Acadians were the first permanent residents in North America. They have succeeded in preserving their mother tongue (French) and their culture since 1609 despite being surrounded by a vast English-speaking majority.

References

Amusement Parks and Attractions (IAAPA). *http://www.iaapa.org/*

Ashworth, G. (2010). Romantic modernism: Nostalgia in the world of conservation. *International Journal of Heritage Studies*, 16, 240–241.

Beritelli, P. (2005). Activity-based market segmentation: A behavioural approach. *Tourism*, 53 (3), 259-266.

Boyd, S. (2002). Cultural and heritage tourism in Canada: Opportunities, principles and challenges. *Tourism and Hospitality Research*, 3(3), 211–234.

Census, (2006). *Community Profile.* http://www.statcan.gc.ca/start-debut-fra.html.

—. (2011). *Community Profile.* http://www12.statcan.gc.ca/census-recensement/2011

Clavé, S.A. (2007). *The Global Theme Park Industry.* Cambridge, ME. CABI.

—. (2010). Leisure parks and destination redevelopment: The case of PortAventura, Catalonia. *Journal of Policy Research in Tourism, Leisure and Events*, 2(1), 66-78.

Cohen, E. (2007). 'Authenticity' in tourism studies: Après la lutte. *Tourism Recreation Research*, 32(2), 75–82.

Desjardins, P. (2009). *Personal Interview with the Chairman.*

Doucet, M.F. (2009). *Personal Interview with the General Manager.*

Economic Planning Group. (2006). *Le Pays de La Sagouine Operational Review.* Halifax: Economic Planning Group.

Gordon, A. (2009). Pioneer living 1963 style: Imaginations of heritage in a post-war Canadian suburb. *International Journal of Heritage Studies*, 15, 479–493.

Inglis, D., & Holmes, M. (2003). Highlands and other haunts: Ghosts in Scottish tourism. *Annals of Tourism Research*, 30, 50–63.

LeBlanc, M. (2011). *Résultats de l'enquête sur le web auprès des visiteurs au Pays de la Sagouine.* Dieppe: Groupe stratégique NuFocus.

Lee, T.J., Li, J. & Kim, H.K. (2007). Community residents' perceptions and attitudes towards heritage tourism in a historic city. *Tourism and Hospitality Planning & Development*, 4 (2), 91-109.

Leiper, N. (1997). Big success, big mistake, at big banana: marketing strategies in road-side attractions and theme parks. *Journal of Travel & Tourism Marketing*, 6 (3-4), 103-121.

Lovelock, C., Wirtz, J., Lapert, D., & Munos, A. (2008). *Marketing des services : 6ᵉ édition.* Paris: Pearson Education.

Maillet, A. (1971). *La Sagouine.* Montréal: Leméac.

Milman, A. (2009), Evaluating the guest experience at theme parks: An empirical investigation of key attributes. *International Journal of Tourism Research*. 11(4), 373-387.

Nowacki, M.M. (2009). Quality of visitor attractions, satisfaction, benefits and behavioural intentions of visitors: verification of a model. *International Journal of Tourism Research*, 11(3), 297-309.

NuFocus (2009). *Plan de marketing du Pays de la Sagouine*. Dieppe: Groupe stratégique NuFocus.

Pays de la Sagouine. (2010). *Le Pays de la Sagouine, visiteurs cumulatifs*. Bouctouche: Pays de la Sagouine.

Pays de la Sagouine. (2011). *http://sagouine.com/index.php?option=com_content&view=article&id =1&Itemid=11&lang=en*

Sawler, H. (2009). *Le Pays de la Sagouine A Sustainable Future*. Charlottetown: Forerunner.

Schneider, B., & Bowen, D. (1995). *Winning the service game*. Boston: Harvard Business School Press

Timothy, D.J., & Boyd, S.W. (2003). *Heritage tourism*. Harlow: Prentice Hall.

—. (2006). Heritage tourism in the 21st century: Valued traditions and new perspectives. *Journal of Heritage Tourism*, 1, 1–16.

Tourism and Parks, (2010). *Economic Impact and Tourism Expenditures in New Brunswick in 2008*. Fredericton: New Brunswick Department of Tourism and Parks.

Wall, K. (2011). A sliver of the true fort': imagining Fort Edmonton, 1911–2011. *Journal of Heritage Tourism*, 6(2), 109-128.

CHAPTER ELEVEN

SHORT-TERM FESTIVALS AS EXAMPLES OF ECO-TOURISM? AN EVALUATION OF THE KIRKWOOD WILDLIFE FESTIVAL, SOUTH AFRICA

NIGEL WEBB, TANYA SPEYERS AND NICOLE GOOSEN

Abstract

Growing disillusionment with mass tourism has meant that eco-tourism has become popular. This popularity has led to many tourist events being labelled 'eco-tourist'. Such labelling, specifically in relation to festivals, is analysed using a two-pronged approach. The first investigates the essential qualities of both eco-tourism and festivals to determine whether the former can be inscribed on the latter. The second assesses the Kirkwood Festival according to a set of eco-tourism criteria. For this second approach, data were collected from festival management, attendees and associated businesses. Although the festival was shown to adhere to eco-tourist criteria linked to community promotion and preservation, it did little to contribute to environmental awareness and local economic development.
Keywords: Kirkwood Wildlife Festival, eco-tourist criteria, eco-tourism.

1. Introduction

Eco-tourism has two major distinctions. First, it is considered to be the fastest-growing sector within the tourist industry (Campbell, 2002; Ceballos-Lascurain, 1996). Second, it is increasingly viewed as an alternative to mass tourism which is now being seen as destructive (Fennel, 2008). Both this growth and popularity have led to a situation where a wide range of tourist activities have sought to adopt an eco-tourist focus. Festivals in South Africa are a case in point and will be elaborated upon below.

A number of possible consequences emerge from the appropriation of an eco-tourist focus by other tourist activities. One of these is that the notion of eco-tourism is continually being stretched to fit new situations. Another is that eco-tourism is constantly having to be defended against dilution, and finally, that the use of the label 'eco-tourism' is simply used as an advertising gimmick to give a certain activity more currency. All of these consequences are at the heart of the investigation concerning the Kirkwood Wildlife Festival (KWF).

Thus, the purpose of this chapter is to determine whether the essential elements of eco-tourism can be legitimately appropriated by short–term festivals such as the KWF in such a way that it can be considered a valid example of eco-tourism. In order to accomplish this, the essential features of both eco-tourism and festivals will be analysed. This analysis will be followed by a detailed investigation of the KWF itself in which data, collected from festival management, attendees and associated businesses will also shed light on its nature.

2. Eco-tourism and Festivals

The traditional notion of 'eco-tourism' does not normally extend to festivals and other tourist events such as concerts, art exhibitions and sporting events because it was claimed that the site itself was an attraction in its own right (Libasoda, 2009; Weaver, 2001). Typical sites, therefore, included areas of ecological and or cultural significance such as game parks, forests and mountain ranges among others. The idea was that these ventures would contribute directly to the funding of conservation projects (Lindberg, Enriquez & Sproule, 1997:547). Early eco-tourists consisted of male birdwatchers, scientists, wildlife enthusiasts and conservationists who tended to be financially secure, well-educated, had the means for extended visits and were prepared to endure hardship (Fennel, 2008). However, developments in thinking and practice have led to the development of conceptions of eco-tourism involving nature-intensive tourism that both safeguards the environment and impacts on the wellbeing of the local people (Buckley, 2007; Higham, 2007). More specifically, this translates into a nature-based approach which also exhibits ecological, socio-cultural and economic sustainability (Blamey, 1997, 2001; Laing & Frost, 2010; Weaver, 2001).

As the literature promoting eco-tourism has grown, further elements and potential benefits have been added. For example, Buckley (2008) asserts that eco-tourism raises environmental awareness for both the local community members and the tourists in a sense that a platform is created for the distribution of environmental knowledge. Problems faced by local communities are exposed to a wider audience especially with the return of the tourists their home countries. This educationally-orientated form of tourism is designed to make tourists aware of and adopt more environmentally-sensitive attitudes and possibly even adopt environmentally-sound behaviour themselves. The empowerment of the local community is another theme. Borman (2008) indicates that it is this empowerment that actually ensures that the community benefits from eco-tourism projects. He mentions the revitalisation of cultural traditions; improvement in community structure, organisation and leadership; growth in community pride; and the development of new skills in the Cofan Indian community in Northern Ecuador.

There has recently been a movement to extend the notion of eco-tourism even further (Weaver, 2007). One of its latest incarnations is that of an amalgamation of adventure tourism, cultural tourism and eco-tourism, called ACE (Fennel, 2008). This involves attempts to include certain spaces and activities under the broad umbrella of eco-tourism that traditionally would have been excluded. For example, could zoos, urban parks and game auctions be examples of eco-tourism? Weaver's (2007) example is that of viewing recreational angling as an eco-tourist activity. Although angling depletes natural wildlife resources, it is an activity which promotes appreciation of the natural environment and may be less harmful than many other activities as long as the appropriate controls are in place. The blurring and overlapping of these different forms of tourism is a clear example of how the boundaries of eco-tourism are becoming increasingly difficult to discern (Weaver, 2002a). Thus, an opportunity is created for speculation as to whether some activities may be classed as eco-tourism or not, based on broad criteria that are open to interpretation (see Blamey, 1997) and on the fact that eco-tourism is a concept in good currency.

This broadening of eco-tourism has led to concern over the corruption or watering down of 'genuine' eco-tourism principles. For example, Fennel (2008) states that eco-tourism has gravitated towards business-orientated tourism with its utilitarian reasoning and very weak sustainability influences. Furthermore, Honey (2002) laments the fact that eco-tourist principles have become increasingly ambiguous and calls for a new set of clear standards, tools and criteria (Honey, 2002). Wheeler (1991: 96), in turn, is sceptical about the growing popularity of eco-tourism. He believes it to be an elaborate ruse and marketing tool for creating a demand for tourism at a time when mass tourism is under fire:

> By clothing itself in a green mantle, the industry is being provided with a shield with which it can both deflect valid criticism and improve its own image while, in reality, continuing its familiar short tourism commercial march.

In one sense, the dynamic nature of eco-tourism is to be expected. Driven by powerful social forces such as an ever-growing environmentalism and with businesses eager to exploit significant amounts of 'tourist' money, eco-tourism is bound to change. Yet, in another sense, the change must be meaningful and not simply cosmetic. Thus, while this chapter recognises the changing nature of eco-tourism, these changes need to be anchored to environmental and ecological principles otherwise the label 'eco-tourism' means very little. The six principles that have been identified are derived from TIES (1993) and can be stated as follows. Any eco-tourist activity should: have a clear environmental focus; have a minimal impact on the environment; contribute to a growing awareness of conservation; contribute tangibly to the conservation of the local environment; provide economic benefits to the local communities; and be a catalyst for the respect of different cultures.

An aspect of festivals that has received ongoing attention is that of their variety (Richards, 2007). In fact, festivals seem to focus on any aspect that a group deems worth celebrating. Art, language, cinema, theatre, religion and nature are all common themes. The challenge is to make sense of the notion 'festival' in the light of the bewildering array of different types and their increasing focus on the environment. Thus, a short discussion on the essential nature of festivals will be given below.

The term 'festival' is a derivative from the Latin word *festivas*, which is said to signify a social gathering with the purpose of celebration or thanksgiving (Waterman, 1998). Thus, at its core, a festival plays an important role in integrating communities. It does this by providing an ideal space for expressing the close relationship between identity, place and shared histories (Quinn, 2005). Local communities are thus drawn together and strengthened. India, with its vast array of cultural festivals, is a clear example of community gathering around a single event (Rao, 2001). Thus festivals are institutions that reinforce community ties and social cohesion (Coleman, 1988) by providing a focal point for celebration and a regeneration of community pride. According to Owusu-Frempong (2005), African festivals are mechanisms for community gathering and unification. They achieve this by being a source of the traits that encompasses a culture's collective existence and identity. These traits include "knowledge about folklore, history, philosophy, aesthetics, music, dance, art and myth" (Owusu-Frempong, 2005: 732). The rich cultural diversity of South Africa is often showcased in festivals such as the Cape Town Jazz Festival, the Cape Minstrels' Carnival and the Klein Karoo Arts Festival in Oudtshoorn.

Art forms an important part of cultural expression and is thus, by default, an important focus in many festivals. Arts festivals also function as unifiers of history – a dimension which can be seen in the Edinburgh Festival (Prentice & Anderson, 2003). This festival often attracts types of tourist searching for a Scottish identity though socialisation, art, and 'creative tourism' (Prentice & Anderson, 2003). A local example is that of the National Arts Festival held in Grahamstown. It makes theatre, music and even ballet available to an audience that might not have had access to these before.

Another core element of culture is religion. These festivals have sacred connotations such as the many Catholic, Jewish and Hindu festivals celebrated all over the world (Lochtefeld, 2004; Manasseh, 2004). While religious festivals, involving important dates in the church calendar or saints or martyrs, have been practiced for centuries, they can aslo have more sinister connotations (Falassi, 1987). The pagan 'Festival of the Dead' most commonly known today as Halloween, is a case in point.

People and products are also celebrated by festivals. Stratford-upon-Avon that celebrates the works of William Shakespeare and the Bayreuth Festival commemorates Wagner with annual staging of his works. Harvest festivals are celebrated in most cultures. These range from simple thanksgiving services in church to elaborate rituals such as those performed by the Namoos tribe of the Tallensi people on the Golden Coast of Australia. Fortes (1936) was the first to describe this early Australian festival in terms of: ritual sacrifice, the beating of drums, dancing, and socialising. The Ficksburg Cherry Festival is the oldest harvest festival held in South Africa and is characterised by feasting and celebrations at the end of the harvesting.

Few cultures have not been affected by the rise in Environmentalism, and nature-orientated festivals are being established on a regular basis (Natural Life, 2010). These festivals often have an aspect of the environment such as a plant or animal species at the centre, which is then surrounded by cultural experiences and recreation of all sorts. The annual Cherry Blossom Festival in the rural town of Kakunodate, north-eastern Japan, is an example (Sakurai et al., 2011). Bird-watching festivals are now also a fairly common type of eco-festival (US Fish & Wildlife

Service, 2010), but on a wider scale, the USA celebrates its National Wildlife Refuge Week in early October. This week is filled with festivals that include wildlife observation, photography as well as environmental education and interpretation, all conducted in a convivial atmosphere (US Fish & Wildlife Service, 2010). Locally, the Hermanus Whale Festival held in the Western Cape, celebrates the annual mating and calving of the Southern Right whale and classifies itself as South Africa's only enviro-arts festival.

The above review has demonstrated that festivals are innovative events which celebrate a wide variety of aspects. Furthermore, they are dynamic in that they can develop new foci, adapting to what is perceived to be important at the time. The growth of the nature-based festivals is a case in point. The function and the meaning of a festival have been described by Falassi (1987: 2) as follows:

> Both the social function and the symbolic meaning of the festivals are closely related to a series of overt values that the community recognises as essential to its ideology and worldview, to its social identity, its historical continuity, and to its physical survival, which is ultimately what festivals celebrate. (Emphasis added)

Within this conception, a festival can be seen as having the ability to incorporate any "overt values", "ideolog [ies]", "worldview[s]", and "social identity" that a community deems important. There is thus no reason why the values, ideologies and worldviews could not be compatible with eco-tourist principles. The real test, however, is whether particular festivals that claim to be 'eco-tourist' exhibit those principles in practice. This leads directly to the case study, the Kirkwood Wildlife Festival.

Kirkwood is situated in the Eastern Cape in the Sundays River Valley (Fig.1), bordered by the Addo Elephant National Park and in relatively close proximity to a number of other game reserves. It is a largely farming community and plays an important role in citrus production in the country, earning approximately R500million in foreign revenue annually (Kirkwood Wildlife Festival, 2010). The main tourist attraction of this generally obscure town (population 10148) is the annual wildlife festival which in 2010 drew approximately 38 000 people. At the heart of the festival is the game auction, but other activities include food and wine stalls, car shows, conservation exhibitions, traditional dances, and concerts by leading South African artists. The festival which takes place in late June is sponsored mainly by Amalgamated Banks of South Africa (ABSA) and is recognized as one of the largest within the country despite its rural setting.

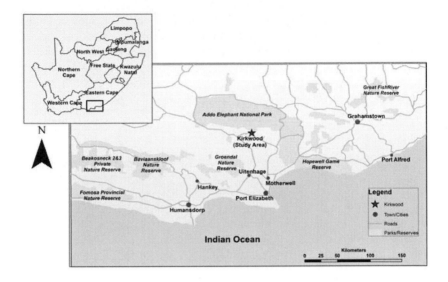

Figure 1 - Kirkwood and its Surroundings (Source: Map drawn by M. Ndou)

3. Methodology

In order to ascertain whether a festival such as the KWF can be classified as an eco-tourism event, a set of criteria was adapted from the main principles of eco-tourism as outlined by TIES (1993). In these terms, a festival would need to: have a clear environmental focus; minimise its physical impact on the environment; provide awareness of the need to conserve the environment; contribute tangibly to the conservation of the environment; provide economic benefits for the local community; and infuse the event with an awareness of and a respect for different cultures. These six statements were then placed in a matrix to allow for a degree of quantification in the form of a rating scale where each criterion is rated using values from 1 to 5. The rating of each statement was done in two separate stages. It was first undertaken by the festival management and then the festival attendees. Because of the disparities in the numbers among the groups, an average value was computed and then assigned to a position on the rating scale. These two sets of ratings are shown side-by-side to indicate the differences.

The economic contribution of the festival was investigated in greater detail. A questionnaire was administered to the festival management; and a random sample of festival attendees, stall holders, local shops and listed local accommodation establishments. Areas of interest included the motivations governing the organization of the event; the effects of the on the hospitality industry; whether small-business development and skills-building occurred as a result of the event; whether employment opportunities were created; the degree to which the local community was involved in the staging of the festival; and the distribution of festival profits.

4. Results

As far as the rating of the festival by different groups is concerned, one would expect the festival organisers to rate all the aspects of the festival highly since they were responsible for the marketing, planning and the execution of the event. Nevertheless, their rankings, and the basis on which they were made, are important to the study. In fact, five of the six criteria were rated highly, with only the economic one being considered moderate. The above views are underpinned by the following additional findings gleaned while conducting the interviews. The stated aim of the festival was to conduct a strong, specialist wildlife festival in the Eastern Cape, and according to the organisers, the festival was environmentally-friendly for two main reasons. First, the physical impact on the environment has been negligible. The local high-school grounds are converted into the festival site every year and provide the necessary infrastructure. The only impact on the site is the erection of temporary stalls and booths which are removed afterwards. Secondly, the festival has received at least two environmental awards with respect to its waste management system.

Two aspects were also mentioned in terms of the conservation of the environment. The awareness aspect was taken on by a specific South African National Parks (SANPARKS) stall where conservation ethics were demonstrated to festival-goers, while the actual conservation aspect rested on the wildlife auction. While the SANPARKS stall promoting conservation was in evidence, it was overshadowed by all the other elements of the festival. In this case, the festival organisers' assessment of its importance is probably exaggerated. The logic associated with the conservation role of the auction is as follows: The festival hosts the second-largest wildlife auction in the country. These proceeds accrue to SANPARKS who are then able to use these to improve conservation within the parks. The festival, then, creates a massive amount of publicity for the auction and creates a convivial atmosphere in which this is able to take place, encouraging conservation.

As far as cultural promotion is concerned, the festival organisers aimed to hold a multicultural festival which sought to transcend the traditional cultural boundaries in South Africa. For example, the opening function was a mix of the Xhosa, English and Afrikaans cultures conveyed by theatre, music and dance. Traditional Xhosa face-painting was also offered during the festival and an effort was made to broaden the spectrum of entertainers for the event. Although considerable effort was expended to provide a multicultural atmosphere, a large amount of entertainment available was focused on the Afrikaans culture. Again, the views of the organisers tended to be exaggerated because the festival seemed to be only moderately successful at providing an integrated event.

It would be logical to assume that the ranking of festival by the festival-goers would be lower than that of the organisers which was indeed the case. The most important reason for this difference is that the aims, ethos and theme of the festival would be less clearly perceived by this group than the former one. Furthermore, festival-goers might have varied and mixed motivations for attending such an event which has nothing to do with the stated aim and ethos. Yet, if the essence of the festival escapes the festival-goers, it cannot be considered a success, however enjoyable it might have been. The particular ratings of both groups are provided in Table 1, below.

In this case, the environmental and conservational issues were rated low, while the economic and cultural benefits were rated high. Non-tangible assets such as the fact that the festival "puts Kirkwood on the map" were also mentioned. The role of the festival in creating an awareness and a respect for culture had the highest rating of any of the measures. The cultural aspect of the festival was of great importance, with 72% of the visitors viewing this as the dominant feature of the event. The fact that the majority of the festival-goers were Afrikaans-speaking and that the majority of the entertainers were also Afrikaans, means that this strong cultural emphasis is rather narrow.

Table 1 - Ratings of the Kirkwood Wildlife Festival

Criteria (The extent to which the KWF)	Rating scale							
	Low		Moderate		High		Very High	
	M[1]	FG[2]	M	FG	M	FG	M	FG
Has a clear environmental theme		2					5	
Has a minimal impact on the environment		2					5	
Provides an awareness of the need for conservation				3	4			
Contributes tangibly to environmental conservation				3	4			
Provides economic benefits to the local community			3			4		
Provides awareness of and a respect for culture							5	5

[1]Festival management; [2]Festival-goers

4.1. Economic analysis

In interviewing festival attendees, 81% of respondents stated that all their spending would take place at the festival. Very few had any intention of taking part in activities outside of the festival grounds as their sole purpose in travelling to Kirkwood was to engage in the activities and support the shops provided at the festival itself. The nature of the Kirkwood festival is that it is an event which has a defined geographical area, the school's sports grounds. This discourages interaction between the festival-goers and the town itself, limiting tourists' experiences to the festival grounds as there is no motivation to explore further when all tourists needs are catered for at the festival.

The majority of the businesses within the town (60%) claimed that the festival's economic effect on their businesses was insignificant. Out of those that did view it as a significant generator of business, the owner of a liquor store and a bakery had had their contracts for the festival successfully renewed unlike the others. Thus, unless particular businesses could successfully negotiate a contract with the festival management and move their business to the festival grounds, they could not benefit as all activities are contained within the festival grounds. All the businesses also indicated that no additional employment was created during the period of the festival – having little stake in the festival meant that the hiring of extra staff was not necessary. This correlates with Crompton and Mackay's (1994) study which states that it is unlikely that businesses will hire new employees for a festival period as increased business demand would only last for a few days. Existing employees are more likely to be requested to work overtime. Local business development as a result of the festival would not appear to be significant.

It must be noted that a limited number of accommodation establishments exist in Kirkwood, ten being listed. These are fully booked during the festival period to the extent that additional accommodation is provided by the school, and homes are opened up to visitors. The owners of nine establishments were interviewed, and it was found that a combined total of approximately R56 000 was spent by tourists on accommodation. Totals per establishment varied considerably, with those providing accommodation for sponsors and stall holders securing the greatest profit.

The short time period over which the festival takes place considerably limits the window of opportunity for the generation of significant economic benefits. Those establishments hosting festivalgoers generally did not receive guests for longer than two nights. This particularly affects smaller establishments. However, it was acknowledged that overall the festival provided a significant, if short, burst of economic benefits for most establishments. It was also found that the same customers returned and booked year after year with accommodation almost fully booked at least six months in advance. An interesting finding was that the informants were of the opinion that the festival had also attracted an increased number of visitors to the town outside the festival period.

The direct involvement of local residents in the festival can be gauged via assessing the involvement in stall holding and employment generation. Of the 320 stalls, festival management estimates that approximately 20 belong to Kirkwood residents. The survey conducted confirmed this low percentage, with only six percent of the stalls representing local ventures. The small population needs to be taken into account in this regard.

Nevertheless, the fact that the majority of stalls represent non-local businesses implies that the profits entering the local community via stall holding at the festival are relatively insignificant.

In terms of job creation and the provision of skills to underprivileged communities, it would appear that the festival falls short of this goal. The nature of the festival means that it usually requires a small number of full-time organisational and management personnel and a relatively large number of temporary, menial labourers. Specifically, two experienced volunteers carry out all the organisational tasks on a permanent basis while 350 temporary jobs for the less-advantaged are available two weeks prior to the festival. The value of any employment to the underprivileged is obvious. However, local economic development requires that job generation for local residents be created on a more permanent basis.

The Forum for the Future (1998) lists community enterprise as one of the essential activities for local economic development to take place. According to festival management, community enterprise at the festival is operational. This includes community organizations or individual community members taking advantage of the opportunity the festival provides for community development. This is encouraged by the festival by providing certain enterprises or organizations with stalls free of charge. For instance, the local Afrikaans Christian Women's Association runs a stall which raises money for various projects in the area. These include raising funds for the old age centre and children's havens. In contrast with other stalls, there is assurance that the profits generated in this case will be used in a direct way to benefit the community.

The Kirkwood Festival is listed as a Section 21 company. The implications of this are that profits remaining after the deduction of expenses are used as a float from one year to the next or otherwise put back into the community through the funding of appropriate programs such as charity organizations. Generally, in the case of the Kirkwood Festival, approximately one third of the capital is given back to a board-approved community project. Past recipients have included the *Mayibuye Ndlovu* Development Trust which seeks to empower communities living on the borders of the Addo Elephant National Park, *Isipho* Aids Trust, *Valleihof* Centre for the Aged, as well as municipal projects. The approximate amount put back into the area has been in the region of R70 000 for the 2009 festival, more than a third of the total profits.

5. Conclusion

The first conclusion of this chapter is that there is no fundamental obstacle to a festival being an example of eco-tourism provided that the festival does not separate itself from core eco-tourist principles, examples of which have been outlined above. A major implication is that it is possible to determine whether a festival complies with the principles or not. Yet this is far from easy. Immediate questions that arise involve the level of compliance. At what level must a principle be adhered to? How many principles need to be complied with? There are no easy answers to these questions.

The second conclusion is that as an eco-tourist event, the KWF is weakest where it should be strongest, namely, its environmental and conservation focus. While these particular elements can be discerned, they are muted. On the other hand, the cultural element of the festival stands out. This begs the question as to whether the KWF is an arts festival that includes a number of eco-tourism elements to give it added status.

As far as the economic contribution of the festival is concerned, it does contribute to the social upliftment of the local area by ploughing back profits into the poorer sections of the community. Otherwise it faces a dilemma. If it had to adopt a stronger local economic development strategy, it would need to be a vehicle for greater local capacity-building, ongoing employment and the involvement of local businesses. Yet, to do this it would mean substituting these for the high-profile pavilions, products and musicians that are brought into the area that function as a draw-card for the crowds.

From a theoretical point of view, it seems that there is no reason why a short-term festival cannot be an example of eco-tourism. Practically, this is far more difficult to achieve. But, by rethinking its strategy, there is no reason why the KWF could not move closer to an eco-tourism ethos.

References

Blamey, R. (1997). Eco-tourism: The search for an operational definition. *Journal of Sustainable Tourism, 5,*109–130.

—. (2001). Principles of eco-tourism. In D.B. Weaver, K.F. Backman, E. Cater, P.F.J. Eagles, & B. McKercher, (Eds.). *The Encyclopedia of Eco-tourism.* (pp. 5-22). NY: CABI.

Borman, R. (2008). Eco-tourism and conservation: The Cofan experience. In A. Stronza & W.H. Durham (Eds.) *Eco-tourism and Conservation in the Americas* (pp. 21-29), Wallingford: CABI.

Buckley, R. (2007). Impacts positive and negative: Links between eco-tourism and environment. In R. Buckley (Ed.) *Environmental Impacts of Eco-tourism* (pp.5-14), Wallingford: CABI.

Campbell, L.M. (2002). Conservation narratives and the 'Received Wisdom' of eco-tourism: Case Studies from Costa Rica. *International Journal of Sustainable Development, 5*, 300-325.

Ceballos-Lascurian, H. (1996). *Tourism, eco-tourism and protected areas: The state of nature-based tourism around the world and guidelines for its development.* IUCN: Geneva and Cambridge.

Coleman, J.S. (1988). Social capital in the creation of human capital. *American Journal of Sociology , 94*, 95-120.

Crompton, J.L., & MacKay, S.L. (1994). Measuring the economic impact of festivals and events: Some myths, misapplications and ethical dilemmas. *Festival Management and Event Tourism 2*:33-43

Falassi, A. (Ed.) 1987. *Time out of Time: Essays on the Festival.* Mexico City: University of Mexico Press.

Fennel, D. (2008). *Eco-tourism* (3rd ed.). NY: Routledge.

Fortes, M. (1936). Ritual festivals and social cohesion in the hinterland of the Gold Coast. *American Anthropologist , 39*(4), 590-604.

Forum for the Future. (1998). Local economy programme, 'Sustainable Local Economic Development': A new agenda for action. Forum for the Future.

Higham, J. (2007). Eco-tourism: Competing and conflicting schools of thought. In J. Higham (Ed.) *Critical Issues in Eco-tourism Understanding a Complex Tourism Phenomenon. (*pp. 1-20). Oxford: Elsevier.

Honey, M. (2002). *Eco-tourism and Certification Setting Standards in Practice.* Washington: Island Press.

Kirkwood Wildlife Festival. (2008). Condensed business plan for 2008.

—. http://www.savenues.com/attractionsec/greater-addo.htm Accessed on 23 September 2010.

Laing, J.L. & Frost, W. (2010). How green was my festival: Exploring challenges and opportunities associated with staging green events. *International Journal of Hospitality Management 29*, 261–267.

Libosada, C.M. (2009). Business or leisure? Economic development and resource protection: Concepts and practices in sustainable eco-tourism. *Ocean & Coastal Management, 52*, 390–394.

Lindberg, K., Enriquez, J., & Sproule, K. (1997). Eco-tourism questioned: Case studies from Belize. *Annals of Tourism Research, 23*(3), 543-562.

Lochtefeld, J.G. (2004). The construction of the Jumbha Mela. *South Asian Popular Culture , 2* (2),103-126.

Manasseh, S. (2004). Religious music traditions of the Jewish-Babylonian diaspora in Bombay. *Ethnomusicology Forum*, 47-73.

Natural Life (2010). Celebrating sustainable living with natural life festivals and expos. *Natural Life Magazine*, p. 33.

Owusu-Frempong, Y. (2005). Afrocentricity, the Adae festival of the Akan, African-American festivals, and intergenerational communication. *Journal of Black Studies, 35* (6), 730-750.

Prentice, R., & Anderson, V. (2003). Festival as creative destination. *Annals of Tourism Research, 30* (1): 7-30.

Quinn, B. (2005). Arts festivals and the city. *Urban Studies, 45* (5/6): 928-943.

Rao, V. (2001). Celebrations as social investments: Festival expenditures, unit price variations and social status in rural India. *Journal of Developmental Studies , 38* (1): 71-97.

Richards, G. (2007). The festivalization of society or the socialization of festivals? The Case of Catalunya. In G. Richards, (Ed.) *Cultural Tourism: Global and Local Perspectives* (pp.257-280). NY: Harworth.

Sakurai, R., Jacobson, S.K., Kobori, H., Primack, R., Oka, K. & Komatsu, N. (2011). Culture and climate change: Japanese cherry blossom festivals and stakeholders' knowledge and attitudes about climate change. *Biological Conservation, 144*(1), 654-658

TIES (The Iinternational Eco-tourism Society). (1993). Eco-tourism Definition and Principles.
<http://www.eco-tourism.org/site/c.orLQKXPCLmF/b.4835303/k.BEB9/What_is_Eco-tourism_The_ International_Eco-tourism_Society.htm> Accessed 23 September 2010.

U.S. Fish & Wildlife Service (2010). Conserving the Nature of America. http://library.fws.gov/Pubs/conserving00.pdf Accessed 7 December 2010.

Waterman, S. (1998). Carnivals for èlites? The cultural politics of arts festivals. *Progress in Human Geography 22*, 54-74.

Weaver, D.B. (2001). Eco-tourism as mass tourism: Contradiction or reality? *Cornell Hotel and Restaurant Administration Quarterly,* April: 104-112.

—. (2002). Asian eco-tourism: patterns and themes. *Tourism Geographies 4*(2), 153-172

—. (2007). *Eco-tourism.* Milton: John Wiley.

Wheeller, B. (1991). Tourism's troubled times: Responsible tourism is not the answer. *Tourism Management 12*(2): 91-96.

Chapter Twelve

The Polish Tourism to Israel: An Overview

Dorota Szczepanowicz-Balon, Magdalena Kubal and Agnieszka Gajda

Abstract

Every year more and more Poles chose Israel as vacation destination, but it is difficult to determinate the exact number of people who go as religious versus recreational tourists. Travel agencies recommend pilgrimage expeditions in combination with recreational offers. A significant number of people want to see Israel, not only for the Holy Land, but also for its beaches and the sun. This chapter presents analysis of Israel's tourist offer, addressed to the Poles, as publicised by travel agents and tour operators, on the Polish market in 2010-2011. Their offer is still addressed mainly to pilgrims; there are rather few options for Poles to see and experience Israel beyond its religious attractions. This chapter discusses also the recent campaign by Israel, which advertised itself not only as a place of pilgrimage, but also vacation destination, and its resonance among the Polish tourists. **Keywords:** Polish tourists, travel advertising campaign, tourism offer.

1. Introduction

Today's Israel attracts millions of tourists from all over the world. Their number continually increases on yearly bases (Figure 1), and the various forms of stay in this country are continuously being developed. Tourists are offered various products; they are provided with more interesting and diverse forms of exploring the country. Israel adapts to the needs and expectations of different groups of tourists. Israel is also the Holy Land, which means religious tourism associated with all the three largest monotheistic religions in the world. Every year the Holy Land is visited by millions of tourists, among whom the Poles are certainly prominent (Figure 1). The earliest descriptions of their presence in the Holy Land date back to medieval times, when in 1147 Polish knights accompanied German knight on his way from Frankfurt/Main to Byzantium during the Second Crusade. Unfortunately, very little information survived from that period. First of all, the written sources about western European crusades rarely mentioned Poland, as the country was not involved in the 'protection' of the Holy Land (Bystroń 1930). It should be noted that at that time the Kingdom of Poland was not a stable Christian country and paganism was still alive and present in everyday life. Consistently over the next centuries, Poles visited the places associated with Jesus Christ's life and activity.

Figure 1 shows the number of Polish tourists travelling to Israel in the years 1990-2010. Since 1990 the Ministry of Tourism in Israel keeps detailed statistics of tourism and tourists ("Migration and Tourism" Israel Central Bureau of Statistics, 2011). Tourism itself is an important branch of the Israel economy ("Economy: Sectors of the Israeli Economy" 2010) and unstable political situation of the region results in changes in the variability of tourist traffic. The graph shows increasing trend of interest among the Polish people. Political situation in Israel, especially military conflicts, results in suspension in tourism and/or decrease of interest caused by the lack of safety. Such situation occurred in years 2001-2003 during 2nd Intifada. The decrease is visible in the chart.

Travel offices started to organize Polish group trips to Israel in 1990's and the number of agencies specializing in organizing pilgrimages to religious destinations began to emerge. A number of significant political determinants had direct impact on the growth of tourism from Poland to Israel. The most important was establishing diplomatic relations between foreign affair ministries of the Republic of Poland and the State of Israel (February 27th, 1990). On the same day the first international agreement about aerial traffic was signed and it entered into force September 21st, 1991. Growth of travels to Israel was also related to social and economic reasons like relatively stable growth of income among the Poles, a general interest in travelling and intense advertisements of Israel as a tourist destination. Other political changes that made it possible for Poles to visit Israel included: freedom of movement from Poland and the abolition of entry visas to Israel that contributed to the security of travel.

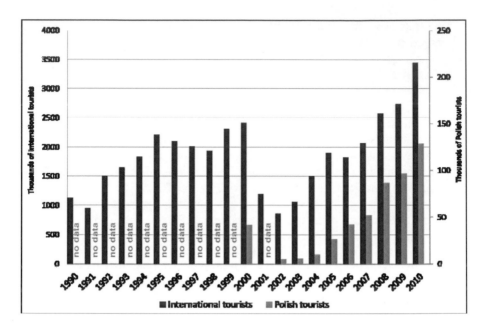

Figure 1 - The Number of Tourists Travelling to Israel (Source: www.cbs.gov.il.)

2. Current Research on Polish Tourism to Israel

The issue of Polish tourism in/to Israel was rarely researched in Polish and foreign literature. There are a lot of books devoted to tourism in Israel and guidebooks describing this country both for the Polish and foreign publishing markets (Gać 2008; Murphy-O'Connor 1999). No academic centre in Poland pays special attention to the issue of tourism in/to Israel. Individual articles by different authors touching upon the subject appear only occasionally. Examples include the work of Bury (1998) describing tourism in Israel and Polish tourists' interest in such trips; Rab-Przybyłowicz (2010) in turn analysed the phenomenon of optional excursions to Israel for Polish tourists vacationing in Egypt; Szczepanowicz (2011) focused on religious tourism of Poles to Israel. The topic of Polish tourism to Israel does not attract much attention from foreign academic centers, either. In Israel, the only academic to undertake such a study was Collins-Kreiner (2008, 2010a) with her research team of Kliot, Mansfeld, and Sagi (2006). They conducted a survey of tourists in/to Israel (Collins-Kreiner, 1999, 2006, 2007, 2010b; Finney, Orwig &

Spake 2009), among whom there was a Polish group. Articles and publications describing the spiritual dimension of pilgrimages to the Holy Land are definitely more popular than the secular experiences of travel.

3. Theoretical Background

This chapter involved an extensive review of the tourist products on offer by the travel agencies in Poland for people wanting to visit Israel. For the purpose of this study, we need to describe our understanding of term: tourist product. Territorial marketing and tourism marketing effectively use and implement the notion of 'a tourist product'. For the purposes of this study, we adopted Altkorn's rather broad definition of 'everything and anything that is the subject of purchase by tourists' (2006). The importance of a tourist product is twofold; while in the narrower sense a tourist product may refer to a single service, a much broader approach encompasses the wide variety of attractions available to tourists as well as the style of management of a given touristic area. It is the whole experience of the journey and stay abroad – from the moment of leaving the place of residence to the moment of return. A tourist product takes into account the consumer's needs and benefits, and therefore it can refer to the experience of staying in a particular place (tourist destination) or using a given tourist service.

A tourist product has a specific structure. It consists of the core of the product referring to the main motivation of a trip (e.g., a desire to relax), and the actual product treated as a service that is essential for achieving the benefits resulting from the core of the product (e.g. accommodation, lodging, guide, tourist attractions (Altkorn, 2006). It is the sum of tourist values, services, goods and facilities (tourist management) that allow tourists to use the tourist attractions and purchase goods and services. The extended product consists of additional or 'extra' features: speaking in marketing terms it is what differentiates a given tourist product from others available on the competitive tourist market. A single service is often referred to as a simple tourist product; an example of a complex tourist product is a compilation of services known as a 'package holiday'. The concept of 'a tourist product' defined in this way becomes the basis for the analysis of tourist offers (complex tourist products) and the offer of Israel (created through advertising). The study analyses tourist offers designed for the Polish tourists. According to Kurek (2008), excursions can be divided into categories: Pilgrimages and Non-pilgrimages (recreational, exploratory, sightseeing, and health tourism).

In the chapter, they are divided into two main groups: pilgrimages and non-pilgrimages. In addition, they are classified in terms of length of stay: short, medium, long term and type: stationary and touring. This creates a matrix of different aspects of various tourist offers that we juxtapose against each other in the analysis.

3. Methodology

The study was conducted in two time periods: from February to April 2010 and from March to May 2011. The purpose of the division of the research period was to capture the period of Polish tourists' highest interest of in the offers of trips to Israel offered by travel agencies in Poland. Work on a small scale included an analysis of offers of travel agents and pilgrimage tourist offices offering tourist trips to Israel. These are offers of travel agencies from across the country, with both Polish and foreign capital. They offer pilgrimage tours, but also those that focus on getting to know recreational places. We analyzed offers found in printed catalogues as well as those posted on travel agents' websites. Comparison of the offers was based on the trip's duration, character of the trip and the programme.

Conducting our research in two time periods allowed us to observe that the typically recreational offer of travel agencies had diminished in the second period. For example, the Oasis Tour travel agency in 2011 withdrew its recreational offer to Israel around the area of the Mediterranean and the Red Sea. This was caused by the low attractiveness of the offer (as perceived by the clients and visible via the actual bookings) as a result of the high pricing of such tourist packages. More attractive recreational offers in the area of the Red Sea are those available from Egyptian tour operators, advertising trips in the catalogues of Polish tour operators. Egyptian travel offers have a distinguished space on the Polish market due to their accessibility, mass character and low prices.

The offer of twenty-two travel agents was analyzed. The programmes of trips were divided into short trips (lasting from 1 to 5 days), medium-length trips (from 6 to 9 days) or long trips (lasting over 10 days), respectively. Additional features included touring trips – themed excursions such as 'getting to know Israel better' (Figure 2A and 2B) or optional trips (offered in addition to the residence in the main destination). The results of the study allow us to formulate our first conclusion, i.e. that the offer of travel agencies in Poland is dominated today by pilgrimage and sightseeing tours. The offers of recreational stays are present among those offered by travel agents, but they are much less popular because of their lower affordability. Trips to Israel from Egypt are much more competitive (Figure 2C); they are made available on the "first minute" and "last minute" bases and therefore – at a lower price. Very popular among Polish tourists are offers which include recreational stays at the Red Sea in Egypt and a wide range of optional: recreational, sightseeing and pilgrimage short excursion to Israel. Preliminary results of the research corroborate our initial observation: it is the pilgrimage trips to Israel that are most popular among the Polish tourists; their offer is also most extensive and well developed on the Polish market. The variety of pilgrimages exceeds the current sightseeing and recreational offer.

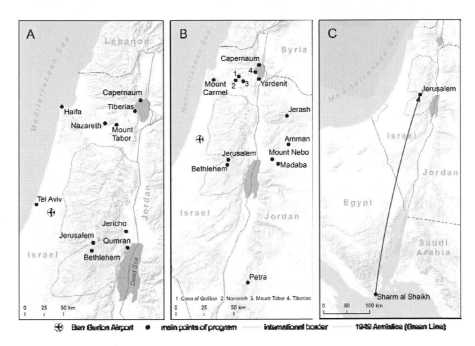

Figure 2 - A spatial and Formal Model of Travel Agents' Tourist Offers of Trips to Israel (Source: own calculations based on travel agents' offers)

4. Results

Since 1990, Poles travelling to Israel have been observed on a mass scale. That is also when that pilgrimage and tourist agencies have started to emerge in Poland. Initially, tourism products on offer were basically pilgrimages. It took years and a number of advertising campaigns for the Poles to develop an interest in Israel not only as the Holy Land. Many travel agencies, responding to the needs of Polish tourists, introduced one- or several-day trips to Israel into their offer. The major tour operators organizing trips to Israel include Komisariat Ziemi Świętej (Commissariat of the Holy Land), Centrum Travel, Biuro Pielgrzymkowe Ojców Pallotynów (the Pallottines' Pilgrimage Office) in Warsaw, Patron Travel, Nomada, Triada, Exim, Trade & Travel Konsorcjum, Katolickie Biuro Pielgrzymkowe (Catholic Pilgrimage Office) in Warsaw, Szczecin, Katowice, Tarnów, Alfa Star, Alfa-Tour, Apostolos, Ave, BTP Frater, GM Travel, Itaka, Rrainbow Tours, Awertour.

The variety of offers on the tourist market is so large that almost everyone who wants to visit Israel can do so in accordance with their expectations, financial capacity and needs (be it spiritual and recreational). One just needs to set the destination, communicate the expectations to the organizer and possibly add own suggestions as to the points that should be included in the programme of the trip. These offers can be divided into those of recreational, health, exploratory and religious nature. Offers can be divided into recreational tours, medical tours, sightseeing tours and pilgrimages. Depending on the demand, travel agents propose one-day offers (mostly as optional trips from Egypt), weekly, bi-weekly and longer ones. The latter are often connected with sightseeing opportunities in neighbouring countries.

Our analysis of recreational offers by travel agencies on the Polish market demonstrates a lack of diversity of this type of tourist products. After analyzing the offers of twenty-two travel agents and pilgrimage offices, only four were found to offer stays at the Red Sea and the Mediterranean. One of these offices has an offer that was active in 2010, and which was suspended in 2011. The products are still displayed on the website but with a note that the offer is no longer available. Another travel agent advertises a recreational stay in Israel, but it does not specify the components of the offer or the needs it can satisfy. The client is referred to a telephone consultant. Two other travel agents offer recreational stays in Israel, at the Red Sea. They lure their customers with medium-length or long stay, with an option to purchase optional trips such as a one-day trip to Jerusalem.

Israel is famous for its access to the Dead Sea, the lowest situated and the most salty reservoir of water in the world. The resorts situated on its coast, both in Israel and Jordan, have been visited by tourists wishing not only to rest, but above all – by those with health problems. The local microclimate and the health benefits of the Dead Sea attract people with skin problems, rheumatism and asthma. Stays in these resorts are also recommended to those who have reduced immunity, are stressed and/or tired. Health tourism in the Dead Sea region is very popular among domestic and foreign tourists. Most offers are prepared bearing in mind basically foreign tourists, who not only have their health needs satisfied, but can combine them with leisure and recreation.

Among the offers of the trips to Israel, we can find some which focus on recreation in the area of the Dead Sea. The majority of them are offered by pilgrimage offices; they combine a stay at the seaside and a pilgrimage. This is usually structured in following way: either a 12-day tour (with sightseeing in the morning and time for swimming in the sea in the afternoon), or a 14-day one, (with seven days of sightseeing and seven days of resting at the sea). Among the offers available from travel agents we found 7-, 8-day, or 14-, 15-day stays at the Dead Sea. This combined type of an offer seems more interesting than a typical recreational and/or sightseeing offer.

The majority of the travel offers to Israel available on the Polish market are exactly those that combine sightseeing with pilgrimage. All of twenty-two travel agents that we analyzed have such an offer in their portfolio. Many programmes do not differ from each other, but also from year to year more and more options and standard trips associated only with pilgrimage trips are revised or are supplemented by sightseeing trips (to different destinations in Israel, Table 1), not only for pilgrims. Tourists have an opportunity to see Israel during an optional trip (short term) or a medium-length stay (6-9 days, medium term) or on long trips (lasting more than 10 days, long term).

Table 1 - A: Different Places of Interest in Israel Advertised as Destinations for Optional Trips

Selected Places of Interest	A				B			
	An optional one-day coach trip	An optional one-day coach-and-plane trip	An optional two-day coach trip	An optional three-day coach-and-ferry trip	8 days–a lay travel agent	8 days–a Catholic travel agent	8 days–a lay travel agent The Holy Land & Sinai	8 days–a Catholic travel agent Holy The Holy Land + Jordan
The Dead Sea	+	+	+					
Jericho			+					
J - The Basilica of the Holy Sepulchre	+	+	+	+	+	+	+	+
J –The Christian Zion	+		+			+	+	+
J –St Anne's Church						+		+
J –The Way of the Cross	+	+	+		+	+		+
J –The Wailing Wall	+	+	+		+		+	

The Polish Tourism to Israel: An Overview

Site								
J –The Temple Mount		+			+			+
B - The Basilica of the Nativity	+	+	+	+	+	+	+	
B –The Shepherds' Field	+	+	+			+		
B –The Milk Grotto			+					
Bethany		+	+					
Jericho		+		+				
Caesarea Maritima				+				
N - The Basilica of the Annunciation	+	+	+	+				
Cana of Galilee	+	+	+					
Boating on Lake Tiberias	+	+	+	+				
Tabgha	+	+	+	+				
Jardenit		+	+	+				
Mount Tabor	+	+	+					
J – The Mount of Olives panorama					+	+		+

J – The Mount of Olives sanctuaries						
J –The Garden of Gethsemane	+		+			

J – Jerusalem B – Bethlehem N - Nazareth

(Source: Own study based on www.triada.pl , www.alfastar.com.pl, www.odyseo.pl); B: Selected items of programmes of medium-length trips to Israel (source: own study based on www.terrasanctwa.pl, www.triada.pl, www.centrumtravel.pl, www.bp.ecclesia.org.pl)

Table 1-A illustrates a sample of programmes of short trips to Israel from Egypt (1- and 2-day ones), but also from Cyprus (a 3-day one). These can be coach trips, coach-and-plane trips or coach-and-ferry trips. The latter provides the least tourist attractions in Israel itself, in spite of lasting three days, since the ferry crossing takes up much of the time of the whole optional trip. The price includes travel from/to the place of stay, HB meals, insurance, Polish tour guide, departure tax (Israel), incoming tax to (Egypt), entrance fees. 2-day tour from Egypt includes also accommodation for one night. Prices do not include tips, lunches, drinks and own expenses.

The offers presented in Table 1-A do not differ much from each other in terms of their programme. All of them offer sightseeing visits to the most attractive places and monuments. Tourists choosing a short-time offer to Israel are generally satisfied that they will visit the Basilica of the Nativity in Bethlehem, the Basilica of the Holy Sepulchre, follow the Stations of the Cross, see the Wailing Wall in Jerusalem and, most importantly, the panorama of Jerusalem from the Mount of Olives, known from postcards, photographs, and folders. This option is the most satisfying for tourists.

Short trips, however, have a lot of disadvantages. They are characterized by haste and fatigue, because tourists spend the night before the tour in the coach, which is not comfortable and quite tiresome; or they spend the night on the ferry, where they have a lot of attractions and little time to sleep and rest. In both cases, the fatigue negatively influences the perception and assimilation of information provided by the guide; it contributes to a weaker orientation in the area, difficulty with recollecting images, sounds, as well as increased irritability. Most of the tourists are also overwhelmed by the excess of emotions, because in most cases it is their first visit to Israel.

Table 1-B demonstrates the differences between the programmes of medium-length trips to Israel, including those offered by Catholic and lay travel agents. Catholic travel offices tend to treat trips like pilgrimages, hence they provide spiritual care in the form of the priest and an opportunity to participate in a daily Holy Mass. Lay travel agents offer only sightseeing visits to holy places (mainly Christian ones) as a tourist attraction and supplement their programmes with places not associated with religion.

All medium-length trips listed in Table 1-B are tours, with the possibility to increase the number of visited places and reduce the time of daily transfers. Sightseeing begins in the morning and ends early in the evening, which gives pilgrim-tourists an opportunity to relax after a busy day, or a possibility to get to know something extra, on top of what has been offered in the programme (either individually or in a smaller group). The Polish tourists tend to have fewer problems with communicating in a foreign language. This fact is associated with individual independence and ability of self-organizing one's free time. This fact makes it possible to independently explore places not included in the tour programmes and take part in the daily life of 'the locals'.

The offers presented in the Table 1-B differ by single places in the programme. All of them include the most significant places and monuments. The basic programme is usually supplemented with additional attractions. The tour operator continuously shapes the programme and adds places according to the preferences and wishes of the group that the specific product is supposed to address. Some programmes include more spiritual sites that are important for tourists travelling to Israel because of spiritual reasons. Other programmes include more sightseeing sites, not associated with Christianity but with the history and culture of Israel.

The average tourist who chooses the medium-length trips to Israel, makes detailed analysis of the offers (tourist products available on the market) and before the actual departure chooses the one that fits best his/her expectations. Accurate selection of the programme and the character of a trip guarantees greater chance for satisfaction at the end of the event.

In contrast to short trips, medium-length ones do not have that many disadvantages. Although the programmes are very rich they give the opportunity of the everyday regeneration during the night thereby they reduce the fatigue during the day. The detailed analysis of the tourist offers of travel agents is completed by a complex tourist product in the form of a tourist package. It is an original composition of various tourist assets (values and attractions) and services, connected to the destination where it takes place.

Currently, the Israeli government is increasing its efforts to promote Israel as a recreational tourism destination. These activities are directed primarily towards countries with noticeable interest in Israel as a pilgrimage destination, e.g. Poland. Such a form of tourism differs significantly from the current idea of the state of Israel as a pilgrimage destination and a country entangled in an ongoing military conflict that prevails in Poland. It is therefore a novelty in the offer of Polish travel offices. Polish tourists are not the first to appreciate the recreational and leisure qualities of the coast of Israel. Such a form of tourism is very popular with tourists from all over the world. This opinion is supported by English-language commercials broadcasted on television and posted on the

Internet, which reach tourists from around the world. It is also in the interest of the Israeli government, which itself struggles with the image of a country at war and involved in violent national and religious conflicts (Fleischer & Buccola 2002). The steps taken in order to achieve this aim are associated with the organization and financing of a new tourist product which is recreational tourism in the Mediterranean region of Israel and the Dead Sea coastal zone. A good example would be a documentary from a photo shoot of models in bikinis, funded by the Israeli government, advertising the beaches of Tel Aviv, which was published on the YouTube website. In the Video tab on the website of the Israeli Ministry of Tourism we can find places where these shots were taken. However, when we tried to log into the website recently (10.01.2012) we noticed that the film had been removed. Instead, a message appears that the removed commercials would be made public again in the near future.

The rather popular advertisements of Israel posted in the Internet are very different from the perception of Israel so far. The selection of content, form, images and language creates a new recreational tourist product, completely different from the elements of the original pilgrimage tourist product. Satisfaction of other needs met by these tourist products requires a selection of different marketing tools to promote and develop the content that is being advertised. Advertising scenarios aim to promote Israel as a state of peace, relaxation and beautiful women. This is the assumption behind the content presented in the media. Many messages have sexual overtones; the authors of the spots associate Israel with the beaches, warm sea, fun and beautiful women in bikinis or in military uniforms. These adverts include catch phrases and word-riddles in English. The translation always refers to the state of Israel, as the Holy Land, but the picture clearly shows the combination of ambiguous content. The spots promoting Israel as a vacation destination are very popular amongst Internet/You Tube users what is demonstrated by high number of hits.

The advertising campaign, carried out in Poland, has an extremely different connotation. It is supported by the Israeli government and addressed to the Polish tourists. It was carefully prepared, well thought out and adapted to the needs of the Poles, designed exclusively for the Polish market. The aim was to promote Israel not only as the Holy Land, but also as a site for excellent vacations. The campaign was held under the title "Holiday Promised Land". It can be assumed that Israel wanted to challenge the most popular vacation destinations for the Poles.

In this campaign, Israel was presented as an attractive, year-round tourist destination. In Polish cities of Warszawa, Krakow, Katowice and Lodz over 200 billboards were hung. Israel was also promoted on the radio, press and the Internet. In addition, a dedicated website www. goisrael.pl was launched. Campaign lasted until February 2011, its budget was ca. 700 000 USD. These activities were supplemented by a road show, during which a representative of the Ministry of Tourism, Israel - Yehuda Shen held a series of meetings with representatives of Polish travel agents in six major Polish cities: Krakow, Katowice, Wroclaw, Poznan, Gdansk and Warszawa. The business partners were Israeli airlines ELAL and charter airline Sundor.

The analysis of the above campaign contributes to the discussion how a change of image of a particular place can be implemented. Israel from being associated with pilgrimages is now an emerging recreational tourist destination for the Polish people. It should be emphasized that we are dealing with two extremely different forms of tourism: pilgrimage and recreational, that meet extremely different needs: the Sacred and the Profane, representing two different recipients of the tourism products. Tourism development history in the Mediterranean demonstrates that the sun and sand tourism model (Aguilo, Alegre, & Sard, 2005) and hedonistic attitude of tourists should not be literally translated into advertisement. The advertisements which portray women as objects of sexual desires (plainly for their bodies), overstress relaxation and enjoyment above all may however backfire. In Poland, they created an image of Israel much different from the intended one. This new direction of tourism promotion, different from the previous image of pilgrimage tourism in Israel, has been distorted and may consequences well into the future. Polish tourists had and still have full access to the contents of both campaigns promoting recreational tourism in Israel. There is no detailed study on the influence on the Poles and their individual decisions of choosing Israel as a tourist destination.

5. Conclusion

The aim of this chapter was to review the different ways in which Polish tourists travel to Israel by analyzing the tourist offers by travel agents in Poland. Israel today is a tourist destination for millions of visitors from all over the world. Travel agencies prepare a wide range of tourist products that are designed to meet the needs of a wide range of tourists. The analysis carried out shows that Israel offers a tourist product designed for tourists, who are characterized by new, different from the pilgrimage ones, motives of coming. Tourists are offered various tourist products, often richer in their programme and attractions, guaranteeing various forms of exploring the country's tourist values.

Israel is a tourist destination which is open to foreign tourists not only as a pilgrimage destination but also is working continuously on developing a new face as a country of leisure, recreation, relaxation and sightseeing. For a Polish tourist this side of Israel had remained unknown until recently. Today, recreational vacations in Israel are offered by 22 travel agencies and tour operators. The fact that travel agents open up to sightseeing or recreational trips indicates that also in Poland the demand for sightseeing and recreational-sightseeing tourist products has become more evident. The analysis of travel agents and their offers reveals that this form of tourism slowly becomes more and more interesting for the Polish customer. However, its ever-growing popularity cannot be attributed only to one set of factors as it would be an oversimplification. This phenomenon requires further detailed studies.

In conclusion, our study demonstrated that for the Polish customers the recreational tourism to Israel is not a simple phenomenon. It consists of a plethora of different options including short optional excursions to Israel, (that take place during longer stay in Egypt or Cyprus), medium- and long-term sightseeing/recreational tours. Catholic travel agencies offer tours that include sacred sites, places important for Israeli culture and they provide pastoral care. Lay travel agencies usually have offer similar places of interest, but their programme significantly differ from pilgrimage tours. They seem more concerned with the length of stay and comfort so as to reduce the fatigue that results from visiting certain sites. In the portfolio of the Polish tour operators, it is the pilgrimage and sightseeing offers that prevail. There is a visible lack of SPA offers. Both pilgrimage and sightseeing programmes are tours. Recreational programme is present in the offers but it is much less popular mainly because of the high price. Very popular among Polish tourists are vacation offers to the Red Sea coast in Egypt, together with a wide range of optional tours to Israel. The tourist has an opportunity to see Israel on the tour as a tourist/pilgrim, on the optional excursion (short trip), medium-length or long-term trips. Pilgrimage offers to Israel are still much better developed and overtakes the sightseeing and recreational offer.

In the second part of the chapter, two distinctive campaigns, promoting Israel as a recreational destination were analyzed. First campaign focused on the message that Israel was trying to send out to the world in general. The second was particularly directed at the Polish people, Polish customers. While the Polish advertising campaign was rather specific and focused on promoting the recreational side of Israel alongside the traditional pilgrimage destination, the international campaign was directed at a specific, narrow audience: young, well-educated and independent people. Perhaps the offer could be extended to include a wider range of visitors, regardless of their age, marital status, education and wealth. Creating a tourism product should not be based only positive or negative associations. Proper planning and developing of the branding process should involve creation of a strong image of the tourist product, which undoubtedly will be subjected to the process of product life cycle on the tourist market. This raises the question for further discussion - how language of the controversial advertisement can attract tourists and whether it is effective? Changing trends in tourism may require us to take steps in designing flexible advertising and promotional campaigns, but are there any limits of such activities?

References

Aguilo, E., Alegre, J., & Sard, M. (2005). The persistence of the sun and sand tourism model. *Tourism Management, 26,* 219–231.

Altkorn, J. (2006). *Marketing w turystyce.* Warszawa: Wydawnictwo Naukowe PWN.

Bury, M. (1998). Walory turystyczne Izraela i zagraniczny ruch przyjazdowy. *Prace Instytutu Geograficznego seria B Geografia Społeczna i Ekonomiczna,* t. XVI, 38-50.

Bystroń, J.S. (1930). *Polacy w Ziemi Świętej, Syrii i Egipcie w latach 1147-1914.* , Kraków: Księgarnia Geograficzna Orbis w Krakowie.

Collins-Kreiner, N. (2010a). Current Jewish pilgrimage tourism: Modes and models of development. *Tourism, 58*(3), 259-270.

—. (2010b). The geography of pilgrimage and tourism: Transformations and implications for applied geography. *Applied Geography, 30,* 153–164.

—. (2008). Religion and politics: New religious sites and spatial transgression in Israel. *Geographical Review, 98*(2), 197-213.

—. (2007). Evaluating tourism potential: A SWOT analysis of the Western Negev, Israel. *Tourism, 55,* 51-63.

—. (2006). Graves as attractions: Pilgrimage-tourism to Jewish holy graves in Israel. *Journal of Cultural Geography, 24*(1), 67-89.

Collins-Kreiner, N., & Kliot, N. (2000). Pilgrimage tourism in the Holy Land: The behavioral characteristics of Christian pilgrims. *GeoJournal, 50,* 55–67.

Collins-Kreiner, N. (1999). Pilgrimage holy sites: A classification of Jewish holy sites in Israel. *Journal of Cultural Geography, 18*(2), 57-78.

Collins-Kreiner, N., Kliot, N., Mansfeld, Y., & Sagi, K. (2006). *Christian Tourism to the Holy Land. Pilgrimage during Security Crisis, New Direction in Tourism Analysis.* Hampshire: Ashgate Publishing.

Economy: Sectors of the Israeli Economy. (2010). Israel Ministry of Foreign Affairs. http://www.mfa.gov.il/MFA/Facts+About+Israel/Economy/ECONOM Y-+Sectors+of+the+Economy.htm (accessed November 29, 2011).

Finney, R.Z., Orwig, R.A., & Spake, D.F. (2009). Lotus-eaters, pilgrims, seekers, and accidental tourists: How different travelers consume the sacred and the profane. *Services Marketing Quarterly,* 30, 148–173.

Fleischer, A., & Buccola, S. (2002). War, terror, and the tourism market in Israel. *Applied Economics,* 34, 1335-1343.

Gać, J. (2008). *Ziemia Święta. Kulturowy przewodnik śladami Jezusa.* Kraków: Wydawnictwo WAM.

Kurek, W. (Ed.) (2008). *Turystyka.* Warszawa: Wydawnictwo Naukowe PWN.

Migration and Tourism. (2011). Central Bureau of Statistics. http://www.cbs.gov.il/www/yarhon/e1_e.htm (accessed May 13, 2011).

Murphy-O'Connor, J. (1999). *Przewodnik po Ziemi Świętej.* Warszawa: Oficyna Wydawnicza Vacatio.

Rab-Przybyłowicz, J. (2010). Wycieczki do Miejsc Świętych jako uzupełnienie oferty wypoczynkowej Egiptu. In Z. Kroplewski, A. Panasiuk (Eds.), *Turystyka Religijna,* 378-389, Szczecin.

Szczepanowicz, D. (2011). Turystyka religijna elementem turystyki kulturowej na przykładzie wyjazdów polskich grup turystycznych do Ziemi Świętej. *Turystyka Kulturowa,* 5/2011, 17-28.

Internet resources

https://www.alfastar.com.pl. (accessed May 13, 2011)
https://www.alfa-tour.pl. (accessed May 13, 2011)
https://www.apostolos.pl. (accessed May 13, 2011)
https://www.ave.turystyka.pl. (accessed May 13, 2011)
https://www.awertour.pl. (accessed May 13, 2011)
https://www.bp.ecclesia.org.pl. (accessed May 13, 2011)
https://www.cbs.gov.il. (accessed May 13, 2011)
https://www.centrumtravel.pl. (accessed May 13, 2011)
https://www.consorcjum.com.pl. (accessed May 13, 2011)
https://www.eximtours.pl. (accessed May 13, 2011)
https://www.frater.pl. (accessed May 13, 2011)
https://www.goisrael.pl (accessed May 13, 2011)

https://www.gmtravel.pl. (accessed May 13, 2011)
https://www.itaka.pl. (accessed May 13, 2011)
https://www.nomada.org.pl. (accessed May 13, 2011)
https://www.patrontravel.pl. (accessed May 13, 2011)
https://www.pielgrzymek.pl. (accessed May 13, 2011)
https://www.pielgrzymki.katowice.pl. (accessed May 13, 2011)
https://www.pielgrzymki.tarnow.pl. (accessed May 13, 2011)
https://www.rainbowtours.pl. (accessed May 13, 2011)
https://www.terrasancta.pl. (accessed May 13, 2011)
https://www.triada.pl. (accessed May 13, 2011)
https://www.twojepielgrzymki.com.pl. (accessed May 13, 2011)

CHAPTER THIRTEEN

THE TOURIST PROJECT OF THE SETAP GROUP FOR THE INTERNATIONAL BID OF IDEAS FOR MASPALOMAS COSTA CANARIA

IVÁN ALVAREZ AND ALESSANDRA CAPPAI

Abstract

The city of Maspalomas began building in 1961[1], year of the celebration of the International Bid of ideas for Maspalomas Costa Canaria. The group of French architects and city planners SETAP where awarded first place in the bid. The project stood out due to its high quality details and the respectful distribution with the landscape. The analysis of the professional work of SETAP, the academic experience of working with the ateliers of the École Nationale des Beaux-Arts, and the bid, are the ideas developed in this investigation. **Keywords**: Urban tourism, Maspalomas Costa Canaria, atelier ATEA-SETAP, Ecole Nationale Superior de Beaux-Arts.

1. Introduction

At the beginning of the seventies, in the south of Gran Canaria Island, the land commonly known as Maspalomas became the place where the new tourist city started to get built. This city was going to be the object of the greatest number of direct and indirect tourist activities of the island. This would promote and transform the main economic engine of the island.

The Maspalomas estate, with an extension of 2,000 hectares and a length of 17 km of coast, was the property of Mr. Alejandro del Castillo y del Castillo. The owner, advised by the architect, Mr. Pedro Massiu, and constantly accompanied by the architect from Madrid, Mr. Manuel de la Peña Suárez, was the person who had the intuition of creating and giving shape to a new international tourist center[2] by the name of Maspalomas Costa Canaria.

To that end, it was necessary to create a bid for ideas from architects and city planners from around the world. The preparation for the official announcement of the International Bid of ideas for Maspalomas Costa Canaria was done under the auspices of the International Union of Architects (UIA) in Paris and the Higher Council of Architects of Spain (CSAE) in Madrid.

The 9th of January of 1962 the international jury announced the eagerly awaited project. The first prize went to the French atelier SETAP (Société pour l'Étude Technique d'Aménagements Planifiés) with a plan that exceeded all of the prospects of every single member of the jury, who decided, unanimously, that the project was superior to the ones submitted by the rest of the participants[3].

The ATEA and SETAP atelier, managed by the architects Guy Lagneau, Michel Weill and Jean Dimitrijevic, until this time was in charge of important projects in the field of architecture, such as the Museum of La Havre (1959), and city planning, such as the study of the outskirts of Paris or the city of Cansado (1958) in Mauritania. The SETAP, installed in Paris, is structured in study groups known as ATEA+SETAP or ATEA +AART, where each one of the departments can develop activities simultaneously, jointly or independently[4]. The relationship of some atelier integrants who taught at the École National Supérieure des Beaux-Arts (ENSBA) and the École des Ponts et Chausséss in Paris was essential in distinguishing some of the peculiarities of the project presented by the SETAP for the Maspalomas bid.

2. The ATEA + SETAP in Paris

The first architectural works were developed by the architects Daniel Badani, Guy Lagneau, Michell Weill and Jean Dimitrijevic in Paris during the 1949, in a building constructed around 1920. The Atelier, divided into eight spaces, a reception, offices, model rooms, etc. It was equipped with distinguished furniture designed by Marcel Gascoin and Finnish chairs model Alvar Aalto (*L'architecture d'aujourd'hui*, 29) that could be dismounted. This Atelier served to start an activity that later in 1953 resulted in the founding of the society ATEA and SETAP.

The offices for the development of architecture and planning would take the name of ATEA (Ateliers d'Etudes Architecturales) and SETAP (Société Technique d'Aménagements Planifiés). The atelier was managed by Guy Lagneau (architect-city planner), Michel Weill (architect-city planner), Jean Dimitrijevic (architect-city planner), Renzo Moro (architect), Henri Coulomb (architect-city planner), Paul Cordoliani (architect), Pierre Ropion (office manager), Philippe Gennet (lawyer-city planner) and Ivan Seifert (city planner). They created a structured and a multidisciplinary atelier for projects that went from an architectonic scale to a wider territorial distribution.

2.1. Structure of the Atelier ATEA+SETAP

The studies and assignments elaborated by the ATEA+SETAP group had to follow an internal methodology of work adapted to the atelier's model and to the type of jobs that they received. In this manner, ATEA+SETAP depending on the type of project began with a "Conseil d'administration" for jobs relating to: technical services; regional, urban, operational or decentralization developments; and administration; or from the "Architectes Conseillers Techniques de la SETAP" for jobs relating to: architecture; tourist development; habitat; community equipment; industrial architecture; investigation and bids.

Depending on the type of job, the "Conseil de coordination equipe ATEA + SETAP" would be the first to prepare the prospecting guidelines for the development of the project. Once the guidelines were established and after deciding which of the four big areas of work would follow: Architecture, technical services; development; and administration; they continued with the project process until the elaboration of the final documentation, before the "Exterior Experts Council", where it was reviewed by external engineers.

2.2. Organization of the Atelier ATEA+SETAP

ATEA and SETAP had complementary activities; they had a common organization and a permanent team whose activities belonged to the following areas:

1. Analysis, coordination, synthesis, study proposals in the areas of geography, demography, economy, finance, city planning, regional and rural development, planning and industrial decentralization.
2. Conception, coordination and executive management of the architecture works.
3. Conception, coordination and executive management of the technical studies related to architecture and engineering.

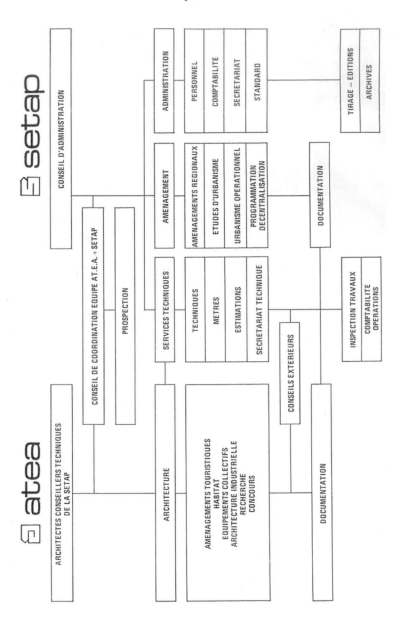

Figure 1 - Structure of Work Stages Depending on Type of Project[5]

Both departments of the Atelier ATEA and SETAP could intervene together, simultaneously or separately, each having their own permanent personnel available[6]. ATEA and SETAP complete this organization with the common and permanent cooperation of different engineers and consultants, as occurred on several occasions with the cooperation of Jean Prouve, among others.

2.3. Tourist development: 1961-1972

Of the 17 tourist plans elaborated by the atelier between 1961 and 1972, the Maspalomas project in 1961 became the first tourist development done by SETAP. The plan estimated a capacity of 40,000 beds and a population density of 60 habitants per hectare. In the same manner, in 1972 the city of Maspalomas became the last tourist project designed by the atelier. In this occasion, it was a consultation by the Maspalomas Costa Canaria company as to how to achieve a 200,000 bed capacity.

The participation of the atelier in numerous tourist planning projects meant working in countries like Spain, Portugal and France. Among the tourist projects and studies elaborated, it is worth mentioning the ones done for Maspalomas (1961), the plan for Mourillon a Tulún in France (1963), the proposal for Vilamoura in Portugal (1965), and the residential assembly of the Marinas de Cogilon in Portugal (1965).

The Maspalomas plan in 1961 stands out due to its fantastic geometry of undulating silhouettes and for its high landscape value, besides having respected the dune system. The project estimated a total capacity of 40,000 beds and an average population density of 60 habitants per hectare in a 2,000 ha extension. The green spaces and the urban settlement units were active elements for the organization and structuring of the coast territory.

On the Mediterranean coast, the strategy employed for the development of the coast of Mourillon en Tulún in 1963 was located at the foot of Mourillon cornice and possessed a 2 km length of coast shore. The project defended the creation of a series of artificial beaches; the creation of spa and recreation equipment; the implementation of luxury residential areas; the building of secondary and tertiary activities that suited the reconversion of the jobs; and the enhancement of the links and exchanges with the region (*Urbanisme*, 100).

In 1965, the tourist project for the town of Vilamoura in Algarve, at the hands of the company LUSOTUR, elaborated a plan with a multidisciplinary team composed of MM. Carver, L. Baker, J. Cactano and Jean Dimitrijevic. The plans and studies were elaborated by C. L. Baker, SETAP, GEFEL and Hidrotecnica Portuguesa Lda. The project stood out for its organic setup and proposed a collection of residential and tourist units that were interconnected, interpreted and managed as a single unit (*Urbanisme*, 101). The proposed structure has meant that the dimension of the planned program has been divided into eight great development areas, connected and intertwined by the road network and green spaces.

The example of Las Marinas de Cogolin will serve as a model of a plan meticulously elaborated and built in the same manner. In 1965, the atelier ATEA and SETAP in cooperation with the engineers Vernet and Paul, and the technical assistants of the "Financial Society for the tourist industry", planned a port complex with an area of 40 ha, of which the recreational port was to take up more than half of the space and with a capacity for 1,500 mooring spots. The rest of the program was defined by 600 houses, and commercial, technical and recreational equipment (*Techniques et Architectures*, 34). As with the other plans elaborated by the atelier, the structure is organized by three groups of changeable settlements, where each one is strategically placed with regard to the port, understood as the real "amusement"[7] and from which all intervention gravitated.

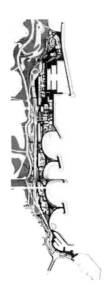 

Left. Figure 2 - Development plan of the coast of Mourillon en Tulún[8]. 1963. Right. Figure 3. Model of the tourist project in the International Bid of Maspalomas Costa Canaria[9]. 1961.

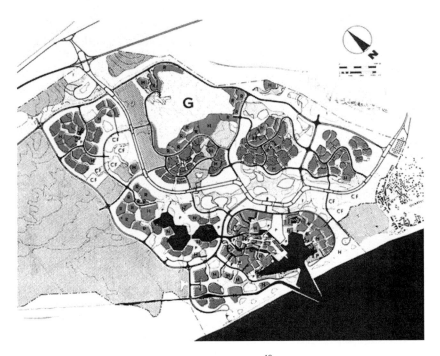

Figure 4 - Tourist development plan of Vilamoura[10]. 1965

3. Methodology Training in the École d'architecture of Paris, ENSBA 1956-1959

The École Nationale Supérieure des Beaux-Arts (ENSBA) in Paris was the education center where the directors of the ATEA and SETAP: Guy Lagneau, Michel Weill y Jean Dimitrijcvic, received their training, as well as other contributors that were part of the atelier. Its directors in the decade of the 50's became part of the group of professors at the ENSBA, creating the Lagneau-Laffaille atelier. The training as urban planner of Guy Lagneau and Michel Weill continued at the Institut d'Urbanisme of the Université of Paris, and Jean Dimitrijevic, architect and technology specialist, went on to the Massachusetts Institute of Technology (M.I.T.).

The ENSBA during the year in which the atelier SETAP won the Maspalomas bid (1961) was an active participant in the creation of a reform to university education in Paris. Some of the most important concepts of the reform proclaimed by the architect and professor Marcel Lods[11] are collected in his first writings, by means of the 1956-1959 education program of the ENSBA, such as:"... l'Ecole tentera de former des esprits ouverts á l'universel..."[12] and "...chaque élément de la création fait partie d'un tout indissociable."[13].

Some of those ethical objectives helped establish the educational guidelines in the ENSBA and adapted to the demands of the Artistic Education General Management[14] of France.

The new reform in education, as stated in the texts of architect Marcel Lods, should guarantee a solid artistic and technical education for students. With the new teaching system, the ENSBA became a center for art and architecture. Marcel Lods described this new spirit of education as: "L'Association pour la création d'une École d'Architecture et d'un Centre expérimental d'Architecture et d'Art"[15]. These words captured the attention of the Secretary of Education in Paris and the Secretary of State of Fine Arts. Only in this manner could the new study plan of the ENSBA reflect architectural studies in three cycles: Propaedeutics (two years); architectural studies (four years); and "stages" (one year).

Students that started the propaedeutics course had to prove their abilities, values for spatial imagination and sensibility to colors and shapes, with activities such as: conferences, practical exercises of application in groups through photos[16]; and seminars on design and construction of models.

The second cycle of education corresponded to the architecture courses with a duration of four years. The work of territorial planning and organization were taught the second year with Guy Lagneau as a teacher.

In addition to the theoretical lessons, practical projects were carried out in the ateliers. The workshops were composed of a maximum of thirty students, teachers and assistants. The objective of the projects was to develop the student's knowledge of culture and methods of artistic expression.

Some organization charts of the ateliers at that period showed the methodology applied on student education. In the education program of 1952-53, they analyzed how the atelier "Lafaille-Lagneau", in collaboration with Jean Dimitrijevic, realized constant reviews of the students' projects. The last stage of the project was assessed by the Managing Committee that awarded them with the education diploma.

During the time they had for the elaboration of the project, training was complemented with theoretical classes and conferences taught by external teachers of the ENSBA.

4. Events, Projects for the International Tender of Maspalomas Costa Canaria

The southern area of Gran Canaria Island, after several attempts of exploitation at the beginning of the 50's with the exploitation of small tourist interventions, among which we can emphasize the proposal of landscape gardener, Nicolás María Rubió, the proposal for the Maspalomas Hotel by the architect Manuel Martín Fernández de la Torre in the Oasis area, and the design of a Parador type by architect Eduardo Laforet (Pescador 1999, pp. 216-217) served as first intuitions for the development that later transformed the Maspalomas area in an international center.

After the first International Bid of Ideas in Spain with tourist purposes, nominated as "Elviria residential area" (1960), the second experience corresponded to the International bid of Maspalomas Costa Canaria (1961). Its developers, Mr. Salvador Guerrero in the case of the "Elviria residential area", and Mr. Alejandro del Castillo y del Castillo[17] for "Maspalomas Costa Canaria" were motivated at the time by the New Plan for the Development of the State by the creation of tourist centers and the recent creation of the Ministry of Tourism[18] in Spain.

Some of the architectural magazines of global recognition[19] announced the "Maspalomas Costa Canaria" bid during 1961. Accompanied by the national press, they revealed the extraordinary qualities of the place for the implementation of a tourist center, with headlines such as "Maspalomas, punto de atracción mundial" (*Falange*, 1961) or "Maspalomas, la mejor playa de Europa" (*Falange*, 1961). The wide coverage of international disclosure that the bid manifest produced among architects of all over the world brought to the event the construction of a tourist imaginary for the city of Maspalomas that was yet to be built.

The development of the bid follows the guidelines established in the "Project regulations for International architecture tenders" as reflected in the attachment of "Project regulations for International architecture and urban planning tenders"[20] published by the U.I.A. in 1955. The regulations were composed of a total of 53 articles, divided in 9 chapters, of which emphasis can be placed on some of the mandatory areas, such as: inscription and admission of participants; awarding of bonuses, compensation and indemnities; copyright; UIA cooperation, and organization and publicity of the bid.

In order to know the steps that were to be followed during each of the phases of the bid, the developer visited the organizers of the "Elviria" tender in Malaga. In the elaboration of the document that set forth the basis for the tender, important people inside the local and national sphere, such as Mr. Simón Benítez Padilla specialist in geological studies, Mr. Felipe Gracia (meteorologist of the Spanish Air Force in the Canary Islands) for the study of the climate in the area, and Grabados Topográficos S.A. in Madrid for the topographical study had their participation. The degree of detail that was included in the basis was such that the judges praised the work done by the company Maspalomas Costa Canaria.

During the admission period between the 1st of June and the 1st of August of 1961, the registration enrolled 148 participants from all over the world[21]. The day of the reception of the projects was the 1st of December and the result of the jury was announced the 9th of January, 1962.

The jury, as described by the international tender regulations of the UIA, had to be formed by members of different nationalities, with the recommendation that one of them be named by the UIA so that the regulations were abided. In this case, the jury was composed of Van der Broek (president) Holland; Pierre Vago (UIA member) France; Luis Blanco Soler and Antonio Perpiñá Sebriá, Spain, Franco Albini, Italy and Manuel de la Peña Suárez (secretary), Spain.

The jury's decision unanimously established that the winning project was the atelier SETAP. The deliberation took place in the Guanarteme warehouse which housed during the days of 4-9 of January, 1962, the 80 proposals presented. According to the UIA's periodical publication in 1962, of the 80 projects received[22], two were disqualified for not fulfilling article 11, regarding the date of delivery and the anonymity of the projects.

The remaining 78 projects were evaluated according to the criteria established by the jury for the following parameters:

1. Respect the dunes, the oasis, the landscape and the beaches, avoiding
2. excessive use of the delta,
3. Creation of a tourist center, not a city,
4. General composition of quality, not quantity,
5. Creation of a tourist center of attraction and entertainment, situated to the west of the oasis and in its surroundings,
6. Distribution and classification of the tourist groups with a good
7. disposition of the road network and accesses to the beaches,
8. Provision and organization of the systems of open spaces,
9. Development of the stages and their execution possibilities,
10. Analysis of the different services.

After deciding the evaluation parameters for each project, 3 elimination rounds were done. In the first one, 46 projects were discarded; in the second one, 12; and 8 in the third one. Finally, 12 projects were remained, for which only 7 received an award or some recognition. The SETAP project that pursued a territorial organization model had, as one of its main objectives, the achievement of an organized urban structure. To do that, one of the project's characteristics was the shape and city model, which was based on: concentration of services; the grouping of installations and tourist equipment as independent units. The units of grouping equipment or housing units were joined and interconnected by a network of roads and green spaces.

The peculiarity of working by units characterized the plan in a zoning system. The theory, developed by the professor André Gutton at the ENSBA, defined the functions that man needs in a city and that must be part of the urban landscape, grouped in 4 concepts (habitat, work, leisure and movement). The city model (Gutton, 1952) of A. Gutton for 50,000 habitants has some similarities with the Maspalomas project. A model built by: variable units, separation of functions; the tracing of the road network; the concentration of use; the plasticity used in the designs; and the prevalence of green as a natural element of the city, define the city proposed by A. Gutton and projected by SETAP at Maspalomas.

In the SETAP project, with an extension of 2.000 hectares, only half of which could be used for building, with a global population density of 60 habitants per hectare and a total population of 60,000 inhabitants. This urban model characterized the intervention with a high value and respect for the landscape. The population was distributed in seven units or sectors as follows: San Pedro (7,700 pop.); Pasito Blanco (6,300 pop.); City of Maspalomas (12,300 pop.); Los Ingleses (9,800 pop.); San Agustín (12,200 pop.); Campo Internacional (4,400 pop.); and San Fernando (7,000 pop.). Each of the sectors was equipped with tourist service infrastructures, roads and green spaces.

The distribution of each of the urban groups had as an objective the organization of the housing units. The large variety of tourist accommodations presented the following in their projects: luxury hotels, lower category hotels, motels, luxury villas, bungalows, apartments, leisure areas. It was a differentiating aspect in regards to the other proposals presented. Among the leisure equipment were piers for leisure boats, vehicle stations, restaurants and a racecourse.

Nevertheless, in this occasion, I have only outlined some of the general aspects of the report that describes the SETAP project. Of the existing publications, the ones by the French magazine Urbanisme (*Urbanisme*, 87) and of the author Ignacio Nadal Perdomo[23] in the book *El Sur de Gran Canaria: entre el turismo y la marginación* are the most accurate in the detailed description of the project.

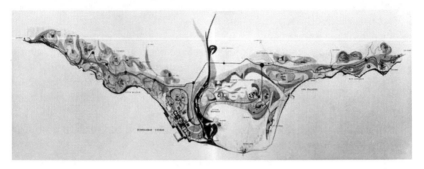

Figure 5 - Plan presented to the tender in January 1962 by the S.E.T.A.P group (Source: provided by Pedro José Franco).

Of the SETAP plan, only the first intervention in San Agustín (1962) was respected, with the building of the restaurant "La Rotonda" and the Apartments "Los Caracoles" by the architect Manuel de la Peña Suárez. The rest of the interventions were planned by a General Organization Plan by Manuel de la Peña and some partial plans that had little to do with the initial project of the atelier SETAP. The other urban planning operations during the 60's and 70's responded to the expectations of the first massive tourism waves that had chosen the city of Maspalomas for vacation.

Notes

[1] The result of the bid was announced in January 1962; however, 1961 was the year in which the material presentations, participant inscription and projects that were presented to the bid took place.

[2] (Taped) Interview given to the author of Mr. Alejandro del Castillo (son of the developer) on the January 4, 2008, Las Palmas de Gran Canaria. Duration: 132 min.

[3] In 1961, a similar bid had been announced in Malaga in which four of the jury members coincided. In this occasion, the first prize did not mean that the second prized was not awarded as in the case of Maspalomas due to the quality of the first prize winner.

[4] All the information about functions and relationships between different departments of atelier AS was founded at *Cité de l'Architecture & du Patrimoine*, in AS; ATEA+SETAP, *Brochure c.v atea+setap*; pp 5-18, edn, s.ed., Archives (IFA) Dossier ATEA-SETAP.133 Ifa 12/1.

[5] AS; ATEA+SETAP, *Brochure c.v atea+setap*; edn, s.ed., Archives (IFA) Dossier ATEA-SETAP.133 Ifa 12/1. page 3.

[6] The number and division of permanent personnel is: URBANISM 12 Sections-6 ETAM; ARCHITECTURE 12 Sections-21 ETAM; TECHNICAL STUDIES 12 Sections-4 ETAM; MANAGEMENT SERVICES 3 Sections-8 ETAM; COMMON SERVICES 1 Section-7 ETAM. (The meaning of the acronym ETAM is unknown). AS; ATEA+SETAP, *Brochure c.v atea+setap*; edn, s.ed., Archives (IFA) Dossier ATEA-SETAP.133 Ifa 12/1. page 4.

[7] Term used by the architect Jean Dimitrijevic to explain the project. Interview (taped) given to the author to architect Jean Dimitrijevic, October, 2008, Paris. Duration: 56 min

[8] L'aménagement du Litoral du Mourillon, par l'Atelier d'Architecture Lagneau, Weill, Dimitrijevic (1967), *Urbanisme*, 100, 50-51.

[9] Biaugeaud, J. (1961), Personal document of the author, provided by Pedro José Franco López, photo of the model, Maspalomas Costa Canaria project, S.E.T.A.P. group (3) b/n; 23x17cm. edn, s.ed, s.l.

[10] L'aménagement touristique de vilamoura, algarve-portugal, par C.L. baker, J.caetano et J.dimitrijevic.(1967). *Urbanisme*, 101, 52-53.

[11] Marcel Lods was an architect and urban planner, founder of the Association Beaudouin et Lods and teacher responsible for the atelier Lods-Hernant-Trezzini at the ENSBA.

[12] "... the École tries to develop a spirit open to what is universal..." École d'architecture de Paris, Archives (IFA) Dossier Lods. 323 AA 14/2. Nouvelle École; Construction-premiers documents 1956-1959, page 18.

[13] "... each element of the creation is part of an indivisible all". Archives (IFA) Dossier Lods. 323 AA 14/2. Nouvelle École; Construction-premiers documents 1956-1959, page 18.

[14] Marcel Lods was an architect and urban planner, founder of the Association Beaudouin et Lods and teacher responsible for the atelier Lods-Hernant-Trezzini at the ENSBA.

[15] "The association for the creation of an Architecture School and an experimental Center of Architecture and Art". Archives (IFA) Dossier Lods. 323 AA 14/2. Nouvelle École; Construction-premiers documents 1956-1959, w/o num. (introduction document).

[16] This technique was used by the SETAP Group to develop the Maspalomas project. Interview (taped) given to the author to architect Alain Naman (contributing city planner in charge of the Maspalomas Costa Canaria project in the SETAP group), the 7th of July, 2009, Paris. Duration: 38 min.

[17] See introduction of the article. Mr. Alejandro del Castillo y del Castillo had knowledge of the Elviria tender because of the architect Mr. Pedro Massiu. Nevertheless, the architect Manuel de la Peña is the one who always accompanied him and managed the projects of the tender, due to his relations in Madrid and his language knowledge.

[18] Minister Manuel Fraga de Iribarne had a great interest in this type of private initiatives that meant the development of the State Plan. Also, the Minister of Housing José María Martínez y Sánchez Arjona will visit the installations of the

tender and will have knowledge of the Maspalomas plans and the Las Palmas plan, 1962.

[19] The French magazine L'architecture d'aujourd'hui announced in its pages of the tender, notes of the development for the Maspalomas Costa Canaria tender in the different issues published in 1961.

[20] Members of the UIA committee: Paul Vischer (Switzerland), Pierre Deprés (France), Patrick Abercrombie (United Kingdom), Georges Candilis (Greece) Werner March (Germany); as observers were Pierre Vago y Robert Lebret. UIA, February, 1955.

[21] The journalist Francisco García Torres, in the newspaper La Falange, on the 1st of October, 1961, announced after the closing of the enrollment, the participation of 148 competitors (8 Japanese, 3 Israeli, 3 Turkish, 2 Yugoslavian, 1 Algerian, 1 Uruguayan, and others from countries like: Portugal, France, Italy, Monaco, Switzerland, Poland, Denmark, Belgium, Germany, Sweden, Holland, United States, UK, Mexico, Argentina, Finland, Canada, etc.). The main nationalities that participated were French, Polish and Dutch. However, the geographer Ignacio Nadal Perdomo in 1983 described the participation of 141 competitors of 24 countries with representation of 30 Spaniards, 25 French, 20 Polish, 8 Dutch, 8 German and 7 Japanese. In Nadal Perdomo, I. & Guitián Ayneto, C., 1983, El Sur de Gran Canaria: entre el turismo y la marginación, C.I.E.S., Lanzarote, page 80.

[22] The UIA's periodical magazine in 1962 published the participation in the Maspalomas Costa Canaria tender of 80 competitors. Nevertheless, Ignacio Nadal Perdomo in his book El Sur de Gran Canaria: entre el turismo y la marginación, after conversations with the Maspalomas Costa-Canaria company, describes that 81 projects were handed in and that in the end half of them were discarded because they worked on the dune areas.

[23] Nadal Perdomo, I. & Guitián Ayneto, C., 1983, El Sur de Gran Canaria: entre el turismo y la marginación, C.I.E.S., Lanzarote, pages 82-87 (Text created through the French magazine Urbanisme (#87) and the documentation presented regarding the SETAP project in the Association of architects in Las Palmas).

References

Alvarez León, I. (2011). The tourist project of the Setap group for the international bid of ideas for Maspalomas Costa Canaria. *ARA Journal of Tourism Research*, *3*, 15-23.

Archives IFA (1958). Dossier Lods. 323 AA 12/1

—. 14/2. *Nouvelle École; Construction-premiers documents 1956-1959*, w/o num.

—. Anonymous s.a., AS; ATEA+SETAP, *Brochure c.v atea+setap*, Paris, Dossier ATEA-SETAP.133 Ifa 12(1), 3-18.

Biaugeaud, J. (s.a). *Doc of the author, courtesy Pedro J. Franco López*. Unpublished manuscript.

Cappai, A. (2012). *Planning for tourism in Costa Smeralda.* Paper presented at 6th Conference of the International Forum on Urbanism IFOU. (2012, 25th to 27 th of January). Barcelona. Spain.

Del Castillo, A. (January 2008). *Interview given to the author of Mr. Alejandro del Castillo (son of the developer),* Las Palmas de Gran Canaria. Duration: 132 min.

Dimitrijevic, J. (October 2008*). Interview given to the author of Mr. Jean Dimitrijevic (son of the developer),* Paris. Duration: 56 min.

Fernández Perdomo, O. (1999). La urbanización Campo Internacional de Maspalomas: El final y el comienzo de un modelo. J.S. López. In *Arquitectura y Urbanismo en Canarias 1968-1998* (103-126). Las Palmas de Gran Canaria: Universidad de Las Palmas de Gran Canaria.

Franco López, P.J., & Mendoza Quintana, A.T. (2004). *Maspalomas: las raíces del progreso 1964-2004: los inicios de la zona turística: homenaje a los pioneros del trabajo hostelero.* Gran Canaria: PeJota / TeeMe.

Gutton, A. (1952). *Conversations sur l'architecture: Cours de théorie de l'architecture professé à l'école nationale supérieure des beaux-arts,* Paris: Vincent, Fréal & Cie.

L'aménagement du litoral du mourillon, par l'atelier d'architecture lagneau, weill, dimitrijevic.(1967). *Urbanisme, 100,* 50-51.

L'aménagement touristique de vilamoura, algarve-portugal, par C.L. baker, J.caetano et J.dimitrijevic.(1967). *Urbanisme, 101,* 52-53.

Les marines de cogolin: Dans le golfe de st-stropez; arquitecto Dimitrijevic, Jean. (1971). *Techniques Et Architectures, 34,* 87-91.

Maspalomas, la mejor playa de Europa. (1961, 20th of June). *Falange* newpaper, page 3.

Maspalomas, punto de atracción mundial (1961, 1st of October). *Falange* newpaper, page 5.

Nadal Perdomo, I., & Guitián Ayneto, C. (1983). *El sur de gran canaria: Entre el turismo y la marginación.* Lanzarote: C.I.E.S .

Naman, A. (July 2009). Contributing city planner in charge of the Maspalomas Costa Canaria project in the SETAP group, *Interview given to the author of Mr. Alain Naman (son of the developer),* Paris, Duration: 38 min.

Pescador Monagas, F. (1997). *Viaje a través del patio.* Las Palmas de Gran Canaria: Ayuntamiento de Las Palmas de Gran Canaria.

Proyecto de Reglamento de los Concursos Internacionales de Arquitectura. (1955). *UIA Union Internationale des Architectes, 6,* 25-26.

Un grand Project touristique aux îles Canaries: Mas palomas par la S.E.T.A.P.(1965). *Urbanisme, 87,* 16-18.

Un Atelier d'architecture a Paris (1950), *L'architecture d'aujourd'hui*, *29*,
    page 11.

CHAPTER FOURTEEN

FEMINIZATION OF A MUSIC INDUSTRY: EXPLORING THE RELATIONSHIP BETWEEN TOURISM AND MUSIC CULTURE IN GOA, INDIA

MTAFITI IMARA AND RANJEETA BASU

Abstract

In this chapter, we posit an interdisciplinary framework derived from economics and music to achieve two objectives: to understand the relationship between tourism and feminization of the music industry in Goa, India; and to understand the resultant effect on the wellbeing of female musicians and music culture of Goa. Empirical evidence has shown that international trade has led to increased demand for female labor. This phenomenon is called the feminization of the labor force. The question that this project addresses is how this increased demand has affected women musicians in terms of their own wellbeing but also in terms of changes in music culture. We measure these changes in terms of artifacts, performance practices, aesthetics, and spiritual significances. **Keywords**: Feminization, wellbeing, music culture, cultural levels.

1. Introduction

"Goan history is a mosaic shaped from every conceivable historical activity which stimulates culture. It is a kind of tapestry woven from Indian traditions of most profound value mixed with the finest elements of European renaissance." (Shirodkar, 1988, p. iii)

In the creation of a fine tapestry or quilt there are various elements and processes that come into play, the least of which being a consideration of how color, texture, shape and overall form can be combined as a single entity with potentially multiple functions. It could be hung on a wall and intended as provocation of thought. It could be a floor-covering intended to enhance the décor of a highly trafficked room. It could also function as bedding meant to keep a child protected from cold nights and imagined fears. A quilt can also function as a meta-narrative, the recycling and regenerating of identity by bringing together disparate and often discarded fabrics. It can tell a story of the second-order that encompasses both the individual agent situated in, and reacting along with a community (Tobin & Dobard, 1999). Thus, it is a useful metaphor for interpreting and bringing together a range of theoretical approaches to assess problems of our contemporary social and cultural life. One such problem is the understanding of the relationship between economic decisions and processes and the cultural life of a community.

In this chapter, we have two objectives: 1) to understand the relationship between tourism and feminization of the music industry in Goa, India; and 2) to understand the resultant effect on the wellbeing of female musicians and the broader music culture of Goa. These objectives are grounded in certain basic assumptions that were generated in a dialogic process involving both theory and practice of music and economics, as well as fieldwork in Goa over a four-year period. As part of our study we conducted structured interviews with 26 female musicians who actively participate in the tourism industry in Goa. Additionally we examined websites and promotional videos on Goan tourism. In the following sections we will convey their perspectives on how they act and react to tourism as well as provide an analysis of how their stories are interwoven into the tapestry of Goan music culture. But first the assumptions - the thread that connects all of the different elements: 1) there is an organic relationship between wellbeing and culture, whereas the well being of an individual is at once contingent upon, and influences the degree of cultural vitality of a community; 2) cultural change can be assessed by observing and describing transformations and functions of specific levels of cultural expression and production; 3) tourism is both an economic and a cultural activity. Musicians, as agents of change, act and react to tourism within both the economic space and the cultural space. Their actions ultimately contribute to cultural change.

2. Background

When Goan author Maria Couto stated, "globalization is not new to Goa," she was reflecting on the fact that the world has been coming to Goa for centuries[1]. She spoke of the long-standing geopolitical and cultural significance of Goa to successive waves of diverse peoples who have come to conquer, convert, extract, frolic, conduct pilgrimage, be a tourist, or simply settle into an environment often characterized by *sossegado* – a calmness and peacefulness that can only be found in a collusion of physical place and mental space. At various times in its history Goa has been controlled by the Vijaynagar Empire, the Bijapur Sultanate, the Estado da Índia Portuguesa, and since 1962, the Republic of India. It was however, the 450 years of Portuguese presence that truly sets Goa apart from the rest of India. Although its location at the western edge of the Western Ghats and the eastern edge of the Arabian Sea makes it a strategic location for shipping and trade; and despite its fertile soil that yields coconut, cashew-nut, mango and rice - as well as precious minerals extracted from the same - it is tourism that is Goa's main industry. Moreover, it is its Portuguese-ness that has come to be the major feature of "the tourist gaze" (Urry, 1990). In this chapter we focus on aspects of the gendered nature and conditioning of the tourist gaze.

3. Relationship between Feminization and Tourism

There seems to be some agreement amongst scholars about the implicit connection between export orientation of the economy and increased female employment. But at this point two divergent paths have emerged in the literature. One school of thought argues that trade liberalization results in fragmentation of the production process and the *deskilling* of the labor force (Kabeer & Mahmud, 2004; Pearson, 2007). They call it *female marginalization* by inclusion and segregation into low paying jobs (Fernandez-Kelly, 1983; Purcell, 1997). In addition, a majority of these jobs (e.g. cleaning or serving within the hospitality industry) perpetuate traditional gender roles (Momsen, 1994; Moore, 1995). Another school of thought articulates this as *female-led industrialisation* where women are included in the process and have much more input into decisions about work conditions (Safa, 1995). These authors argue that with trade liberalization women in developing countries will benefit: (i) they will be more likely to find employment; (ii) they will have access to market income; and (iii) have more control over their lives (Cone, 1995; Swain, 1993).

The female marginalization school of thought provides one explanation for the increased demand for female musicians. They would argue that as tourism expands, tourism venues compete for scarce tourist dollars by either offering a unique experience or by offering the same experience at a lower price. If the focus is on price competition, then venues catering to tourists aim to provide a homogenized product at the lowest price. The process of homogenization to facilitate mass consumption often leads to deskilling of the labor process and firms demand low wage, low skilled labor, which in many instances happen to be women due to gendered societal constraints and the subsequent lack of opportunities. In the case of the music industry, tourist venues demand low wage, low skilled musicians who can perform a standard repertoire of popular songs. Our findings suggest that the story does not quite unfold in that manner in Goa. According to the women we interviewed there are proportionately more women working in the music industry over the last decade. Although there may be other factors, this trend is coincident with the growth in tourism. Tourist venues are trying to cut costs and they do that primarily by decreasing the size of the bands they hire. The increased availability of digital technologies has made it possible to substitute live musicians with recorded tracks. In the process of reducing the number of musicians, vocalists tend to be the last to get cut. Since most, if not all, of the female musicians participating in the tourism industries are vocalists they benefit from this trend.

Demand for labor also depends on tourist preferences and expectations regarding the tourist experience (Urry, 1990). To understand how tourist preferences are affecting demand for female musicians we focus on: (i) the way in which Goa is being packaged and sold to tourists by the tourism industry and the state government of Goa; and (ii) the changing mix of the tourist population in Goa. Post-colonial and post-structuralist literature has characterized the promotion of tourist venues as a socially constructed narrative where the tourism industry "invites first world western tourists to consume third world places and people as pleasure products." (Aitchison, 2001). There are several studies that have deconstructed this narrative using feminist discourse analysis of tourism promotion materials (Marshment, 1997; Patil, 2011). We studied the Goa Department of Tourism's promotion video and the tourism promotion materials available on the Goa Tourism Development Corporation's (GTDC) website. This is the chief medium for cultivating the tourist gaze. The overall theme is one of 'having fun' and representing a trip to Goa as "a balm on the busy mind to enjoy days of freedom on Goa's magnificent beaches". The Goan tourism industry attracts tourists by representing a social space whereby 'anything goes", i.e. a relaxation of social norms. To the domestic tourists, Goa's 'Portuguese-ness' is packaged as being exotic. Goa is called the "Rome of the East". There is also an appeal made to domestic and international tourists that Goa is a destination for tourists from around the world. The GTDC invites tourists to "swim with the tide of fellow visitors from all around the globe". The promotional video mainly includes images of tourists, both white (European) and brown (Indian), having fun at the beach, on cruises, engaging in a variety of adventure activities. Most of the tourists, both men and women are young, athletic, dressed in swimwear in direct contrast to the few depictions of local Goans. The local 'Goans', both men and women, are depicted dressed in traditional clothing, engaging in Goan festivals and rituals both Hindu and Catholic. There were also images of local Goans either cooking or serving food or playing music for the tourists. These Goans were always shown *serving* the tourists and were always male. Ultimately, the videos and promotional materials depict Goa as a place where tourists don't have to adhere to the strict social dress codes and norms of behavior that exist in the rest of India.

Tourist expectations and preferences differ based on factors such as age, sex, country of origin and language. About 70% of tourists coming to Goa are male. As compared to international tourists, the percentage share of domestic tourists visiting Goa from the rest of India has been increasing in recent years. The fact that Goa has a lower drinking age as compared to the rest of India is an added attraction. As evidenced by the promotion videos, part of the attraction for domestic male tourists is the promise of the racialized, sexualized "other". In this case the other happens to be international tourists who, given the 'anything goes' expectation, dress and behave in ways that might be considered sexually provocative within the broader context of Indian social mores. There is an inversion of the 'tourist gaze' where the gazer becomes the one gazed upon by the domestic other.

The 'anything goes' attitude also spills over into tourist expectations regarding female vocalists. Sexuality is woven into the fabric of labor demand for certain types of jobs (Adkins, 1995). Jobs in the hospitality and entertainment sectors have always been about serving the needs of tourists and meeting their sexualized expectations. Given that most of the tourists in Goa are male, it is clear that tourist managers are responding to a limited yet cultivated set of tourist preferences and expectations. The rising number of domestic tourists has brought with it a changing expectation regarding Goan women vocalists. Many of the women we interviewed complained about sexual harassment they faced from domestic male tourists. In addition, all of the women we interviewed mentioned the rising demand for popular Bollywood songs. Many of them mentioned the specific demand for *item numbers*[2], which are laden with sexualized images which objectify women. The demand for item numbers provides another explanation for the rising demand for female vocalists.

The supply side of the market is also gendered. Patriarchy constrains women's ability to supply labor in certain occupations to serve the needs of capital. This relationship hinges on the positioning of women's labor as "natural" thereby subject to exploitation, e.g. the primary responsibility for childcare is still considered the domain of women. This is a major concern of many of the women we interviewed – in contrast to the males interviewed in earlier fieldwork. The women who have children talked about the need to fulfill childcare and other domestic responsibilities before they could work outside the home i.e. double burden. Given the social stigma associated with women working in restaurants and bars and the late night hours, women musicians who want to participate in the tourism industry tend to face opposition from their families, neighbors and the broader community. Most of the women we interviewed said that they could not have become musicians without the support of their family. Most of them have male chaperones that accompany them to the tourist venues. Many spoke of a male family member who informally played the role of manager to their careers and/or were members of the band. However they all agreed that these gender norms are changing and becoming more tolerant of women working at these venues. Some of them mentioned that the popularity of television shows like *Indian Idol* has made being a vocalist more acceptable and more glamorous. But despite these changes, the social constraints for women working in this industry remain formidable.

4. Relationship between Feminization and Music Culture

McClary (1991) posits a critical postmodern feminist perspective for the re-examination of assumed tenets of gender construction in music culture. She argues that music can be read as public discourse within which gendered realities are often constructed, contested and negotiated (McClary, 1991). Women are, and have always been, forces within the music industry – including performers/workers embedded in the complex of tourism. The increase in the number of women musicians in Goa's tourism industry is a quantitative change that requires a re-examination of assumptions about qualitative changes within its music culture. Toward that end we posit the notion of *cultural levels,* a composite view taking into account that culture can be expressed as material objects, actions, ideas about what constitutes best practices, and meaning derived from the exigencies of life and its resultant identities. These levels are respectively termed: artifacts, performance practices, aesthetics, and spiritual significances. Cultural change can be assessed in terms of how these levels affect or 'act' on each other.

The artifact level refers to the material/physical tools of music-making. In addition to the musician herself as a producer of sound, this also includes musical instruments, semiotic derivatives and digital technologies. According to the women we interviewed most managers of tourist venues insisted that having a female vocalist was a necessary condition for hiring a band. In order to cut costs there is an increasing trend towards vocalists using recorded tracks instead of singing with a live band. The main change to Goan music culture, as well as definitive change in the timbres or instrumentation is a movement away from traditional bands that included 'blowers' or horn players. We now see an increasing number of female led chapatti bands[3] and female DJs in Goa. Amongst our interviewees, 16 regularly sing with ensembles and 8 with chapatti bands. The chapatti vocalists are usually younger, sing in hotels, and have contracts. They also make more per month than those that sing in a traditional/instrumental band in local restaurants. Chapatti band singers earn on average Rs.65000 per month versus Rs.42000 per month for band singers. Chapatti band singers on average have less training, yet sing full time, versus band singers that sing fewer nights per week on average. Accordingly, chapatti singers were satisfied with the amount of work they were getting, while most band singers wanted to work more. Albeit artificial to the music-making process, several band singers indicated that they might not be the 'right' body-type (and youthfulness) to imitate or emulate the Bollywood prototype that sings to pre-recorded tracks. These findings suggest that the increased demand for female musicians has undercut the aesthetic standards of this community in favor of a tourist driven notion of 'aesthetic labor[4]' (Warhurst, Nickson, Witz, & Cullen, 2000). Female vocalists are increasingly being hired for their physical attributes rather than their musicianship which has led to a deskilling of the labor force. Essentially, their bodies (the visual object) have eclipsed their voices (the aural subject) in importance. The emphasis on the body implies that their increased earnings are short lived and are inversely related to age. In the long run this could lead to a disincentive for women vocalists to acquire greater musical proficiency.

The demand for "item numbers" (subsequently performed in the chapatti format) is expressed directly by the tourists to the singers, or indirectly through restaurant and hotel managers - who often require performers to have this particular genre of Hindi songs in their repertoire. Although most Bollywood songs are in Hindi, most Goan Catholics do not speak Hindi fluently - in contrasts to English or their native Konkani. The response to this demand is therefore mixed. Some of the musicians we interviewed said that they accommodated this demand by learning popular Bollywood songs, as it would generate more opportunities to work. Others were conscientious about not being able to perform with the proper accent. Oddly enough, many of this latter group said that they do, in fact, accommodate requests from international tourists (attempting to sing in other foreign tongues) but not from domestic tourists. We found that those singers who were the most accommodating typically got more opportunities to perform/work.

Thus, the performance practices also reflect a differential in how Goans view and accept different tourist groups. Notably, there is some tension between groups that accommodate these language demands and groups that promote Konkani, signaling a contestation of Goan identity. The manner in which songs are performed in the chapatti format are also markedly different than with a band, given there is no interaction between the singer and the 'musical' accompaniment or between the musical accompaniment and the audience. More focus is therefore placed on the singer's body movement and other rehearsed gestures, narrowing the possibility for improvisation and engaging the audience. Given that gender is often constructed along a visual paradigm, some postcolonial feminist theorists have sought to describe how female empowerment could be a corollary to performance practices in which women have inverted this paradigm to become "subjects"; taking control over their bodies and thusly adopting a disposition of resistance or an "oppositional gaze" (hooks, 1992; Springer, 2008). Examining the tourist space of *La Habana Cuba*, Armstead (2008) discusses the possibility of cultural space being created and expanded by sound, rather than through the "classificatory eye's orientalist gaze". She asserts, "focusing solely on the visual we miss music-making as a potential avenue for agential action and resistance" (Armstead, 2008, p. 131). Armstead argues that some women musicians[5] use their music (sound) to educate and define these tourist spaces that would otherwise restrict their physical presence. There is some indication that some women musicians in Goa are also trying to create a cultural space wherein they can assert their identity as Goan. For example, one of the women we interviewed has developed a radio show where she features local musicians performing in Konkani expressing themes that are pertinent to the Goan experience. Their audience is not tourists but other Goans. She believes that local Goan musicians need a cultural space where they can *reinvent* their identity in and on their own terms.

In Goa, the tourist cultural space is complicated by distinctions made between foreign and domestic tourists. It is not the model that positions the hegemonic orientalist gaze solely from the vantage point of the westerner toward the global south. Although Goa is increasingly becoming "metro", and folding into the fabric of greater India, there is still a lived experience of difference, that manifests between Goan Catholics and Goan Hindus (internally); and between Goans and other Indians. This can be seen, as previously suggested, in current polemics around the debates of Konkani vs. English in the schools[6]. This can also be discerned in the performance practice of Goan female musicians. Several of the Goan interviewees acknowledged the importance of the visual to their livelihood, stressing its influence as beyond the importance of the "sound" or their individual musicianship. This nexus between musical training, experience, and difference is demonstrable in the performance practices. We found that 11 had no formal training, six had on average reached grade 6 on the Trinity college music exams, while the remaining four had received some training in Hindustani classical music. Within our sample, the singers with training were typically younger (average age 27) versus those without training (average age 38).

In other words, the younger group had more training but less experience. The older group had more experience but less training. But with the focus upon the visual or how one looks, the value of music education is marginalized, whereas the "experience" of differentiating themselves from other Indians was most reflected in comments made by the "older" women. In other words, this latter group shared a greater awareness of the "gaze" while performing in venues dominated by the domestic tourist. This particular "aural landscape" is only partly constructed by playback technologies, reflecting a mode of performance not aligned with either their education or experience, but with specific patterns of consumption (Thompson, 2002). The capacity to utilize one's music skill, such as in Armstead's model, is diminished.

Demands for Bollywood music have also challenged Goan aesthetic sensibilities. It has had an effect upon a community that is proudly linked to a legacy of 'good' musicianship. The Goan musicians' relationship with the rest of India, particularly Bollywood, has here-to-fore been privileged – with Goans making profound contributions in all areas of music performance, arranging and composition – in part due to its unique relationship with the West (Fernandes, 2012). However, pedagogical modalities and methods of transmission of musical knowledge have changed in recent decades. Music education is no longer offered in a widespread fashion, but is channeled through a few institutions, such as

the Kala Academy (Basu & Imara, 2009). Coincident with this process is
a shift from focus on musicianship to extramusical concerns invariably
dominated by "visual imagery". Our informants reported that a female
vocalist is considered a necessary and desired element in the music
presentation more or less accommodating of male tourist preferences.
This infers a greater awareness on their part that performance is inextricably
tied to 'femaleness' vs. an ideal of musicianship and that music training
plays a decisive role in decision-making authority within the music
industry. Repertories and best practices that were once derived from
within the Goan community, as well as expectations of what constitutes a
'good' performance, are increasingly being determined outside of the
Goan community. This is particularly the case if a Goan artist has less
affinity with domestic tourists, as compared to foreign tourists. The
narratives of sexually available women embedded in many of the
Bollywood item numbers (Nijhawan, 2009) may be inconsistent with
values and social expectations for women in the Goan community. In
terms of moral sensibility or spiritual significance, the ramifications for
her 'acting' in this way may signify social transgression and challenge
Goan identity. Foreign female "musicians" on the other hand, need not be
as concerned as the Goan counterparts, with the stigma attached to singing
"item numbers" or any such material that may be of dubious, if not
ambiguous moral character within the Goan community.

In response to the question "do you think that tourism has challenged
Goan identity" one respondent said, "Goan identity has been challenged
by the Portuguese for 500 years and then the Indians since 1962". Another
musician said that Goa was growing into a "metro area" accommodating
people from many different parts of India and the rest of the world.
Initially, she said there was some resistance to this current phenomenon,
but "over time Goans will adapt and assimilate to these changes like they
have done time and time again". Nonetheless, it appears that the influence
of domestic tourists is perceived by Goans as being a hegemonic
relationship if not by degree, but qualitatively different than Goans'
relationship with foreigners. The fact that Goans have experienced – as
compared to other parts of India - a difference between Portuguese settler
colonialism and British economic extraction may account for their
susceptibility to accommodation and/or cultural change. Firstly, there is a
demonstrable affinity for, if not deference toward, the white/European.
Conversely, there is evidence in some of their statements of a disdain for
the "brown Indian". Secondly, the Goan musical affinity to Western
music aesthetics, which was linked to a tradition of western music
education, is being challenged by a deskilling effect of less talented

musicians. Thirdly, the requests made by the Indian male tourists are often sexualized and challenge the moral sensibilities of Goans. For example, the Indian (domestic) male tourists often misguidedly conflate the western attire of many Goan Catholic women with the image of the western women as being sexually accessible. These processes subvert the gaze of the other which is traditionally associated with First World gazing upon the Third World (Urry, 1999). They also challenge spiritual significances that have served as a binding force for the Goan Catholic community, as both the individual's sense of self and the community's identity is determined by how meaning is constructed by these life (musical) experiences.

5. Relationship between Feminization and Well-Being

For many years there has been a debate in the literature regarding the impact of international trade on women working in trade related industries. On the one hand, trade has provided jobs to many women (female led industrialization thesis) but on the other hand these jobs have come at an enormous price (female marginalization thesis). Part of this debate is explained by the fact that the two sides conceptualize wellbeing very differently. In this chapter we seek to reconcile this debate by using a broader measure of wellbeing to assess the impact of tourism on the wellbeing of women musicians working in the tourism industry. In recent years there has been a significant amount of work done in the area of wellbeing. As economists we have tended to measure wellbeing only in terms of income. But many researchers have shown that beyond a certain level of income, further increases in income do not always lead to increases in wellbeing (Diener & Seligman, 2004; Easterbrook, 2003). Expanding the notion of wellbeing has required economists to work with philosophers (Nussbaum, 2000) and psychologists (Kahneman, Krueger, Schkade, Schwarz, & Stone, 2004) to develop notions of wellbeing that go beyond income considerations.

For the purposes of this project we have borrowed from the work of Sen (1999), Seligman (2011) and DuBois (1903) to develop our own notion of wellbeing. Sen introduces the idea that wellbeing is related to an expansion of 'capabilities'. The ability to get an education, to have access to drinking water, healthcare, safe working conditions, or to be free of harassment might be examples of activities or 'functionings' that we might value as a community. An individual's 'capabilities' are all the possible combinations of functionings that she is able to achieve (Sen, 1999). Seligman developed a dashboard approach to wellbeing called PERMA, which combines objective and subjective measures of wellbeing. This acronym stands for positive emotion, engagement, relationships, meaning and accomplishment. He believes that as human beings all of these factors affect our wellbeing. Experiencing positive emotions on a daily basis is important but it needs to be balanced with a sense of purpose and achievement. According to Seligman, we need to feel engaged with our community, with each other and with our jobs to improve our wellbeing. According to DuBois wellbeing depends upon three factors: sustaining a passion, making a living, and serving humanity. In this chapter we use a composite measure of wellbeing to understand the impact of tourism on the wellbeing of women musicians working in the tourism industry. We decided to focus on the extent to which tourism had enhanced the capability of the women we interviewed: (a) to make a living; (b) to follow their passion and make music the way that they wanted to do it; (c) to derive meaning from the same.

Almost all of the musicians we interviewed said that music was the chief way in which they expressed their passion and creativity. For a majority of them music was their sole occupation. Most of them said tourism does give them more pay and opportunities to perform but tourism does not give them the opportunity to sing the kind of songs they want to sing. Some of them also recognize that tourism is an unstable source of income because of the nature of the tourism industry, but also because they recognized that part of the demand for their services is conditional on their age and appearance. They are aware of the small window of opportunity afforded to them in this industry.

In response to the question whether tourism increases their capability to make music the way that they want to about equal number of women said 'yes' and 'no'. Those who said 'no' wanted to grow as a musician and sing /compose their own music. They wanted to find their own voice and develop their musicianship by doing more concerts versus performing at tourist venues. They feel that they are forced to sing the same song over and over (repetitive labor/monotony) and don't get a chance to play their own music. Those who said 'yes' were happy to be able to make a living doing what they love to do; composing their own music often inspired by their religious faith. To quote one of the musicians we interviewed, "I sing for my supper and I sing for the Lord." They have found another outlet for their music, which satisfies their passion in a way that performing at a tourist venue does not.

6. Conclusion

We started this project trying to understand the relationship between tourism and feminization of the music industry in Goa, India; and to understand the impact of feminization of the music industry on the wellbeing of female musicians and music culture in Goa. We found that tourism has led to increased demand for women musicians in Goa in part due to the pressures of price competition and in part due to sexualized and racialized expectations of primarily domestic male tourists. These expectations have led to changes in music culture, as evidenced by: the increasing number of female-led chapatti bands; performance practice and repertoire shifts towards Hindi songs in general and item numbers in particular; diminished aesthetic standards largely determined by tourists; and challenges to Goan identity as musicians are pressured to conform to demands for music popular in the rest of India. Tourism has increased the ability of almost all of the women musicians we interviewed to make a living but for most of them it has not enhanced their ability to make music the way they want to. Creating opportunities for women musicians to receive more musical training, compose and perform their own music will go a long way towards improving the wellbeing of women musicians. The women we interviewed demonstrate pragmatic acquiescence combined with agency. Even though new patches of fabric have been added to the cultural milieu, these women continue to view the patches through the prism of *sossegado* – creating a tapestry that is uniquely Goan.

Notes

[1] This interview was conducted in her Aldona village home June 2009. Dr. Couto received the Padma Shri Award in 2010 for her work on Goan history and culture.

[2] Item numbers or " Item songs are big-budget song-and-dance numbers that are played on television countdowns [they] run for several months at a time, and work as snappy advertisements for a film and original music scores with their quick cuts and sexy imagery". (Nijhawan 2009, p. 99)

[3] Chapatti bands are vocalists performing with minus one recorded tracks. Chapatti refers to a flat bread, a staple food of India, likened here to the CD carrying the recorded track.

[4] "Refers to the skills of looking, conversing, and behaving in a manner appropriate upon the specific stage where it is enacted" - Warhurst et al (2000)

[5] For example, the female rap group Las Krudas used their music to challenge racial and gender inequalities in Cuba.

[6] See Naik, P. (1999) *Goan Catholics and the Konkani Language* (excerpt from presidential address at the 22nd All India Konkani Parishad at Belgaum) Retrieved from http://www.goa-world.com/goa/music/goan_catholics_and_the_konkani.htm

References

Adkins, L. (1995). *Gendered Work, Sexuality, Family and the Labour Market*. Philadelphia: Open University Press.

Aitchison, C. (2001). Theorizing other discourses of tourism, gender and culture: Can the subaltern speak (in tourism)? *Tourist Studies,* 1(2), 115-131.

Armstead, R. (2008). Las Krudas, spatial practice, and the performance of diaspora. *Meridians: Feminism, Race, Transnationalism*, 8(1), 130-143. journal name????

Basu, R., & Imara, M. (2009). *From the Perspective of Music Practitioners in Goa, India: How has Tourism Policy impacted Music Culture?* Unpublished manuscript.

Cone, C. (1995). Crafting selves: The lives of two Mayan women. *Annals of Tourism Research*, 22(2), 313-327.

Diener, E., & Seligman, M. (2004). Beyond money: Toward an economy of well-being. *Psychological Science in the Public Interest, 5*, 1-31.

Du Bois, W.E.B. (1903). *The Souls of Black Folk*. NY: Bantam Classic.

Easterbrook, G. (2003). *The Progress Paradox: How Life Gets Better While People Feel Worse*. NY: Random House.

Fernandes, N. (2012). *Taj Mahal Foxtrot: The Story of Bombay's Jazz Age*. New Delhi: Lustre Press.

Fernandez-Kelly, M.P. (1983). *For We are Sold, I and my People: Women and Industry in Mexico's Frontier*. Albany: SUNY Press.

Goa Department of Tourism. (2012). Retrieved January 20, 2012 from website:
http://www.youtube.com/watch?v=p9DjB7nCgkU&feature=related

Goa Tourism Development Corporation. (2012). Retrieved January 20, 2012 from website:
http://www.goa-tourism.com/

Hooks, B. (1992). *Black Looks: Race and Representation*. Boston: South End Press.

Kabeer, N., & Mahmud, S. (2004). Globalization, gender and poverty: bangladeshi women in export and local markets. *Journal of International Development, 16*(1), 93-109.

Kahneman, D., Krueger, A., Schkade, D., Schwarz, N., & Stone, A. (2004). A survey method for characterizing daily life experiences: The day reconstruction method. *Science*, 306, 1776-1780.

Marshment, M. (1997). Gender takes a holiday: Representation in holiday brochures. In M. Thea Sinclair (Ed.), *Gender, Work and Tourism*. London and New York: Routledge.

McClary, S. (1991). *Feminine Endings: Music, Gender, and Sexuality*. Oxford: University of Minnesota Press.

Momsen, J. (1994). Tourism, gender and development in the Caribbean. In V. Kinnaird, & D. Hall (Eds.), *Tourism: A Gender Analysis*. Chicester: John Wiley.

Moore, R. (1995). Gender and alcohol use in a Greek tourist town. *Annals of Tourism Research*, 22(2), 300-313.

Nijhawan, A. (2009). Excusing the female dancer: Tradition and transgression in Bollywood dancing. *South Asian Popular Culture*, 7(2), 99–112.

Nussbaum, M.C. (2000). *Women and Human Development*. Cambridge: Cambridge University Press.

Patil, V. (2011). Reproducing-resisting race and gender difference: Examining India's online tourism campaign from a transnational feminist perspective. Signs, 37(1), 185-210.

Pearson, R. (2007). Reassessing paid work and women's empowerment: Lessons from the global economy. In A. Cornwall, E. Harrison, & A. Whitehead (Eds.), *Feminisms in Development: Contradictions, Contestations and Challenges*. London and New York: Zed Books.

Purcell, K. (1997). Women's employment in UK tourism: Gender roles and labour markets. In M.T. Sinclair (Ed.) *Gender, Work and Tourism* (pp.   ). London and New York: Routledge.

Safa, H. (1995). Gender implications of export-led industrialization in the Caribbean basin. In R. Blumberg, C. Rakowski, I. Tinker, & M. Monteon (Eds.). *Engendering Wealth and Wellbeing: Empowerment for Global Change*. Boulder: Westview Press.

Seligman, M. (2011). *Flourish*. NY: Simon & Schuster.

Sen, A.K. (1999). *Development as Freedom*. NY: Anchor Books.

Shirodkar, P. (Ed.). (1988). *Goa: Cultural Trends*. Panaji, Goa: Directorate of Archives, Archaeology and Museum.

Springer, J. (2008). "Roll It Gal": Alison Hinds, Female Empowerment, and Calypso. *Meridians: Feminism, Race, Transnationalism*. 8(1), 93–129. journal name???

Swain, M.B. (1995). Gender in tourism. *Annals of Tourism Research*, 22(2), 247–66.

Thompson, E. (2002). *The Soundscape of Modernity: Architectural Acoustics and the Culture of Listening in America, 1900–1933*. Cambridge, MA: MIT Press.

Tobin, J., & Dobard, R. (1999) *Hidden in Plain View: A Secret History of Quilts and the Underground Railroad*. NY: Random House.

Urry, J. (1990). *The Tourist Gaze: Leisure and Travel in Contemporary Societies*. London: Sage.

Warhurst, C., Nickson, D., Witz, A., & Cullen, A. (2000). Aesthetic labour in interactive service work: Some case study evidence from the "new" Glasgow. *Service Industries Journal*, 20(3), 1-18.

CHAPTER FIFTEEN

THE MULTIDISCIPLINARY LITERATURE OF CLIMATE CHANGE AND SKI TOURISM

O. CENK DEMIROGLU, HALVOR DANNEVIG AND CARLO AALL

Abstract

The interaction of climate change and tourism has received increased attention from scholars in recent years, as tourism is expected to be one of the most vulnerable industries to climate change as well as a major emitter of greenhouse gases. The scope of study in this chapter is ski tourism, which is already under visible impact by and is thus going through adaptation to climate change. This chapter aims to point out the major disciplinary clusters of this specific literature, focusing on the spatiotemporal development of the research and the inherent multidisciplinarity within. Finally, we briefly discuss the progress of the literature towards transdisciplinarity and underline the research gaps in terms of space, methodology, and further problems. **Keywords:** Climate change, interdisciplinarity, ski tourism, SkiKlima.

1. Introduction

Tourism over the last decades has evolved into one large global industry, whose ever growing interaction with economy, society, politics, culture, technology, and nature has required the scholarly study by researchers of different backgrounds, mostly social sciences, making it a highly multidisciplinary subject. As a result; the tourism literature is made up of not only monodisciplinary studies but also an increasing number of interdisciplinary ones, needed for a better understanding of the related topics. One last hot topic, climate change and tourism, has even called for a closer collaboration of social sciences with physical sciences, widening the spectrum of disciplines acting on the subject. Moreover; besides relating the physical disciplines, particularly climatology, to the social ones, a transdisciplinary form of interdisciplinarity is also said to be in effect (Pröbstl & Unbehaun, 2006), through attempts for hybridization of climate change and (ski) tourism research, where scholars of diverse disciplines as well as non-scientific parties, such as businesses and politics, need to aim for a crossdisciplinary collaboration that encourages them to have empathy for each other's field and an ultimate problem orientation in a holistic way.

Throughout this chapter, we aim to present the body of climate change and ski tourism literature, based on a census of publications derived from an extensive bibliographical survey, while we also categorise the literature according to the dominant disciplinary profiles. In doing so, we attempt to provide the readers with a comprehensive guide over this highly salient topic, and act as a walkthrough for prospective research efforts.

2. Studies on Climate Change and Ski Tourism

Climate change is expected to lead to a loss in areas covered by snow and a shorter snow season in most regions (IPCC, 2007, pp. 339-383). Regarding its impacts on tourism, ski industry as "the most directly and the most immediately affected" subsector has been "the first and the most studied aspect" embedded in a "geographically and methodologically diverse literature" (Scott *et al.*, 2012, pp. 201-202). A recent survey on this literature by Scott *et al.* (2012) has a selected review of some 30 peer-reviewed studies about 13 countries, considered on the bases of impact assessments (pp. 201-211), supplier perception and adaptation (pp. 272-274), and demand response and adaptation (pp. 326-330). As an addition to this review, Dawson and Scott (2010) have categorised 32 major studies for ski areas in ten countries, most (26) of them being solely focused on supply. Lastly, an earlier bibliography of climate change and tourism research by Scott *et al.* (2004) stands out as an essential source, especially for tracking the earliest publications on the subject.

Based on our survey of the literature, we have identified 300 academic publications that directly deal with climate change and ski tourism in 30 countries. The below figure depicts how the literature has grown over the last four decades, considering its breakdown to the major studied regions and predominant disciplines. 51% of the studies (152) analyse ski tourism in the European Alps, with most emphasis on Switzerland and Austria, while the rest are equally distributed for North America, where Great Lakes and New England states and provinces are the main scopes, and other diverse ski destinations of the world such as Northern Europe, Eastern Europe and Oceania. The paradigm, mostly centred around the "Northeast American" and the "Alpine" schools, is highly interdisciplinary in the broadest sense, as 131 (44%) of the studies tend to possess a blend of physical and social analysis efforts. The rest 37% mostly come from climatologists and meteorologists as natural (physical) science studies, while the remaining 19% are characterised as social science studies that focus on supply and demand behaviour but do not incorporate, yet may acknowledge, a physical module. Increasing the scale of such classification would result in identifying more inter-disciplinarity within the literature, as the paradigm is shifting between not only the natural and the social sciences, but also their branches.

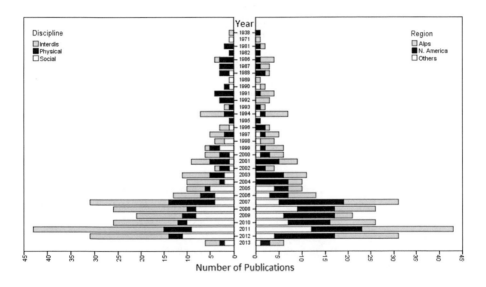

Figure 1 – Historical Trends in the Number of Publications for Climate Change and Ski Tourism Literature

In this chapter, we are not able to cover all studies, thus limit our review to some selections that point out the spatial and disciplinary diversity of the literature, with the most emphasis on peer-reviewed articles but also exceptions for any publication that covers untouched spaces and issues of the literature. Yet we provide the researchers with an occasionally updated geo-bibliography of the above figure on SkiKlima (Demiroglu, 2011), where all studies of the topic are compiled and sorted by their year of publication and clustered spatially on an interactive map with the placemarks graduated according to the disciplinary categories.

2.1. Natural science studies

Natural science studies that examine climate change and skiing come mostly from a background of relevant earth sciences such as meteorology, climatology, hydrology, and, in general, physical geography. These studies look into the exposure and sensitivity of the supply side of the issue rather than the demand, and do not necessarily focus on ski tourism, but the snow cover as its ultimate resource.

Among the many studies that examine snow cover and related changes for the North American ski areas, one could mention analyses for Ontario (Scott *et al.*, 2002), New England (Scott & Dawson, 2007), Colorado (Lazar & Williams, 2008), Washington and Oregon (Nolin & Daly, 2006), and as peripheral as Alaska (Yu *et al.*, 2009) and Arizona (Bark *et al.*, 2010). The "reassessment" of climate change impacts through incorporation of the snowmaking module (Scott *et al.*, 2002), has been the major innovation for the physical studies of the last decade, leaving those studies solely based on natural conditions outdated and giving the edge to the users of the module in the form of more valid results that yield realistically less vulnerability issues for ski resorts. Scott and Dawson (2007) have further utilized this modelling approach as a physical basis to their on-going socioeconomic and integrated research on New England in the Northeast USA. Bark *et al.* (2010) have followed the same approach with altered climate models for the two major low latitude, high altitude resorts of Arizona, discovering a "technical snow(making) reliability" challenge already by the middle of the century, resulting in a suggestion for moving the resorts even higher, preferably onto the shaded sides.

The other four North American studies have not incorporated snowmaking in their analyses, but anyhow provided us with precursors for these less scholarly mentioned but business-wise important ski destinations of western North America. The modelling by Lazar & Williams (2008) have touched upon a not-at-all studied but important aspect of snow, its quality, disclosing the future news for the popular ski resort Aspen, finding out that it would maintain its characteristic fresh powder snow quality. The hydrological model, developed by Nolin and Daly (2006), for the Pacific Northwest, has outlaid that the low lying ski resorts of the Cascade and Olympic Ranges are at stake as long as the future form of precipitation is to fall as rain than snow. Last but not the least, the study of the Alaskan ski resort, Anchorage, by Yu *et al.* (2009), have shown that even those very high latitude ski resorts are also subject to the change, as their analysis of past climate data from 1942 to 2005 has depicted a shortening of the natural ski season by 9 days.

The European Alps is the other destination than North America, where a vast number of physical studies on the effects of climate change on ski areas exist, with most of the focus on the two conventional ski destinations, Switzerland and Austria, and few studies on France, Italy, Germany, and Slovenia. A comprehensive example here is the universal analysis of natural snow reliability that has been carried out for Switzerland, Austria, France, Italy, and Germany (Abegg *et al.*, 2007). The 100-day rule by Witmer (1986) has been taken as the working tool here to determine which ski areas comply with the viability factor stating that "in order to successfully operate a ski area, a snow cover sufficient for skiing should last at least 100 days per season" with the "sufficient" snow cover being considered as one with a minimum depth of 30 cm (p. 29). A spatially complementing version of such analysis, which looks into the past rather than the future trends of the line of natural snow-reliability, has later been administered also for the neglected eastern parts of the Alps in Slovenia (Ogrin *et al.*, 2011). Overall the combined results have shown that the number of the Alpine ski areas with sufficient natural snow-reliability fall from 666 to 493 under a $1°$ C warming scenario, and further down to 392 under a $2°$ C warming scenario. Regarding the case of Slovenia, data from the three meteorological stations representing the ski areas below 1000 m a.s.l. has signified an observed reduction in the duration of a sufficient snow cover by 12 to 40 days in conjunction with a $1.3°$ C to $1.4°$ C warming trend between the 1961-1990 and 1979-2009 normals.

Among other ski destinations that were physically analysed solely for their exposure and sensitivity to climate change are Australia, New Zealand, and South Korea in the Asia-Pacific Region. Galloway (1988) launched one of the first studies on this issue, regarding the unconventional but locationally troubled ski destination of Australia, mainly concerning its domestic tourism. This pioneering model had then yielded that the duration of the snow season (number of days with snow cover at any depth) at the three largest resorts would fall from 135, 130 and 81 days to 60, 60 and 15 days, respectively, under a $2°$ C warming and a 20% less precipitation scenario. More than two decades later, a study (Hendrikx & Hreinsson, 2012) on the neighbour New Zealand, where skiing is practiced more commonly owing to higher latitude and altitude, also modelled the future of ski climate, incorporating this time the vital component of snowmaking. Their results for 10 ski areas disclosed that the range of snow days with depth over 30 cm would fall from 0-223 to 0-187 by the 2040s and to 0-155 by the 2090s. Their snowmaking model also showed a reduction in the number of snowmaking hours by 18-47% by the 2040s and 41-83% by the 2090s, yet still indicating a future (technical) snow-reliability for the ski areas as they would maintain at least 100 days of operations. On the contrary, the results for the Korean Yongpyong Ski Resort (Heo & Lee, 2008) depict a loss of the 120 days long ski season down to 106, 84, and 62 for the 2010-2040, 2040-2070, and 2070-2100 periods, respectively. The snowmaking availability is not as promising for Yongpyong as for New Zealand, since a major reduction in the number of production days is expected, especially for the October-November period.

2.2. Social science studies

Studies approaching climate change and ski tourism research with a social science perspective will to provide us with a disclosure of the societal dimension of the issue. Most qualitative research focusing on the demand side of the problematic is embedded here, while exploration efforts towards stakeholders on the supply side are also present. Thus, the studies almost solely concentrate on the adaptive capacity, as opposed to the exposure and sensitivity orientation of the physical studies. The works employing various methods, such as demand surveys, econometrics, interviews, and focus groups, at the first step try to understand the awareness and perception levels of the stakeholders towards the issue of climate change and ski tourism, and further dig into to their attitudes and desired or realized adaptive behaviour.

Among the studies solely about the supply side of the human aspect of climate change and ski tourism, one could list cases from Austria (Wolfsegger *et al.,* 2008), Switzerland (Hoffmann *et al.,* 2009), Germany (Hoy *et al.,* 2011), France (Duchosal, 2007), Sweden (Engström & Leffler, 2012), and Finland (Tervo, 2008). The results on the perceptions of operators for low-lying ski areas on the Austrian Alps show that there is a strong faith in the future of snowmaking adaptation overcoming the fear of climate change in the very long-term. Likewise, the attitudes of the tourist offices in Northern French Alps and ski resorts in Mid-South Sweden were more or less the same with an understanding of the threat. In the low-lying, non-Alpine ski areas of Saxony in Eastern Germany, the downhill ski tourism businesses do also carry concern over the issue, but stay uncertain due to the perceived lack of scientific consensus, while not failing to engage in the adaptation measures such as business diversification as, given the low altitude, their resources have been among the first to be exposed to climate change. In Switzerland, the survey on 124 ski lift operators has revealed that, instead of the actual vulnerability to the effects of climate change, the awareness towards climate change itself has indeed been the major determinant for corporate adaptation decisions. In Finland, entrepreneurs perceive an interannual variability rather than a warming trend of the climate change, and moreover, some acknowledge the phenomenon as an opportunity in the form of less extreme cold days that suspend tourist flows, while they state that this advantage is mostly valid for the very northern parts of Finland, jeopardizing the competitiveness of remaining businesses.

As opposed to the body of studies on suppliers, "little research has been conducted to examine the influence of climate change on skier demand", as recently noted by Dawson *et al.* (2011, p. 390), underlining a vital gap to be fulfilled towards an integrated understanding of adaptive capacity, vulnerability, and adaptation. Studies that look directly into tourist behaviour, regardless of climate models or analogues, come from the US Northeast (Dawson *et al.*, 2011), Austria (Unbehaun *et al.*, 2008), Finland (Landauer *et al.*, 2009), Australia (Pickering *et al.*, 2010), and Slovenia (Vrtacnik Garbas, 2007). A part of the pioneering interdisciplinary work by König (1998) has set the stage for most of these studies in guiding them towards the exploration of skier adaptation in the form of temporal, spatial, and functional substitutions. The follow-up study (2007) to that of König (administered in 1996) for a large Australian ski resort revealed that an increase in awareness was on the nail in the past years (from 78% to 87%) and the tendency of the skiers to ski less frequently in Australia in a warmer climate had substantially increased from 75% to 90%. In the US, on-premise skier surveys, administered to 1,158 subjects at six ski areas, indicated that the likelihood of changing skiing behaviour parallel to poor snow conditions increased especially for the medium involvement segment that made up 47% of the representative sample.

In Austria, it was found out that among the 540 respondents surveyed, most tended to choose visiting high altitude areas perceived to be snow-reliable, with a tolerance for 10% additional cost and two hours additional driving. Above those thresholds, they would suspend skiing. In Slovenia, the 2004-2005 survey on 855 respondents, 92.5% of whom expressed their awareness towards climate change, disclosed some interesting results. For instance; a seasonal shift, in the form of less snow in December and more in April, could not ensure the same volume of business as 38% of the subjects would have diverted to spring activities. However, more than half of those non-spring skiers were eager for a temporal adaptation if the climatic trend continued. Another detail was the convenient proximity of a spatial substitute. The fact that Slovenian ski resorts are quite remote from their competitors ensured a domestic loyalty, as well as one from the neighbouring Hungarian and Croatian markets. Finally, the Finnish case analysed the behaviour of an often neglected but a highly traditional Nordic segment of ski tourism, the cross-country skiers. The study pointed out some diverse behavioural dynamics among the participants, such that; those attributing cross-country skiing as a tradition, "the social type", were the first to quit during a warming trouble.

Last but not the least, we should mention two other groups of social science papers on climate change and ski tourism: those that integrate stakeholder analyses in terms of both supply and demand sides, and those that make use of such empirical findings in compiling, implicating and categorising adaptation measures. For the first group, the study by Behringer *et al.* (2000) is a good example by performing a comprehensive approach. Their surveys to skiers combined with focus groups involving tourism decision-makers yielded the results that 83% of the demand perceived climate change as a threat, with half the demand expecting its impacts by 2000-2030, while all supply representatives also acknowledged the threat in principle. The adaptive capacity of demand was very flexible with almost the half willing for a spatial substitution and 32% eager to ski less often. Suppliers, on the other hand, did not possess the same capacity, but showed some priority to technical adaptation measures such as snowmaking and moving higher. Likewise, the recent report by Prince (2010) follows this dual approach as well, and secures the position of an important ski destination of the Southern Hemisphere, New Zealand, on the literature map. This work goes further innovative by discussing the issue of climate change mitigation and ski tourism – an essential topic not covered in our very specific paradigm at all.

The latter group of papers on adaptation formulation are quite evident in the literature, especially in the decision trees developed by Elsasser and Bürki (2002, p. 256), and Scott and McBoyle (2007, p. 1415). The preceding study was one of the first to provide us with a figure that compiled the ten common adaptation strategies of the supply side under one roof with the four directions of "maintain ski tourism", "subsidies", "alternatives to ski tourism", and "fatalism". The latter work had an enrichment of those strategies, while addressing the implementers as the "government", "ski area operators", "ski associations", and the "financial sector" and further drawing the line to the demand side with the emphasis on their substitution behaviour for time, space, and activity.

2.3. Interdisciplinary studies

Studies of climate change and ski tourism do meet at an interdisciplinary collaboration of physical and social backgrounds at the largest scale of the scientific spectrum. However; a distinction among the three clusters of studies, especially between the physical and the interdisciplinary, sometimes becomes challenging. For instance, many modelling approaches possess predominantly physical characteristics, but would eventually require the knowledge on the economics of ski tourism, as in the common utilization of the 100-days rule as a breakeven factor, or most analogues would need the empirical findings on behavioural adaptation, or at least some visitation data, to be able to draw conclusions, having the paradigm step from the physical into the social side. Nevertheless, below we provide a brief review of such coined papers with respect to their spatial and scholar clusters.

In the Alps, König and Abegg (1997) had an early test of the 100-days rule for 230 major and 122 minor ski areas in Switzerland against a potentially retreating snowline from 1200 m to 1500 m. The results pronounced only the 63% of the major and the 9% of the minor ski areas to survive the projection. In Austria, and partly in Germany, following the natural snow model of Breiling and Charamza (1999), a set of second generation works evolved as to explore and integrate the future availability and viability of snowmaking (Schmidt et al., 2012), and behavioural dynamics and demographics (Steiger, 2012). Moreover; further innovative attempts were also recently published, introducing the use of agent-based models in integrating and simulating climate change and ski tourism scenarios (Soboll & Dingeldey 2012).

In North America, the certain school around Scott et al. (e.g. 2006; Dawson & Scott, 2010; 2012) dominates most of the interdisciplinary studies, particularly for the ski areas of the Northeast, while some other researchers have also managed to synthesize analyses. Among those; Hamilton et al. (2007) have presented two close-up cases from New England, disclosing interesting dimensions such as the impact of urban snow on skier activity, while in a more recent study; Butsic (2011) found out a substantial loss of residential real estate value around the less snow-reliable ski resorts.

Some other ski destinations where interdisciplinary works have had their foci on are Sweden (Moen & Fredman, 2007), Romania (Surugiu et al., 2011), and Japan (Fukushima et al., 2002). These studies in common are econometric studies looking at the past and/or future relationship of climate and tourism data, such as temperature, precipitation, snow depth, and snow cover duration on the physical side and skier figures, ticket sales, guest nights and alike on the socioeconomic side.

As seen above, the interdisciplinarity of climate change and ski tourism research evolves in a sequential essence of the socioeconomic analyses following the physical phase, whereby the insubstantial volume but significant contribution of the socioeconomic phase builds on and confirms the physical basis. The challenge here could be to move beyond this informatus and become as transdisciplinary as possible. This, in return, would benefit the paradigm with an eclectic methodology and a problem formulation liberated from but nourished by the disciplines and the practices within and around, consolidated through the collaboration of researchers, professionals, and the public who will be oriented directly towards the scholarly, comprehensive and practical solutions of the problem specified in extenso, and ultimately implement the remedies with a bottom-up approach (Pröbstl & Unbehaun, 2006).

3. Conclusion

So far we have tried to cover the paradigm though some selected bibliography, but the online guide, SkiKlima, would further provide the reader with the body of literature as complete as possible. At least our current census representing three disciplinary clusters and 30 countries would be present there, while the rest of the countries with established ski tourism supply but no relevant research would be marked as well in order to highlight the spatial gaps. This cartographic display is especially important in leading researchers to the untouched destinations such as the rapidly emerging China, and the peripheral countries of the cryosphere of a probable, high vulnerability, such as Lebanon, Algeria, and Mexico.

The literature still needs to improve itself in terms of contents and methodology. Content wise; more inclusion and separate handling of climate oscillations in atmospheric/hydrological models seems as a good way to explain the past and future interannual variability of climate versus its long-term change and the consequent, different perceptions of ski tourism stakeholders on the supply side. On the demand side, we encourage a delimitation of the survey towards understanding groups besides the downhill skiers/boarders and cross-country skiers, such as the emerging generation of the Alpine tour skiers, who have the greatest flexibility of all for spatial substitution as they are not generally bounded by lift logistics. Such approach is also needed to understand the frontier of supplier adaptation, and looking into the rare but radical cases of today, such as the "indooring" of the natural ski slope in Isaberg, Sweden (Abbasian *et al.,* 2009) or the instalment of dry base layers as in

Monterreal, Mexico, could be a good starting point. Lastly, the bivious conflict of adaptation versus mitigation should also be addressed in the research. On the one hand, further adaptation to the "tertiary" impact of climate change rising as side effects of some greenhouse gas mitigation policies should be elaborated (Aall & Høyer, 2005). On the other hand, the need for mitigation of emissions resulting from the adaptation measures themselves should be inspected through carbon accounting analyses, considering the different viewpoints of suppliers and consumers and the different types of adaptations in the form of technical, spatial, temporal or functional shifts (Aall, 2010).

Methodologically speaking; improvements on the natural and the technical snow-reliability analyses seem to be required. The most betaken snow-reliability method, the 100-days rule, should be regeneralized or individualized as this financial viability threshold of snow cover duration is quite outdated and represents only the Swiss Alps (Witmer, 1986), and the physical/psychological sufficiency thresholds of snow depth are even more outdated and based on findings from only one Swiss ski resort (Eckel, 1938 in Witmer, 1986, p.193). Regarding technical snow-reliability; wet bulb, instead of the commonly utilized dry bulb, temperatures should be one input so that the thresholds are corrected according to relative humidity when determining snowmaking capacity. In doing these, sources of data collection should not only rely completely on interviews, but rather on fact sheets such as financial statements and technical manuals.

As a final word; the authors believe that some transdisciplinary emphasis on climate change and (ski) tourism research will bring more comprehension, cohesion, and practicability, whenever and wherever it is possible to implement such approach into its utmost holistic integration of physical models, supply and demand socioeconomics, adaptation, mitigation, and the interrelationship of adaptation and mitigation.

Acknowledgements

This work is a part of the research for climate change and ski tourism, administered by Western Norway Research Institute and Istanbul University Geography Department and supported by the Research Council of Norway under the YGGDRASIL (pnr. 21 11 61) and the NORKLIMA (pnr. 22 14 41) Programmes.

References

Aall, C. (2010). Winter tourism in Norway: Adapting or promoting climate change? *Clim-ATIC Study Visit in Åre*, March 15-18, Sweden.

Aall, C., & Høyer, K.G. (2005). Tourism and climate change adaptation: the Norwegian case. In C.M. Hall, & J.E.S. Higham (Eds.), *Tourism, Recreation, and Climate Change* (pp. 209-221). Clevedon: Channel View.

Abbasian, S., Hair Jr, J.F., Pesämaa, O., Rylander, D., & Yolal, M. (2009). Isaberg on the edge of the future by responding to the lack of snow. *The 5th International Symposium on Entrepreneurship in Tourism and the Experience Research Meeting,* 17-21 March. Rovaniemi, FI.

Abegg, R., Agrawala, S., Crick, F., & de Montfalcon, A. (2007). Climate change impacts and adaptation in winter tourism. In S. Agrawala (Ed.), *Climate Change in the European Alps: Adapting Winter Tourism and Natural Hazards Management* (pp. 25-60). Paris: OECD.

Bark, R.H., Colby, B.G., & Dominguez, F. (2010). Snow days? Snowmaking adaptation and the future of low latitude, high elevation skiing in Arizona, USA. *Climatic Change,* 102, 467-491.

Behringer, J., Buerki, R., & Fuhrer, J. (2000). Participatory integrated assessment of adaptation to climate change in Alpine tourism and mountain agriculture. *Integrated Assessment,* 1, 331–338.

Breiling, M., & Charamza, P. (1999). The impact of global warming on winter tourism and skiing: A regionalised model for Austrian snow conditions. *Regional Environmental Change,* 1(1), 4-14.

Butsic, V., Hanak, E., & Valletta, R.G. (2011). Climate change and housing prices: Hedonic estimates for ski resorts in Western North America. *Land Economics,* 87(1), 75-91.

Dawson, J., & Scott, D. (2010). Systems analysis of climate change vulnerability for the US Northeast ski sector. *Tourism and Hospitality Planning & Development,* 7(3), 219–235

—. (2012). Managing for climate change in the alpine ski sector. *Tourism Management,* in press.

Dawson, J., Havitz, M., & Scott, D. (2011). Behavioral adaptation of alpine skiers to climate change: Examining activity involvement and place loyalty. *Journal of Travel & Tourism Marketing,* 28(4), 388-404.

Demiroglu, O.C. (2011). *SkiKlima: A Geo-bibliography of Climate Change and Ski Tourism Research.* Available on-line at http://www.skiklima.com, last updated 10 April 2013.

Duchosal, E. (2007). *Climate change impacts and adaptation to winter tourism: How adapting winter tourism to climate change? Based on a survey realised in the northern French Alps.* Unpublished Master's Thesis, European Tourism Management, Bournemouth University.

Eckel, O. (1938). Ueber die Schneeverhaeltnisse von Davos. *Jahresbericht der Naturforschenden Gesellschaft Graubuendens,* 75, 109-156.

Elsasser, H., & Bürki, R. (2002). Climate change as a threat to tourism in the Alps. *Climate Research,* 20, 253-257.

Engström, D., & Leffler, F. (2012). *Perceptions of climate change at ski resorts in mid-south of Sweden.* Unpublished Bachelor's Thesis, School of Technology and Business Studies, Högskolan Dalarna.

Fukushima, T., Kureha, M., Ozaki, N., Fukimori, Y., & Harasawa, Y. (2003). Influences of air temperature change on leisure industries: Case study on ski activities. *Mitigation and Adaptation Strategies for Climate Change,* 7: 173-189.

Galloway, R.W. (1988). The potential impact of climate changes on Australian ski fields. In G.I. Pearman (Ed.), *Greenhouse: Planning for Climate Change* (pp. 428-437). Melbourne, AU: CSIRO.

Hamilton, L.C., Brown, B.C., & Keim, B. (2007). Ski areas, weather and climate: Time series models for integrated research. *International Journal of Climatology,* 27(15), 2113-2124.

Hendrikx, J., & Hreinsson, E.Ö. (2012). The potential impact of climate change on seasonal snow in New Zealand: part II—industry vulnerability and future snowmaking potential. *Theoretical and Applied Climatology,* DOI: 10.1007/s00704-012-0713-z

Heo, I., & Lee, S. (2008). The impact of climate changes on ski industries in South Korea: In the case of the Yongpyong ski resort. *Journal of the Korean Geographical Society,* 43(5), 715-727.

Hoffmann, V.H., Sprengel, D.C., Ziegler, A., Kolb, M., & Abegg, B. (2009). Determinants of corporate adaptation to climate change in winter tourism: An econometric analysis. *Global Environmental Change,* 19(2), 256-264.

Hoy, A., Hänsel, S., & Matschullat, J. (2011). How can winter tourism adapt to climate change in Saxony's mountains? *Regional Environmental Change,* 11(3), 459-469.

IPCC (2007). *Climate Change 2007: The Physical Science Basis.* Cambridge: Cambridge University Press.

König, U. (1998). *Tourism in a Warmer World: Implications of Climate Change due to Enhanced Greenhouse Effect for the Ski Industry in the Australian Alps.* Zürich, CH: University of Zürich.

König, U., & Abegg, B. (1997). Impacts of climate change on winter tourism in the Swiss Alps. *Journal of Sustainable Tourism,* 5(1), 46-58.

Landauer, M., Sievänen, T., & Neuvonen, M. (2009). Adaptation of Finnish cross-country skiers to climate change. *Fennia*, 187(2), 99-113.

Lazar, B., & Williams, M. (2008). Climate change in western ski areas: potential changes in the timing of wet avalanches and snow quality for the Aspen ski area in the years 2030 and 2100. *Cold Regions Science and Technology*, 51, 219-228.

Moen, J., & Fredman, P. (2007). Effects of climate change on alpine skiing in Sweden. *Journal of Sustainable Tourism*, 15(4), 418-437.

Nolin, A.W., & Daly, C.D. (2006). Mapping "at risk" snow in the Pacific Northwest. *Journal of Hydrometeorology*, 7(5), 1164-1171.

Ogrin, M., Ogrin, D., Rodman, N., Močnik, M., Vengar, R., Smolej, A., & Bunčič, G. (2011). Climate change and the future of winter tourism in Slovenia. *Hrvatski geografski glasnik*, 73(1), 215-228.

Pickering, C.M., Castley, J.G., & Burtt, M. (2010). Skiing less often in a warmer world: Attitudes of tourists to climate change in an Australian ski resort. *Geographical Research*, 48(2), 137–147.

Prince, B.W. (2010). *Climate Change Adaptation and Mitigation in New Zealand Snow Tourism*. Wellington, NZ: Ministry of Economic Development, The Tourism Strategy Group.

Pröbstl, U., & Unbehaun, W. (2006). Climate change in winter sport - a new approach to transdisciplinary research and implementation. *OECD Workshop 2006: Adaptation to the Impacts of Climate Change in the European Alps*. October 4-6, Wengen, CH.

Schmidt, P., Steiger, R., & Matzarakis, A. (2012). Artificial snowmaking possibilities and climate change based on regional climate modeling in the Southern Black Forest. *Meteorologische Zeitschrift*, 21(2), 167–172.

Scott, D. & Dawson, J. (2007). Climate change vulnerability of the US Northeast ski industry. In A. Matzarakis, C.R. de Freitas, & D. Scott (Eds.), *Developments in Tourism Climatology* (pp. 191-198). Freiburg, DE: Commission on Climate, Tourism and Recreation, International Society of Biometeorology.

Scott, D., & McBoyle, D. (2007). Climate change adaptation in the ski industry. *Mitigation and Adaptation Strategies for Global Change*, 12(8), 1411–1431.

Scott, D., Hall, C.M., & Gössling, S. (2012). *Tourism and Climate Change: Impacts, Adaptation and Mitigation. London:* Routledge.

Scott, D., Jones, B., & McBoyle, G. (2004). *Climate, Tourism and Recreation: A Bibliography*. Waterloo, ON: University of Waterloo.

Scott, D., McBoyle, G., & Mills, B. (2002). A reassessment of climate change and the skiing industry in Southern Ontario (Canada): exploring technical adaptive capacity. *16th International Congress of Biometeorology.*

Scott, D., McBoyle, G., Mills, B., & and Minogue, A. (2006). Climate change and the sustainability of ski-based tourism in eastern North America: A reassessment. *Journal of Sustainable Tourism,* 14(4), 376-398.

Soboll, A., & Dingeldey, A. (2012). The future impact of climate change on Alpine winter tourism: A high-resolution simulation system in the German and Austrian Alps. *Journal of Sustainable Tourism,* 20(1), 101-120.

Steiger, R. (2012). Scenarios for skiing tourism in Austria: Integrating demographics with an analysis of climate change. *Journal of Sustainable Tourism,* 20(6), 867-882.

Surugiu, C., Surugiu, M.-R., Frent, C., & Breda, Z. (2011). Effects of climate change on Romanian mountain tourism: Are they positive or mostly negative? *European Journal of Tourism, Hospitality and Recreation,* 2(1), 42-71.

Tervo, K. (2008). The operational and regional vulnerability of winter tourism to climate variability and change: The case of the Finnish nature-based tourism entrepreneurs. *Scandinavian Journal of Hospitality and Tourism,* 8(4), 317-332.

Unbehaun, W., Pröbstl, U., & Haider, W. (2008). Trends in winter sport tourism: challenges for the future. *Tourism Review,* 63(1), 36-47.

Vrtacnik Garbas, K. (2007). The potential influences of climate change on tourist demand in winter sport centres in Slovenia In A. Matzarakis, C.R. de Freitas, & D. Scott (Eds.), *Developments in Tourism Climatology* (pp. 199-206). Freiburg, DE: Commission on Climate, Tourism and Recreation, International Society of Biometeorology.

Witmer, U. (1986). *Erfassung, Bearbeitung und Kartierung von Schneedaten in der Schweiz.* Bern, CH: Geographisches Insitut der Universität Bern.

Wolfsegger, C., Gössling, S., & Scott, D. (2008). Climate change risk appraisal in the Austrian ski industry. *Tourism Review International,* 12(1), 13-23.

Yu, G., Schwartz, Z., & Walsh, J.E. (2009). Effects of climate change on the seasonality of weather for tourism in Alaska. *Arctic,* 62(4), 443-457.

Chapter Sixteen

Effects of Contemporary Morphogenetic Processes on Natural and Tourist Slopes in High-Mountain Area

Joanna Fidelus and Eliza Płaczkowska

Abstract

The aim of this chapter is to compare the effects of natural processes occurring on a slope without tourist impact and on a slope dissected by footpaths. Geomorphologic mapping using GPS was the main method used to study relief transformation on selected slopes. Landforms were measured during different weather conditions from 2009 to 2011. Tourist traffic measurements were carried out by means of tourist counter. In general, the development of landforms depends mainly on weather conditions, geoecological zones and the intensity of tourist traffic. This type of research provides useful information about the negative effects of tourist activity in high-mountain areas. The comparison of two slopes with different usage allows us to recognize the direction of relief development. **Keywords:** Slope processes, tourist management, high-mountain areas, the Western Tatra Mountains.

1. Introduction

High-mountain areas are continuously transformed by various types of morphogenetic processes (Kotarba, 2005; Boltiziar *et al.*, 2008; Krzemień, 2008). Natural processes are controlled by timberline (Troll, 1973; Krzemień *et al.*, 1995) and local environmental conditions. Natural hazards such as avalanches and debris flows are the most typical of processes occurring in high-mountain areas. Avalanches and debris flows contribute the most to mountain relief transformation (Jacobson *et al.*, 1989; Nyberg, 1989; Barnikel & Becht, 2003; Crosta *et al.*, 2003; Decaulne & Saemundsson, 2006).

Special attention was paid to the occurrence and dynamics of processes occurring above the timberline in the Tatra Mountains (Tatras). The slope relief transformation is usually driven by needle ice action, snow avalanche erosion, nivation, debris flow, solifluction as well aeolian processes (Kotarba, 1970; Izmaiłow, 1984). The effects of needle ice action are sliding and creeping of the soil cover. However, these processes do not occur across the entire slope surface. Nivation and deflation are limited to passes and upwind slopes (Kotarba, 1970; Izmaiłow, 1984). Snow avalanches are limited to ravines and concave slopes. The morphological effects of snow avalanches in the Tatra Mountains are not as significant as those in other high-mountain areas (Kotarba, 1970; Rączkowska, 2006). The most important processes occurring in the study area are debris flows, mud flows and torrential flows (Krzemień, 1988; Kotarba, 1989; Krzemień *et al.*, 1995; Rączkowska, 2006). These processes as well as snow avalanches provide a connection between slope and channel subsystems (Kaszowski & Krzemień, 1979; Krzemień *et al.*, 1995). An understanding of the effects of natural processes is important in order to predict slope development trends (Kotarba, 1992, 2005).

Hiking is one of the most important factors that initiate the erosion process. This is the reason why tourist traffic should be limited to protected footpaths and tourist roads. In high-mountain areas, however, tourist infrastructure is difficult to maintain and requires systematic inspections, especially when the intensity of tourist traffic and that of natural processes are high. Anthropogenic degradation remains a current issue, as confirmed by many studies from different mountain areas – for example Mount Rainier National Park (Rechefort & Swinney, 2000) and the Rocky Mountains in the United States (Cole & Monz, 2004), the Babia Góra Massif and the Tatra National Park in Poland (Buchwał & Fidelus, 2008) as well the Bucegi Mountains in Romania (Mihai *et al.*, 2009). Reducing the negative effects of mass tourism requires a recognition of the natural conditions in a given area. In addition, an important aspect of tourist management is the recognition of management methods used in other mountain areas.

The aim of this chapter is to compare the effects of natural processes on a slope without tourist impact and on a slope dissected by footpaths. The recognition of similarities and differences in processes occurring on both types of slopes can provide better a understanding of the entire slope system, its development and various aspects of tourist management.

Study Area

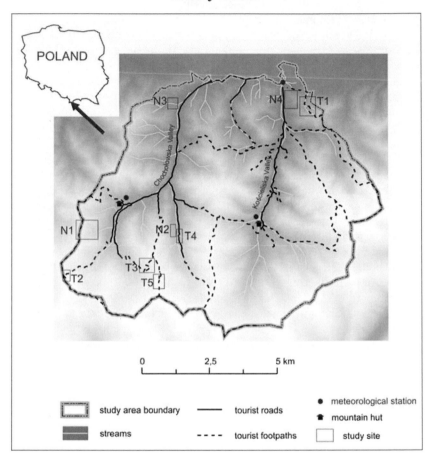

Figure 1 - Study Area with Natural Slope Study Sites (N1, N2, N3, N4) and Tourist Slope Study Sites (T1, T2, T3, T4, T5)

The study area consists of the Western Tatra Mountains within Tatra National Park in southern Poland (Fig. 1). This area includes two lithologically different parts: a crystalline part in the south and a sedimentary part in the north. The crystalline part consists of granitoids and metamorphic rocks. The sedimentary part generally consists of limestone, dolomite and marl (Bac-Mocaszwili *et al.*, 1979). Podzolic rankers, umbric leptosols and orthic podzols occur on crystalline rocks.

However, humic-rendzic leptosols, cambic-rendzic leptosols and umbric-rendzic leptosols occur on calcareous rocks (Skiba *et al.*, 2002). The thickness of the soil cover varies across Tatra slopes. The thickness of moraines is up to 40 m. The thickness of saprolite on slopes without glacial transformation reaches 1 m (Baumgart-Kotarba *et al.*, 2008).

The Tatra Mountains are a high-mountain area. There are two different types of relief: high-mountain relief and middle-mountain relief. Typical landforms in high-mountain relief are glacial cirques and post-glacial valleys with moraine cover. In the lower part of the mountains, typical landforms include deep and narrow V-shaped valleys and rocky slopes (Baumgart-Kotarba *et al.*, 2008). The hydrogeological conditions in the study area vary substantially. There is low retention above the timberline, which is caused by impermeable bedrock and steep slopes. Below the timberline, however, the high density of vegetation improves infiltration conditions (Kotarba, 1992). High-mountain areas are characterized by variable weather conditions. The Western Tatras possess four seasons – niveopluvial (IV-VI), pluvial (VII-IX), pluvionival (X-XI) and nival (XII-III). Annual precipitation reaches 2,000 mm (Kłapa, 1980).

There are three geoecological zones in the study area – a forest zone (below 1,500 m a.s.l.), a subalpine zone (1,500–1,800 m a.s.l.) and an alpine zone (over 1,800 m a.s.l.). The intensity of morphogenetic processes varies across these zones, especially above and below the timberline.

Tatra National Park is the most popular tourist region in Poland and this is the reason why it has a high density of footpaths. The largest tourist traffic occurs from May to September (data from Tatra National Park). The tourist traffic is mostly confined to valley floors and the average daily flow rate is about 2,000 tourists (data from Tatra National Park). There is less tourist traffic above the timberline but this area is much more susceptible to relief transformation. Detailed field research was conducted in the Chochołowska and Kościeliska Valleys (Figure 1).

2. Methodology

Geomorphological mapping using GPS was the principal method used to study slope relief transformation. Geomorphological investigation was conducted by means of topographical maps at a scale of 1:10 000. Measurements of the longitudinal profile and cross sections were made on footpaths and natural slope surfaces. In this chapter, slopes are designated using two different names: natural slope and tourist slope. Slopes with no tourist impact are designated natural slopes and slopes dissected by footpaths are designated tourist slopes. Landforms were measured in different morphogenetic seasons from 2009 to 2011. Tourist traffic measurements were carried out by means of tourist counter made by EcoCounter in summer season 2009. Tourist counter was installed in subalpine belt in rock debris site on footpath from Wyżnia Chochołowska Valley to Pass below Wołowiec. In order to analyze the long-term development of the studied slopes we took into consideration previous studies conducted by other researchers. In order to avoid the influence of natural factors such as geology and geoecological zones, we compared slopes with the same natural conditions.

3. Seasonal Differentiation of Morphogenetic Processes

The type and intensity of slope processes depend upon weather conditions changing throughout the year. There are four morphogenetic seasons in the Western Tatra Mountains. The type and intensity of slope processes are different in each season and for each type of slope usage. A comparison of a natural and a tourist slope was performed using Kłapa's (1980) season classification system. The high density of tourist footpaths in Tatra National Park (1.3 km km^{-2}) is the result of the increasing popularity of hiking in the area. Tourist traffic in the Tatras has increased substantially in the last few decades. The mass tourism effect in protected areas is concentrated along footpaths and in surrounding areas.

3.1. Niveopluvial season

Snowmelt season is important in relief transformation both on natural and tourist slopes. Oversaturation of the soil cover is caused by water from melting snow, which reduces soil cover stability. In these conditions, saturation overland flow occurs (Figure 2A). The result of that is soil creep and shallow landslides. Typical process during this season is nivation, which causes development of nival niches (Figure 2B). They occur in concave slopes filled with snow patches. Concave slopes are also susceptible to the triggering of snow avalanches. An example of this landform can be found in Litworowa Valley. The development of erosive landforms occurs on surfaces without compact vegetation. These are typical for tourist slopes constantly transforming via mechanical impact of tourist traffic. Linear runoff and needle ice action are the most common processes found to occur on tourist footpaths. The effects of needle ice action are slope undercuts and erosive niches (Figure 2E, F).

Figure 2 - Natural and Tourist Slope Processes and Landforms: A – Sheet Flow (N4), B – Nival Niche (N1; Photo by A. Wolanin), C – Torrential Fan (N3), D – Snow Avalanche (N1), E – Needle Ice Action (T4), F – Undercut in Footpath Edge Zone Made by Needle Ice Action (T4), G – Coarse Debris on Footpath as a Result of Extreme Event (T1; Photo by J. Krzeptowski-Sabała), H – Bare Surfaces on Tourist Slope (T3).

3.2. Pluvial season

The pluvial season is characterized by the most intense rainfall of the year. The effect of extreme rainfall is infiltration excess overland flow and saturation overland flow. The most significant relief transformations during this season take place after several days of medium intensity rainfall followed by torrential rainfall. An example of such an event is precipitation of 104 mm in 45 minutes in Staników Valley on June 5, 2007 (Gorczyca & Krzemień, 2008). Field research and data from three meteorological stations located 5–10 km apart indicate highly variable precipitation amounts. Based on this data, it is possible to infer that this rainfall event had a small range. The effects of extreme rainfall in this case were erosive undercuts, deep evorsion hollows as well as the movement of coarse debris (Figure 2G). Relief transformations along other footpath sections are generally connected with incisions as well as small torrential fans, which expand following future rainfall events. However, natural slopes during heavy rainfall are transformed by torrential flows, especially in the forest belt. The effect of this process is torrential fans, which develop as a result of debris movement from upper parts of slopes to valley floors. An example of such an event was a torrential flow observed after a rainfall of 82 mm on September 1, 2010 in Wielkie Koryciska Valley (data from the Institute of Meteorology and Water Management, Figure 2C). Another process connected with extreme events may be lateral stream erosion in the forest belt. When footpaths are located in the vicinity of a channel bank on a tourist slope, the channel bank may be destroyed within a short time. However, on natural slopes, it is mass movements that occur most often. Runoff is the principal process on both types of slopes but it is more significant on tourist slopes. Runoff on natural slopes is limited to surfaces without vegetation, for example, niches resulting from nivation, soil creep, deflation or seepage erosion. In the course of long-term rainfall, episodic springs could become activated. At this time, footpaths and tourist roads turn into small channels. In this case, seepage erosion is activated and intensified on natural slopes. The most important process on both types of slopes in the pluvial season is linear erosion. However, on natural slopes, this process is generally limited to areas with concave cross sections.

3.3. Pluvionival season

This period is characterized by a small amount of precipitation. In this context, the soil cover is quasi-stable and there is little risk of relief transformation. Frequent temperature oscillations about 0°C create good conditions for needle ice action. This process may cause soil movement but it is limited to bare surfaces on both types of slopes (Figure 2H). However, on tourist slopes, the effects of this process are more pronounced because of the mechanical impact of tourist traffic. This season is best for aeolian processes. The principal effects of these processes are deflation niches and gelideflation steps.

3.4. Nival season

This is the least active morphogenetic season of the year. The thick snow cover inhibits natural and anthropogenic process action. These are good conditions for snow avalanches to occur. Snow avalanches can transform both types of slopes. Soil cover degradation and vegetation degradation are the main morphological results of snow avalanches. The next stage is the development of unstable surfaces directly exposed to runoff and needle ice action. An example of such an event is the snow avalanche in Litworowa Valley in 2009 (Figure 2D). Based on the landforms identified, it is possible to infer that direct effects of snow avalanches are not morphologically significant. Snow avalanches trigger activation and intensification processes in other seasons. This is especially true of runoff, needle ice action and nivation. In the case of tourist slopes, snow avalanches can destroy entire sections of footpaths. This may result in changes to the course of an affected tourist footpath.

4. Comparison of Natural and Tourist Slopes Transformations

Slope development depends mainly on bedrock resistance, morphometric parameters and the intensity of tourist traffic. All three factors affect the intensity of relief transformations. Natural slope and tourist slope transformation is not uniform across large surfaces. There exist local surfaces with higher process intensity (Figure 3A). These areas differ in size. In contrast to natural slopes, tourist slope relief transformation can only be linear, resulting from the linear nature of tourist footpaths.

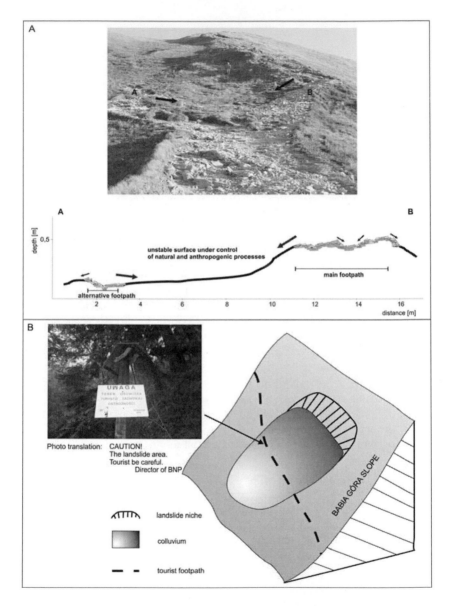

Figure 3 - The Examples of Negative Effects of Tourist Impact: A – The Tourist'
Slope Cross Section (T5). Axis Indicates Main Direction of Relief Transformations;
B – Tourist Footpath in Landslide Area in the Babia Góra Massif (Beskidy
Mountains, Poland)

Morphogenetic process variances between natural and tourist slopes generate different slope transformations (Figure 4). This is directly connected to sediment movement and the development of erosive and accumulation landforms. The changing longitudinal profile on natural slopes results from gravitational processes. The consequence of these transformations is niche development in upper parts of slopes as a result of nivation, mass movement and torrential fans in lower parts of slopes. In addition, the changing local longitudinal profiles and cross sections of natural slopes may be caused by seepage erosion limited to spring niches. However, on tourist slopes, the main relief transformations are related to cross section changes. This is the result of close interactions between tourist traffic impact and natural processes. The mechanical impact of tourists has different types of negative effects (Figure 3A). The most important negative effect is alternative footpath formation. This type of tourist impact produces degraded zones, which are predisposed to further transformation by natural processes (Figure 2H). The result is incisions, evorsion hollows, nival and deflation niches as well as gelideflation steps along footpaths.

Landform evolution contributes to the expansion of denuded surfaces, which undergo further transformation via morphogenetic processes on both types of slopes. Nevertheless, the origin of the denuded surfaces is heterogeneous on both types of slopes. Extreme processes on natural slopes are mainly responsible for the largest relief transformations on surfaces without vegetation. However, on tourist slopes, anthropogenic degradation is the key to the development of bare surfaces.

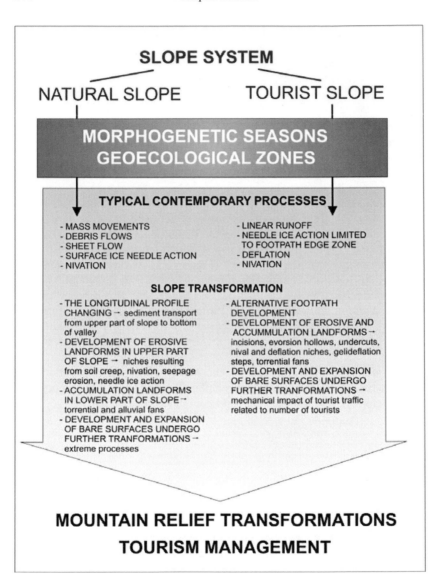

Figure 4 - Natural and Tourist Slope Transformations

5. Natural Controls of Tourism Infrastructure

The high-mountain areas are characterized by different types of human activities. Hiking, skiing, horse riding and grazing can produce major relief changes in mountain areas (Buchwał et al., 2009; Olive & Marion, 2009). One aspect of the management of protected areas should be the marking of tourist footpaths and other areas of tourist infrastructure, which takes into account the natural conditions of the given slope. This issue was investigated by Krzemień (2004, 2008) on the volcanic slopes of the Monts Dore Massif in France. The most common form of human activity in high-mountain areas in Poland is hiking (Prędki, 2004; Buchwał & Fidelus, 2008). A suitable designation of hiking areas and appropriate technical staff are needed for the sustainable development of protected areas. Therefore, a good understanding of a given slope system is important for the proper management of tourist areas. Improper designation of footpaths can destroy the stability of the natural environment, especially in high intensity tourist areas. An example of improper designation would be footpath creation in a landslide area, which in turn can reactivate landslides. This is observed on the tourist slope of the Babia Góra Massif in the Beskidy Mountains (Figure 3B). Another example would be footpath creation in the vicinity of a stream channel bank. This occurred in the Staników Valley. Footpath creation in a snow avalanche area or debris flow paths is also not proper. In this case, tourists passing by could trigger an avalanche, e.g. in the High Tatra Mts. Therefore, if it is not possible to create a footpath in another area, the given tourist region should be closed to tourists until the total disappearance of the snow cover. Another example of natural disturbance on tourist footpath can be debris flow. This process can provide the destruction of tourist infrastructure as it took place on footpath to Rysy Summit in the High Tatra Mts. in 2012.

The management of mountain protected areas is an important aspect of efforts to explore new methods designed to minimize the negative effects of anthropogenic impact as shown by studies of Mount Rainier National Park in the United States (Rechefort & Swinney, 2000). Mihai et al. (2009) studied the Bucegi Mountains in Romania and was able to show close interactions between geomorphological conditions and tourism. The tourist attractiveness of an area is linked to the nature of the local terrain and drives tourist traffic, which in turn generates a specific course of erosive processes. Tourist slopes feature slope sections with numerous polygenetic landforms. The development of these landforms depends on the mechanical impact of tourists. In order to determine the mechanical impact of tourists it is important to identify number of tourists and directions of their movements. One method of determining the intensity and direction of tourist traffic in difficult high-mountain conditions is a tourist counter. In the study area on tourist footpath from Wyżnia Chochołowska Valley to Pass below Wołowiec the dominant direction of tourists is down towards the valley (Fig. 5). Such information could be useful in the management of natural areas and may contribute to the improvement of tourist infrastructure. The same method was used in other protected areas e.g. in the Yosemite National Park (Pettebone *et al.*, 2010).

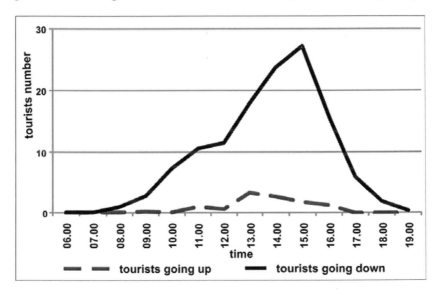

Figure 5 - The Average Number of Tourists on Footpath Section Wyżnia Chochołowska Valley-Pass Below Wołowiec from 21 VIII to 06 IX 2009 (T2)

Complex studies yield a very important approach to a better recognition of environmental issues in high-mountain areas. This approach is particularly important in protected areas where one of the main goals is to maintain the stability of natural ecosystems.

6. Conclusion

High-mountain areas are characterized by a wide variety of relief changes. This diversity depends on natural environment conditions and slope usage. The same types of processes taking place on natural slopes and tourist slopes produce different effects. This differentiation results from the different percentage of bare surfaces on different slopes. Footpaths and tourist roads are the most exposed to relief transformation due to prominent bare surfaces. Moreover, the mechanical impact of tourists contributes to soil and saprolite fragmentation. However, bare surfaces on natural slopes are characterized by rock pavement, which can make them more resistant to erosion. The biggest transformations on natural slopes are made by extreme events whereas on tourist slopes even medium-intense processes can cause significant relief transformations. An interdisciplinary approach is needed in order to gain a better understanding of interactions between particular elements of the natural environment. Hence, scientific research can be used to help improve tourism management methods in protected mountain areas.

Acknowledgement

We would like to thank the Tatra National Park for providing tourist traffic data and the Institute of Meteorology and Water Management for providing rainfall data.

References

Bac-Moszaszwili, M., Burchart, J., Głazek, J., Iwanow, A., Jaroszewski, W., Kotański, Z., Lefeld, J., Mastella, L., Ozimkowski, W., Roniewicz, P., Skupiński, A., & Westwalewicz-Mogilska, E. (1979). Geologic map of the Tatra Mts., 1:30 000. Warszawa: Wydawnictwa Geologiczne [In Polish].

Barnikel, F., & Becht, M. (2003). A historical analysis of hazardous events in the Alps – The case of Hindelang (Bavaria, Germany). *Natural Hazards and Earth System Sciences*, 3(6), 625-635.

Baumgart-Kotarba, M., Dec, J., Kotarba, A., & Ślusarczyk R. (2008). Glacial trough and sediments infill of the Biała Woda Valley (the High Tatra Mountains) using geophysical and geomorphological methods. *Studia geomorphologica Carpatho-Balcanica*, 42, 95-108.

Boltiziar, G., Bugar, G., Hresko, J., & Kohut, F. (2008). The Dynamics of Recent Geomorphic Processes in the Alpine Zone of the Tatra Mountains. *Geographia Polonica*, 81(1), 53-65.

Buchwał, A., & Fidelus, J. (2008). The development of erosive and denudational landforms on footpaths sections in The Babia Góra Massif and The Western Tatras. *Geomorphologia Slovaca at Bohemica*, 2, 14-24.

Buchwał, A., Fidelus, J., & Rogowski, M. (2009). Relief transformation along footpaths in The Riła, Piryn and Western Tatra Mountains. *Landform Analysis*, 10, 18-25.

Cole, D., & Monz, C. (2004). Trampling disturbance of high-elevation vegetation, Wind River Mountains, Wyoming, USA. *Arctic and Alpine Research*, 34(4), 365-376.

Crosta, G.B., Dal Negro, P., & Frattini, P. (2003). Soil slips and debris flows on terraced slopes. *Natural Hazards and Earth System Sciences*, 3(1-2), 31-42.

Decaulne, A., & Saemundsson, T. (2006). Geomorphic evidence for present-day snow-avalanche and debris-flow impact in the Icelandic Westfjords. *Geomorphology*, 80, 80-93.

Gorczyca, E., & Krzemień, K. (2008). Morphologic effects of extreme rainfall event in the Tatras in June 2007. *Landform Analysis*, 8, 21-24 [In Polish].

Izmaiłow, B. (1984). Aeolian process in alpine belt of the High Tatra Mts., Poland. *Earth Surface Processes and Landforms*, 9 (2), 143–151.

Jacobson, R.B., Miller, A.J., & Smith, J.A. (1989). The role of catastrophic geomorphic events in central Appalachian landscape evolution. *Geomorphology*, 2(1-3), 257-284.

Kaszowski, L., & Krzemień, K. (1979). Channel subsystems in the Polish Tatra Mountains. *Studia geomorphologica Carpatho-Balcanica*, 11, 149-161.

Kłapa, M. (1980). Morphogenetic processes and their relation to seasonal weather changes in the vicinity of Hala Gąsienicowa in the Tatra Mts. *Dokumentacja Geograficzna*, 4, (pp. 56) [In Polish].

Kotarba, A. (1970). Investigations of contemporaneous morphogenetic processes in the Western Tatra Mountains. *Studia geomorphologica Carpatho-Balcanica*, 13, 149-161.

—. (1989). On the age of debris flows in the Tatra Mountains. *Studia Geomorphologica Carpatho-Balcanica*, 23, 139–152.

—. (1992). Natural Environment and Landform Dynamics of the Tatra Mountains. *Mountains Research and Development*, 12 (2), 105-129.

—. (2005). Geomorphic processes and vegetation pattern changes case study in the Zelene Pleso Valley, High Tatra, Slovakia. *Studia Geomorphologica Carphato-Balcanica*, 39, 39-48

Krzemień, K. (1988). The dynamics of debris flows in the upper part of the Starorobociańska Valley (Western Tatra Mts.). *Studia Geomorphologica Carpatho-Balcanica*, 22, 123–144.

—. (1999). Structure and dynamics of the high-mountain channel of river Plima in the Ortler-Cedevale Massive (South Tirol). *Prace Geograficzne*, 104, 41-55.

—. (2004). Le role des processus morphogeniques contemporains dans le modelage de Massif volcanique des Monts Dore (Massif Central). *Prace Geograficzne*, 113, 11-25.

—. (2008). Contemporary landform development in the Monts Dore Massif, France. *Geographia Polonica*, 81(1), 67-78.

Krzemień, K., Libelt, P., & Mączka, T. (1995). Geomorphological conditions of the timberline in the Western Tatra Mountains. *Prace Geograficzne*, 98, 155–170.

Mihai, B., Reynard, E., Werren, G., Savulescu, I., Sandric, I., & Chitu, Z. (2009). Impacts of tourism on geomorphological processes in the Bucegi Mountains in Romania. *Geographica Helvetica*, 64(3), 134-147.

Nyberg, R. (1989). Obsrvations of slushflows and their geomorphological effects in the Swedish mountain area. *Geografiska Annaler. Series A, Physical Geography*, 71(3-4), 185-198.

Olive, N., & Marion, J. (2009). The influence of use-related, environmental, and managerial factors on soil loss from recreational trails. *Journal of Environmental Management*, 90, 1483-1493.

Pettebone, D., Newman, P., & Lawson S.R. (2010). Estimating visitor use at attraction sites and trailheads in Yosemite National Park using automated visitor counters, *Landscape and Urban Planning*, 97, 229-238.

Prędki, R. (2004). Le suivi de la degradation des sols dans la zone des itineraries touristiques: L'exemple du Parc National des Bieszczady. *Prace Geograficzne*, 113, 61-72.

Rączkowska, Z. (2006). Recent geomorphic hazards in the Tatra Mountains. *Studia Geomorphologica Carpatho-Balcanica*, 11, 45-60.

Rechefort, R.M., & Swinney, D.D. (2000). Human Impact Survey in Mount Rainer National Park: Past, Present and Future. *USDA Forest Service Proceedings RMRS-P15*, 5, 165-171.

Skiba, S. (2002). Soil map of Tatra National Park. In W. Borowiec, A. Kotarba, A. Kownacki, Z. Krzan, Z. Mirek (Eds.) *Przemiany środowiska przyrodniczego Tatr*. (pp. 21–26). Kraków-Zakopane: Wyd. TPN-PTPNoZ [In Polish].

Troll, C. (1973). The upper timberlines in different climatic zones. *Arctic and Alpine Research*, 5(3), 3-18.

CHAPTER SEVENTEEN

RECREATION PREFERENCES AND LIFESTYLES IN THE CANADIAN ROCKY MOUNTAINS

BARBARA MCNICOL AND JOE PAVELKA

Abstract

This evaluation takes data from three studies conducted by the authors in the Bow Valley of the Canadian Rocky Mountains. Analysis and interpretation targets preferences for amenity attributes of recreation opportunities and how 'lived experiences' contribute to mountain recreation lifestyles of resident groups (permanent and nonpermanent). Results show that while the lifestyle of all residents is strongly linked to a 'recreation connection', there exist significant differences for the preference of recreational amenity attributes between different resident groups. Key to this examination is the recreational opportunities available in and around Canmore and Banff town sites of Alberta as representative of attractive Canadian Rocky Mountain landscapes. **Keywords:** Amenity attributes, recreation, second homes.

1. Introduction

"I find living in the Bow Valley you are able to integrate leisure and recreation into small parts of one's day, rather than just wanting to do it on a weekend or in the evenings. It's all part of the experience (2009 Interviewee, Banff Male)."

This statement reflects the attraction of the Bow Corridor in Alberta to resident recreationalists. It reflects a mountain lifestyle that integrates outdoor recreation attributes and activities into an all-encompassing quality of life. Bow Corridor recreational landscapes are the result of the natural beauty of a montane ecosystem which extends along valley corridors and disappears up the sides of steeply tilted and folded mountains. At higher elevations biodiversity reflects fragile alpine ecosystems located on features carved by a glacial past and, for the present, still covered by snow and receding glaciers and ice fields. Canadian Rocky Mountain landscapes feature some unique flora and fauna (such as grizzly bear and mountain goat), diversified recreational opportunities and a perceived healthy 'lived experience' by visitors and residents alike.

The Towns of Canmore and Banff, situated twenty-five kilometers apart along the Trans-Canada Highway in the Bow Corridor of Alberta, are magnets for amenity migrants: People seeking to escape urban environments and associated problems and move closer to wilderness and mountain recreational landscapes (Gloriosa & Moss, 2007; Moss, 2008). In these locations, and in most of the Canadian Rockies, both permanent resident and second home recreational opportunities are valued for close proximity to protected ecosystems and the internationally recognized ski areas of the five mountain national park system. While the Town of Banff, located in Banff National Park, does not accommodate second home residences due to national park policies (Canadian Heritage, 1999), the nearby Town of Canmore has actively marketed the town-site as a second home and outdoor recreational destination.

Figure 1 - Bow Valley Corridor in Alberta, Canada (Robin Poitras, 2009)

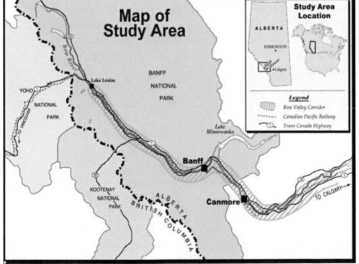

It has been established that second home owners have tended to emphasize different needs than permanent residents of amenity-driven communities (Asgary, Rezvani, & Mehregan, 2011; Brida, Osti, & Santifaller, 2011; Buxton, 2009; McNicol & Buxton, 2009). These differences have generally translated into recommendations about governance and policies for economic development and community growth. An increased accessibility and mobility as well as increased amounts of leisure time have contributed to a growing interest in second home tourism and how second home residents may prove different than permanent residents of these growth communities?

At the same time, differences from comparisons between resident groups are not easily articulated. Groups of circular-patterned migrants, such as second home owners, tend to be sporadic, seasonal, monthly, or weekend users of communities and not easily captured in resident surveys. These nonpermanent and part-time residents often are not present when the survey is circulated or they respond poorly to mail questionnaires due to the factor of distance of the primary residence. Most past resident surveys in the Bow Corridor have been unsuccessful at capturing credible samples of second home residents (Hargroup, 2004) due to low return rates.

This chapter presents in-depth and useful information about second home owners from some of the first successful surveys to capture both permanent and nonpermanent recreational preferences and link these to interview responses of associated lifestyle observations by Banff and Canmore residents. Analysis and interpretation targets preferences for attributes of recreation and how these contribute to mountain recreation lifestyles, or the 'lived experience' of permanent and nonpermanent resident groups.

2. Recreation and Second Homes

The concept of amenity migration was developed and initially used by Laurence Moss in 1994. This concept can directly be linked to tourism hence the often used second home resident label of amenity tourism migrant, yet the goal of the amenity migrant is to reside for a period of time rather than to solely visit the destination. At the same time, these nonpermanent 'tourist residents' seek out places perceived to possess extraordinary natural and cultural resources that were not available within their previous (or permanent) places of residence (Moore, 2006; Moss, 2006a; Moss, 2006b; Stewart, 2000).

Over time, second home issues have firmly manifested as an interdisciplinary subject area. A useful and encompassing compilation of studies has been published by Chraca and Marcouiller (2010) about second home studies as they link to planning and policy recommendations and initiatives. Many of these articles target rural community development and indirectly link results and recommendations around 'recreational lifestyles'. Community researchers and planners often assume that recreation and tourism amenities are important incentives that entice both seasonal and permanent development and growth in rural communities (Dillman, 1979; Knapp & Graves, 1989; Snepenger, Johnson, & Rasker, 1995).

Coverage of studies that link directly recreation, amenity migration and second homes is less prevalent, although most of the important literature refers to second homes as 'recreational properties' without clearly detailing a direct link to recreational attributes or activities (Chipeniuk, 2008). One article that incorporates the social aspects of ecotourism with recreational lifestyles is Buckley (2005) yet, even here, the emphasis is on anecdotal environmental impacts rather than the attributes of recreation.

Geographical location also is closely integrated with leisure and recreation as a motive for mobility and choice of a destination (Glorioso & Moss, 2006). Amenity migration has been rapid to communities in the Canadian Rockies and Alberta since the late 1990s (Buxton, 2009; Chipeniuk, 2005; Godde, Price, & Zimmerman, 2000; Robinson & Stark, 2006; Stefanick, 2010). While some attractive attributes are generically important in most destinations, such as the beauty of natural scenery and surroundings (Glorioso & Moss, 2006), perceived amenities that have attracted and increased the permanent resident population over time are proving different in type than many that are attracting amenity migration of second home owners to the Bow Corridor of Alberta (Buxton, 2009; McNicol & Buxton, 2009).

3. Permanent and Nonpermanent Residents

The Town of Canmore's permanent population is 12,317 individuals (Town of Canmore, 2011) but the total population may increase on busy weekends and in the summer season to about eighteen thousand through the influx of transient labor and second home usage (Buxton, 2009). The overall rate of change for the two populations of permanent and nonpermanent residents is different with recent decrease in the rate of growth of the permanent population to less than 2%, while the rate of growth in second home numbers remains in the double-digit percentage

(Town of Canmore, 2011). Observation suggests that some of this second home growth has more recently been deterred by the global economic down turn, especially for foreign investment real estate markets.

There exist key differences between the permanent residents and the second home owners for population composition and demographic make-up in Canmore. Permanent residents tend to span the 25-54 age cohorts while the majority of second home owners are baby boomers in the 40-65 age brackets (McNicol & Buxton, 2009; Town of Canmore, 2011). The second home market is dominated by residents from urban areas in Canada. In fact, what is often referred to as an active Canadian market is really a majority market composed of people from Alberta's two largest cities: Calgary and Edmonton (McNicol & Sasges, 2008). International second home markets to Canmore are strong for the United States, dominated by California (23%), Texas (14.6%) and Florida (9.2%) residents, and the United Kingdom and Northern Ireland, with 78.2% of these second home seekers from England (McNicol & Sages, 2008).

The Town of Banff has a different population composition and demographic then the Town of Canmore. Residents of Banff must work and prove a 'need to reside' to maintain a permanent residence in the national park town. Second homes are not welcome in the Town of Banff which is located within Banff National Park proper. The population of Banff is 8,244 with 7,251 permanent residents and 933 considered temporary or transient residents (those that stay for short-term periods and work) (Town of Banff, 2011). More than half of the population is between the ages of 20-49 and almost a quarter of the population is between 20 and 29 (Town of Banff, 2011). Permanent residents tend to be parks employees, owners of businesses and fulltime workers for the service and tourism enterprises in the Bow Corridor. Temporary or transient residents work in the food and beverage, accommodation or tourism retail trade (Town of Banff, 2011).

4. Recreation Studies and Methods

This chapter places emphasis on identified categories of recreational amenities in The Bow Corridor of Alberta. Results are presented that confirm significant recreational preferences about the importance of recreational attributes between the two key amenity migrant groups of 1) full-time permanent residents and 2) nonpermanent second home owners in the Town of Canmore. This evaluation divides the results of the nonpermanent second home owner preferences into the three key submarkets of 1) Canada, 2) the United States and 3) the United Kingdom.

This comparative evaluation includes data from the 2004 Recreation Needs survey, of the Recreation Master Plan, of full-time permanent residents in the Town of Canmore with the 2006 Town of Canmore Second Home Owner survey results. Finally, the comparative results are evaluated within the context of 2009 focus group and interview results of selected Canmore and Banff residents. This 2009 research involved five focus groups with Banff and Canmore residents, a five-person qualitative interview study of Canmore second-home owners, and a twenty four person qualitative interview study to investigate the 'lived experience' of recreation and leisure by permanent residents of the Bow Valley. This study interpreted the 'lived experiences' of Canmore and Banff residents: What is collectively referred to here as the recreation connection. These studies are summarized for clarity in Table 1.

4.1. Permanent vs. nonpermanent resident recreation

A main goal of the initial comparative survey study was to gain insight and understanding into the similarities and differences about recreational attribute preferences by different resident groups; both permanent and nonpermanent. This type of comparative analysis requires inferential statistics that use significance testing to understand which differences are credible (or significant) between the resident groups targeted. A Mann-Whiney U non-parametric significance test was used to identify significant differences of preferences between recreational attribute categories comparing permanent and nonpermanent resident groups. Data analysis compared a single multi-response question, included in both the 2004 Recreation Needs survey and the 2006 Canmore Second Home Owner survey, where respondents were provided with a list of recreation attributes and instructed to rate the importance of each attribute toward their recreational needs in the Town of Canmore. Recreation attributes rated for importance by resident groups were:

1. The trails and parks found with the town-site area;
2. The trails and parks surrounding the town for camping and hiking and other recreation opportunities;
3. Drop-in opportunities at the Recreation Centre or other town operated facilities;
4. Festivals and special events;
5. Recreation and leisure in the mountains around the town;
6. Other commercial recreation opportunities (these were not listed for respondents).

Table 1 - Summary of Recreation Studies and Methods

Recreation Study	Population Size	Sample Size	Return %
Town of Canmore Recreation Master Plan Telephone Survey (2004)	Permanent Residents N=400	n=400	
Town of Canmore Second Home Owner Mail Survey (2006)	Canada N=635 USA N=269 United Kingdom N=96	n=328 n=137 n=48	51.65 56.37 50.00
Bow Corridor Lifestyle Focus Groups and Interviews (2009)	5 Focus Groups 5 Second Home Owner Interviews 24 Permanent Resident Interviews		

Data for the category of the attribute of 'trails and parks surrounding the town for camping and hiking and outdoor recreation opportunities' was not evaluated for the permanent resident group since this category was not included in the 2004 Recreation Needs Survey but subsequently added to the 2006 Town of Canmore Second Home Survey.

The number of responses for each option was compared using the Mann-Whiney U non-parametric significance test. The results of the statistical test were studied and all significant relationships were identified based on the alpha value of .05. For each grouping of survey categories all questions with a Z score value of less than .01 were identified as being significantly different, therefore implying that the samples of survey respondents were from two different populations. Table 2 shows numerical distributions of survey results and lists the final comparison of differences between all resident groups (both permanent and nonpermanent) identified in bold with significant differences between groups highlighted in the far right-side column.

4.2. Similarities for recreation attributes

A lack of a significant value between sample groups will reveal similarities about the importance of the recreation attribute amongst the resident groups. Both permanent residents and all second home owners, from all countries, agree on the similar high importance of one attribute: Festivals and special events in this mountain community (Table 2). The Town of Canmore has been proactive in encouraging festivals to the community and annually offers the Highland Games, the Golden Eagle Migration Festival and a very popular summer Folk Festival. These events attract people from the entire Bow Valley Corridor including high weekend numbers from Calgary. They have been ongoing and actively marketed by the Town and should be considered as successful ventures supported by the results from this study.

One attribute, as mentioned in section 5.0, was not included in the survey of permanent residents, this was the 'trails and parks surrounding the town for camping and hiking and outdoor recreation opportunities'. All second home resident groups, however, agree on the importance of the role of the trails and parks surrounding the community for camping and hiking (Table 2). These were the only two attributes that remained similar for their importance as defined by the different resident groups.

Table 2 - Between Resident Group Differences

	Not at all important	Somewhat important	Important	Very Important	Don't Know/ Blank	Significantly Different From:
	n (%)	n (%)	n (%)	n (%)	n (%)	
Trails and Parks w/in Town	7 (2.3)	26 (8.7)	38 (12.7)	225 (75.3)	3 (1.0)	CDN-Perm;
Trails and Parks Outside Town	10 (3.4)	31 (10.4)	63 (21.1)	191 (64.1)	3 (1.0)	
Drop-in Rec	70 (23.5)	84 (28.2)	78 (26.2)	57 (19.1)	8 (2.7)	CDN-Perm;
Registered Programs	109 (0.3)	98 (33.0)	45 (15.2)	34 (11.4)	9 (3.0)	CDN-Perm;
Festivals and Special Events	17 (36.7)	77 (26.0)	110 (37.0)	75 (25.3)	4 (1.3)	
Recreation and Leisure	5 (1.7)	12 (4.0)	59 (19.7)	218 (72.9)	5 (1.7)	CDN-Perm;
Other Commercial Rec.	25 (8.4)	80 (26.8)	101 (33.9)	88 (29.4)	3 (1.0)	UK; US; CDN-Perm;

	Not at all important	Somewhat important	Important	Very Important	Don't Know/ Blank	Significantly Different From:
	n (%)	n (%)	n (%)	n (%)	n (%)	
Trails and Parks w/in Town	14 (3.5)	20 (5.0)	110 (27.5)	256 (64.0)	0 (0.0)	CDN; US
Trails and Parks Outside Town						no comparative data
Drop-in Rec	72 (18.0)	86 (21.5)	114 (28.5)	118 (29.5)	10 (2.5)	CDN; UK; US
Registered Programs	81 (20.2)	74 (18.5)	109 (27.2)	127 (31.8)	9 (2.2)	CDN; US
Festivals and Special Events	54 (13.5)	77 (19.2)	128 (32.0)	141 (35.2)	0 (0.0)	
Recreation and Leisure	23 (5.8)	31 (7.8)	81 (20.52)	264 (66.0)	1 (0.2)	CDN; UK; US
Other Commercial Rec.	89 (22.2)	93 (23.2)	110 (27.5)	75 (18.8)	33 (8.2)	CDN; UK; US

	Not at all important	Somewhat important	Important	Very Important	Don't Know/ Blank	Significantly Different From:
	n (%)	n (%)	n (%)	n (%)	n (%)	
Trails and Parks w/in Town	0 (0.0)	1 (2.3)	9 (20.1)	34 (77.3)	0 (0.0)	
Trails and Parks Outside Town	0 (0.0)	1 (2.3)	8 (18.2)	35 (79.5)	0 (0.0)	
Drop-in Rec	1 (2.3)	19 (41.3)	12 (27.3)	12 (27.3)	0 (0.0)	
Registered Programs	8 (18.2)	20 (45.5)	6 (13.6)	10 (22.7)	0 (0.0)	CDN-Perm
Festivals and Special Events	4 (9.1)	9 (20.1)	15 (34.1)	15 (34.1)	0 (0.0)	
Recreation and Leisure	1 (2.3)	1 (2.3)	3 (6.8)	39 (88.6)	0 (0.0)	CDN-Perm
Other Commercial Rec.	0 (0.0)	8 (18.2)	14 (31.8)	22 (50.0)	0 (0.0)	CDN; CDN-Perm

	Not at all important	Somewhat important	Important	Very Important	Don't Know/ Blank	Significantly Different From:
	n (%)	n (%)	n (%)	n (%)	n (%)	
Trails and Parks w/in Town	1 (0.8)	5 (4.1)	21 (17.4)	97 (78.9)	0 (0.0)	CDN-Perm
Trails and Parks Outside Town	2 (1.6)	6 (4.9)	17 (13.9)	97 (79.5)	0 (0.0)	
Drop-in Rec	29 (24.0)	40 (33.1)	27 (22.3)	21 (17.4)	4 (3.3)	CDN-Perm
Registered Programs	42 (34.7)	38 (31.4)	22 (18.2)	17 (14.0)	2 (1.7)	CDN-Perm
Festivals and Special Events	12 (9.8)	39 (32.0)	38 (31.1)	32 (26.2)	1 (0.)	
Recreation and Leisure	1 (0.8)	6 (5.0)	20 (16.8)	91 (76.5)	1 (0.8)	CDN-Perm
Other Commercial Rec.	6 (5.0)	21 (17.4)	55 (45.5)	39 (32.2)	0 (0.0)	CDN; CDN-Perm

4.3. Differences for recreation attributes

Considerable differences exist about the importance of the remaining recreation attributes between the permanent residents and the Canadian subgroup of second home owners. In fact, the highest amounts of significant differences about recreation attributes are between these two resident groups; these include all but the two categories of similarities listed in Section 5.1 (Table 2). The Canadian second home owners are finding less importance for the opportunities found on the trails and in the parks inside the town-site than are the permanent residents but greater importance for the recreation and leisure in the mountains around the town (Table 2). This suggests that second home owners from Canada, mostly from Calgary and Edmonton, prefer the recreational opportunities in the mountains around the Town of Canmore than do the permanent resident population.

On the other hand, permanent residents place emphasis on the types of recreational opportunities that can be done in town such as using drop-in facilities at the Canmore Recreation Centre as well as the registered programs at the Recreation Centre and other town-operated facilities (Table 2). A key significant difference, therefore, between the Canmore permanent residents and the Canadian second home owners is a higher importance placed on town-generated leisure and recreation experiences and opportunities by the permanent resident group. Permanent residents place importance on these community recreation facilities and activities whereas second home owners in general are less involved in community issues and want to cocoon and have the tendency to prefer time to enjoy their properties over community contact (McNicol & Buxton, 2009).

Of specific note, one deviation from the previous observation is a significant difference between the permanent residents and nonpermanent second home owners over the importance of 'other commercial recreation opportunities'. Most of these commercial opportunities are found within the town-site proper although a few of these, such as dog-sled tours, will be facilitated in the surrounding countryside. In the Town of Canmore, commercial opportunities include heritage and geological museums, art galleries, up-market retail stores, as well as fine dining restaurants and bars. Permanent residents place less importance on these commercial opportunities than do all of the second home owners including those from all three of the second home submarkets: Canada, the United States and the United Kingdom (Table 2). Therefore, another key difference between permanent and nonpermanent resident groups is the level of importance placed on opportunities to experience commercial recreational activities.

Finally, the nonpermanent second home owner sub-markets show fewer differences between and amongst themselves than do the permanent versus nonpermanent resident groups. The only category where second home sub-market groups demonstrate a significant difference over a recreation attribute is when rating the importance of 'other commercial recreation opportunities'. Both second home owners from the United States and the United Kingdom consider these commercial opportunities more important than do second home owners from Canada. This suggests that Canadian second home owners are less interested in 'going out on the town' than the international second home owners. This is most likely due to the reality of international second home owners travelling longer distances to reach their second home destination. Due to distance, they have less opportunity to 'get-away' and use their residences than those that can weekend from Calgary and Edmonton, perhaps heightening their need to be 'tourists' in their adopted town.

5. The Bow Valley Resident Lifestyle

5.1. The Permanent Resident Lived Experience

Interviews and focus groups in 2009 revealed that of the five most common reasons to permanently reside in the Bow Valley, the first, and by far most common response can be summed up as 'mountains'; mountain recreation activities and a general passion for the mountains. Some individuals stated that they were lured to the Bow Valley by one recreational activity (generally skiing) and, in the end, stayed for the inclusive recreational lifestyle. Of importance to this evaluation, when interview participants were asked to discuss whether their motivation to live in the Bow Valley was based on the pursuit of an activity or a specific recreation lifestyle the overwhelming response was lifestyle. Of the twenty-four individuals interviewed for the 2009 study, all but two reported that recreation and a recreation lifestyle was an important reason for residency in the Bow Valley.

Some permanent resident interviewees, while acknowledging the overarching draw of the lifestyle, also reinforced their dedication to an activity (for example, skiing, hiking or paddling sports). Other participants reported that over time they managed to build a lifestyle around one activity, usually skiing. In the 2006 Second Home Owner Survey, when second home owners were asked the importance of their property's proximity to a ski resort there were differences in market responses: United Kingdom respondents felt it was important to their property purchase 55.2% of the time, Canadians felt it was important 63.9% of the time, while Americans answered proximity to a ski resort was important 72.7% of the time (McNicol & Sasges, 2008). This reinforces the pull of skiing to amenity migration in the Bow Corridor of Alberta.

For permanent residents, interviews suggested that a unique aspect of the recreation connection for some residents of the Bow Valley is that they believe recreation can be better incorporated into daily life than in other places they have lived prior to their migration. They refer to this as 'seamless living' whereby the mountain recreation lifestyle is ideally viewed as integrated recreation activity, work, housing, and social life all guided by a mountain dominated theme. Some longer term permanent residents have openly discussed their lifestyle as one that is different from the city, where one is not defined by their career but by their recreation: "You may be a doctor but can you climb 5.10. (2009 Interviewee, Banff Male)". Many participants view their lifestyle as different from life in the city in that it is more relaxed and with a value system counter to the harried life of the city.

5.2. The Second Home Resident Lived Experience

"On a regular basis I go there and I can sit in my house in Canmore and never move. I'd be quite happy to do that and that's the solitude thing, whereas at home, I could never do that (2009 Interviewee, Second Home Owner)."

What is described by this interviewee is what has previously been described as the 'cocoon effect' where second home residents have a greater commitment to their property than to a community (Buxton & McNicol, 2009, p.260). It is suggested that most second home owners may find the act of cocooning more enjoyable than community involvement.

Second homeowners express an interest to participate in recreation activities within the town-site or close to it. This was characterized by one 2009 Canmore interviewee as "a quiet urban respite experience with short forays into the mountains". Activities of expressed importance were front country walks/hikes, grocery shopping, visiting restaurants, enjoying arts/culture and short, mountain hikes. Other, preferences for activities were urban-focused recreation; hikes in town parks and on town pathways, recreation within the condo-complex, Banff town-site visits, shopping and enjoying nightlife. A group of final activities mentioned were outdoor intensive recreation activities in the backcountry and skiing at ski areas. Interviews and focus group results, therefore, indicate that second homeowner recreational preferences tend to be largely concentrated at home and in the town-site for commercial activities with short forays into the mountains surrounding the town-site for more intense outdoor activities such as skiing, hiking or climbing.

6. Conclusion

Amenity migrants have flocked to Canadian Rocky Mountain towns in search of tourism and recreational opportunities. This is most pronounced in the Bow Valley Corridor of Alberta where the Towns of Canmore and Banff, combined with the natural and heritage amenities of Banff National Park and the surrounding skiing opportunities, create some of the most used and recognized tourism and recreation landscapes in Canada. These landscapes draw both full-time permanent amenity migrants and nonpermanent second home residents to mountain and recreational lifestyles. The lived experience in the Bow Corridor of Alberta has a pronounced recreation connection contributing to the quality of lifestyles of all residents.

There exist, however, differences between resident groups about the importance of specific recreational attributes. Full-time permanent residents differ directly from nonpermanent second home owners about some key recreational attributes such as 1) the use of trails and parks within the Town, 2) the importance of drop-in and recreation facilities, 3) the importance of registered recreational programs and 4) a preference for recreation and leisure in the mountains around town. While preferences do not always translate into behaviors there are comments recorded during interviews and focus groups that support the results from the comparative data evaluation.   For example, some of these differences can be directly attributed to the less community involved group of nonpermanent second home owners that prefer to cocoon and enjoy their properties. Second home owners, when they do emerge from their residences, place importance on the trails available to them in and around the town and are much less interested in organized recreation facilities and activities in the town. Both permanent residents and nonpermanent second home owners place similar high importance on established festivals and events. They differ, however, over the importance of 'other commercial activities'. This suggests that further subdivision of this attribute category may uncover significant differences about commercial activity preferences between permanent and nonpermanent resident groups.

While the lifestyles of all residents is strongly linked to a recreation connection, this evaluation shows that there exist significant differences (and some similarities) for the preference of recreational attributes between permanent and nonpermanent resident groups that come to the Bow Corridor of Alberta seeking the recreational amenities of the Rocky Mountains of Canada.

References

Asgary, A., Rezvani, M.R., & Mehregan, N. (2011). Local residents' preferences for second home tourism development policies: A choice experiment analysis. *Tourismos: An International Multidisciplinary Journal of Tourism*, 6(1), 31-51.

Brida, J.G., Osti, L., & Santifaller, E. (2011). Second homes and the need for policy planning. *Tourismos: An International Multidisciplinary Journal of Tourism*, 6(1), 141-163.

Buckley, R. (2005). Social trends and ecotourism: Adventure recreation and amenity migration. *Journal of Ecotourism* 4(1), 56-61.

Buxton, G. (2009). Planning for amenity migration: Can amenity migration pay for itself? In L.A.G. Moss, R. S. Glorioso, & A. Krause (Eds.), *Understanding and Managing for Amenity-led Migration in Mountain Regions* (pp. 103-106). Banff, Alberta: Banff Centre for Mountain Culture.

Canadian Heritage. (1999). *The concept of the eligible resident in Canada's National Park communities: Special places and special requirements* [Brochure]. Banff, Alberta: Parks Canada.

Chipeniuk, R. (2005). Amenity migration in the Bulkley Valley. Proceedings from: *Smithers symposium on mountain community development: Planning for tourism, amenity migration and resorts*. Smithers, British Columbia: University of Northern British Columbia, School of Environmental Planning, Outdoor Recreation and Tourism.

—. (2008). *Defining amenity migration: Results from a survey of experts*. Smithers, British Columbia: University of Northern British Columbia, School of Environmental Planning, Outdoor Recreation and Tourism.

Chraca, C., & Marcouiller D. W. (2010). *Recreational Homes, Amenities, and their Gateway Communities: A Review of the Planning and Public Policy Literature*. Madison, Wisconsin: University of Wisconsin, Department of Urban and Regional Planning.

Dillman, D.A. (1979). Residential preferences, quality of life and the population turnaround. *American Journal of Agricultural Economics* 61, 960-966.

Gloriosa, R.S., & Moss, L.A.G. (2006). Sante Fe, a fading dream: 1986 profile and 2005 postscript. In L.A.G. Moss (Ed.). *The Amenity*

Migrants: Seeking and Sustaining Mountains and their Cultures (pp.73-93). Wallingford: CABI.

Gloriosa, R.S., & Moss, L.A.G. (2007). Amenity migration to mountain regions: Current knowledge and a strategic construct for sustainable management. *Social Change* 37(1), 137-161.

Godde, P.M., Price, M.F., & Zimmerman, F.M. (2000). *Tourism Development in Mountain Regions.* Oxon: CABI.

Hargroup Management. (2004). *Recreation Master Plan.* Canmore, Alberta: The Town of Canmore.

Knapp, T.A., & Graves, P.E. (1989). On the role of amenities in models of migration and regional development. *Journal of Regional Science,* 29(1), 71-87.

McNicol, B., & Buxton, B. (2009). Profiling Canadian and international second home owner cultures in Canmore, Alberta: Implications for community planning and governance considerations and relationships. In L. A.G. Moss, R. S. Glorioso, & A. Krause (Eds.). *Understanding and Managing for Amenity-led Migration in Mountain Regions* (pp. 254-263). Banff, Alberta: Banff Centre for Mountain Culture.

McNicol, B., & Sasges, K. (2008). *Canmore Second Home Owner Survey: Data Analysis and Presentation.* Canmore, Alberta: Town of Canmore, Planning and Development Office.

Moore, S. (2006). Finding a pad in paradise: Amenity migration effects on Whister, British Columbia. In L.A.G. Moss (Ed.). *The Amenity Migrants: Seeking and Sustaining Mountains and their Culture* (pp.135-147). Wallingford: CABI.

Moss, L.A.G. (1994). Beyond tourism: The amenity migrants. In M. Mannermaa, S.Inayatullah, & R. Slaughter (Eds.). *Coherence and Chaos in Our Uncommon Futures: Visions, Means and Actions - Selections from the XIII World Conference of the World Futures Studies Federation,* (pp. 121-128). Turku, Finland.

—. (2006a). *The Amenity Migrants.* Oxfordshire: CABI.

—. (2006b). The amenity migrants: Ecological challenge to contemporary Shangri-La.

—. (Ed.). *The Amenity Migrants: Seeking and Sustaining Mountains and their Cultures* (pp.94-107). Wallingford: CABI.

—. (2008). The mountain amenitymigration phenomenon, why it is happening and our response. In L.A.G. Moss, R.S. Glorioso, & A.Krause (Eds.). *Understanding and Managing for Amenity-led Migration in Mountain Regions* (pp.1-12). Banff, Alberta: Banff Centre for Mountain Culture.

Robinson, B., & Stark, C. (2006).   Alberta's amenities   rush.   In L.A.G.
    Moss (Ed.). *The Amenity Migrants: Seeking and Sustaining Mountains
    and their Cultures* (pp.120-134). Wallingford: CABI.
Snepenger, D.J., Johnson, J.D., & Rasker, R. (1995). Travel- stimulated
    entrepreneurial migration. *Journal of Travel Research* 34(1), 40-44.
Stewart, S.I. (2000).   Amenity migration. Proceedings from: *Trends 2000,
    5th outdoor   recreation   and   tourism   trends   symposium.* Lansing,
    Michigan: Outdoor Recreation and Tourism Association.
Stefanick, L. (2010).   The path to progress or paradise lost? Planning for
    amenity migration in Canadian mountain communities.   Amenity-
    based mountain change and development in an era of increased global
    uncertainty. Proceedings from: *Global change and the world's
    mountains.* Perth, Scotland: Mountain Research Institute.
Town of Banff. (2011).   *2011 Banff Census.*   Banff, Alberta: Town of
    Banff.
Town of Canmore. (2011). *2011 Canmore Census.*   Canmore,   Alberta:
    Town of Canmore.

CHAPTER EIGHTEEN

A DIAGNOSTIC ANALYSIS OF WINTER SPORTS TOURISM IN ROMANIA AND FRANCE IN TERMS OF LOCAL SUSTAINABLE DEVELOPMENT

SORINA CERNAIANU AND CLAUDE SOBRY

Abstract

Sports Tourism is the fastest developing segment of economy around the world. Winter sports activities such as skiing, snow-boarding, ice-skating, climbing, paragliding, etc., with a varied and adapted offer to each type of consumer can be a way of developing tourism. The main purpose of this chapter is to compare the situation of winter sports tourism between Romania and France, in order to see if tourism can be considered as a means of local sustainable economic development. Analysing the data and some examples of mistakes that were made, as well as the strategies for sustainable development allows us to draw a picture of the potential future of this set of tourist activities with really specific characteristics. **Keywords:** Winter tourism, sports activities, sustainable development.

1. Introduction

If tourism is the economic field knowing the highest growth[i] (in 2012, the record number of international tourists was smashed with a billion tourists), sports tourism is the fastest developing side of this sector. Moreover, sports tourism through its diversity (viewing a sports event, participating in a sports event, leisure sports, and visiting places of historical interest sports wise) offers host territories opportunities for socio-economic development.

Winter sports activities such as skiing, snow-boarding, ice-skating, ice-climbing, paragliding, etc., with a varied and adapted offer to each type of consumer, are among the newest sport tourism activities to develop on a massive level – even though recent results contrast with noticeable modifications on a worldwide level, due to climate change. During winter 2011-12 the United States, who had long been the world leader in terms of visitors, have seen their number decrease by 15.8% with 50.97 million skier visits, following the National Ski Areas Association[ii]. This situation has had a positive impact on the European resorts (especially the French), where the amount of snow has been particularly satisfying, thus allowing France to regain its title of first worldwide destination with 55.3 million skier visits (+3% compared to the previous winter) – second best performance after winter 2008-09 when the record number of 58.5 million skier visits was attained (against 57.4 million for the USA)[iii]. It is interesting to point out that in the same conditions, Austria, third worldwide destination for 2011-12, witnessed a 2% decrease compared to the previous winter with 50 million skier visits.

The Chinese market totals two million skiers, a figure expected to reach 20 million by 2025. However there are other countries closer to us who are little known as a winter destination despite their ski area such as Lebanon, Morocco, Greece or Croatia[iv]. Others, especially in Central Europe, do have winter sports resorts – sometimes built long ago. They try to catch up with the lacks induced by the communist era and use winter tourism as a tool for local economic development. Poland manages to attract international visitors. Romania tries to reach this level, thus adding winter sports as a new asset for tourism, along with sea resorts and cultural, historical and religious tourism.

Major European countries, and especially France, possess exceptional quality infrastructure and services able to satisfy the most demanding requirements, being one of the highest figures of total skiers' visits. Concerning the lifts, France has the world's best park, being the leader in innovation and technology.

Regarding Romania, even if it possesses the second largest mountain chain in Europe (Romanian Carpathians), the slope infrastructure is still limited and the services are just not the best. At the same time, it is still little-known as a winter holiday destination. However, the organization of the European Youth Olympic Festival (FOTE) in 2013 is a mobilizing factor for the development of the ski infrastructure in Romania.

The main purpose of this chapter is to compare winter sports tourism between Romania and France, in order to see if tourism can be considered as a tool for local sustainable economic development. Comparing the data and some examples of past mistakes, as well as the sustainable development strategies, allows us to draw a picture of the potential future of this set of tourist activities with really specific characteristics - for it needs a natural environment offering both risk and safety, works in the area and heavy equipment to reach it, the whole in a tough and fragile site.

2. Sport Tourism and Local Sustainable Development

Sports tourism has been one of the most dynamic activity sectors for over 10 years, a sector which activity has not decreased despite the spasms of the economy. Although perfectly identified by tourism professionals, the object of products and strategies, sports tourism is still seeking its identity in the research and higher education communities despite some works have been realized-but are still isolated (Bouchet & Lebrun, 2009; Bouchet & Bouhaouala, 2009; Pigeassou, 2004; Sobry, 2004).

Sustainable development involves various definitions, the most common being the one given by the World Commission on Environment and Development in the report "Our Common Future" (1987): "development which meets the needs of the present without compromising the ability of future generations to meet their own needs".

A well-known definition for sustainable tourism is brought by the World Tourism Organization: "Tourism that takes full account of its current and future economic, social and environmental impacts, addressing the needs of visitors, the industry, the environment and host communities".

Sport tourism is considered as an efficient local development tool even if this statement is sometimes difficult to prove – even though many works have demonstrated the role of tourism regarding local sustainable development and/or the fight against poverty.

The analysts are perplex as for the efficiency on local development of major sport events such as the Olympics. It would not be the sports event triggering the necessary elements to economic growth, but the long term growth of well spotted variables with a self-supporting mechanism. Major sport events are only a pretext to use the media as a resonance chamber as they focus on a definite territory during several weeks. Thinking these events are able to produce a growth mechanism is heading towards great disillusions - and mostly to a massive deficit without any positive effect on the concerned territory.

Quite the opposite, the organization of yearly local sport events, original and very well prepared, the appointment of specialists and amateurs or the progressive and measured development of facilities to welcome tourists and give them the means to live their passion or simply enjoy sport activities, allows the creation of material and human structures (creation of jobs, qualification of the population who can work on site and doesn't need to leave anymore), efficient for a long term social and economic growth. With this progressivity major errors, often irreversible, on the environment can be avoided. These three aspects of the development, economic and social, as well as the preservation of the environment focusing on a definite territory in order to measure the impact of what is done, are just the conditions required for local sustainable development. This is what has been done for the last thirty years in Val Cenis, France, a group of mountain villages gathering means to reach a high hosting capacity and quality while keeping their authenticity. Other resorts came to the sustainable touristic development later mostly because they were issued from the last generation. The best example of sustainable development thanks to sports tourism is located in the Joux Valley in Switzerland (Di Cola, Costa, Bélony & Loze, 2008).

3.1. Winter tourism in Romania

Located in the southeastern part of Central Europe, with a population of about 22 million people and covering a vast area of 237,500 square kilometers, Romania is a country of diversity, characterized by various landscapes, traditions, World Heritage sites and cultural crossroads between Latin culture, Balkan and Orthodox Christianity. The tourism potential is very varied and diverse, characterized by a historical and architectural heritage internationally appreciated, favorable climate, rich flora and fauna, with unique species and ecosystems in Europe. The mountain area in Romania represents 37.9% of total country area, against 25.2% for France (see Table 1).

Table 1 - National Area Covered by Mountain Municipalities

Country	Country area (1,000 km^2)	Mountain area (1,000 km^2)	Mountain area as percentage of total country area
Romania	238.40	90.24	37.9
France (excluding DOM)	549.035	138.465	25.2

Source: Nordregio Report, 2004.

The National Development Tourism Strategy in Romania is a priority due to the benefits offered by the existing tourism potential. In terms of consumption of tourism services in Romania, a study ran by INSOMAR in August 2009 on a sample of 2,502 persons representative for the Romanian population, aged minimum 18, shows that in 2009 only 26% of respondents went on holiday. The same study indicates that only 4.1% of respondents practiced various sports activities during their holidays.

The most important sports activities practiced during winter in Romania are: alpine skiing, snow-boarding, biathlon, paragliding, ice-skating, sledge, ATV rides and rock climbing; skiing is practiced by 80% of tourists staying in a Romanian mountain resort (Pisteur project, 2010).

The development of winter sports tourism is influenced by the weather, temperature and climate conditions. According to a study realized by Pisteur Project in Romania, the ski season in most mountain resorts lasts between 90 and 130 days per year.

By processing data from the Romanian National Institute of Statistics (INS) concerning the arrivals of tourists hosted in structures dedicated to tourist reception we observe that the arrival of Romanian tourists reached a peak in 2008 (5,659,416 arrivals) and was continuously decreasing in the last two years. Concerning the arrival of foreign tourists in Romania, the highest value was recorded in 2007 (1,550,957 arrivals), also followed by a decline during the economic crisis (see table 2).

Regarding the coming of Romanian tourists in mountain resorts, there was an increase of 34.88% between 2001-2008, followed by a decrease of 18.44% directly linked with economic crises. The winter tourism market, mostly domestic, has been heavily struck by the salary cuts measures adopted from 2008 to 2010. In the same time the ratio of Romanian tourists hosted in mountain resorts divided by the total arrivals of Romanian tourists reached a maximum value of 16.83% in 2004, decreasing to 15.41% in 2010.

The percentage of foreign tourists in mountain resorts decreased significantly from 9.61% in 2001 to 6.44% in 2010. Another significant decrease was recorded for the total number of tourists (from 15.39% in 2001 to 13.42% in 2011) (see table 2). These decreases can be the result of the image of the country conveyed by the media, who focus more on the political, economic and social issues rather than on the qualities and positive aspects of the country. One of the reasons for the decrease of Romanian and foreign tourists during winter is due to the uprising of markets such as Poland or Bulgaria, which have a diversified offer and a better value for money, but also to the competition with other countries involved in the winter sports market like Austria, Germany, Italy and Switzerland, each of them trying to stand out on a specific aspect by putting their qualities forward – natural environment, culture, skills, etc.

Table 2 - Arrivals of Tourists Hosted in the Structure of Tourists

Year	Arrivals of romanian tourists in mountain resort	Ratio[1]	Arrivals of foreign tourists in mountain resort	Ratio[2]	Total arrivals of tourists in mountain resort	Ratio[3]	Total arrivals of romanian tourists	Total arrivals of foreign tourists	Total arrivals of tourists
2001	662,088	16.72	87,903	**9.61**	749,991	15.39	3,960,268	914,509	4,874,777
2002	601,643	15.63	98,305	9.84	699,948	14.44	3,848,288	999,208	4,847,496
2003	649,762	16.44	98,068	8.88	747,830	14.79	3,951,718	1,104,975	5,056,693
2004	720,117	16.83	116,181	8.55	836,298	14.83	4,279,023	1,359,494	5,638,517
2005	715,230	16.35	112,722	7.88	827,952	14.26	4,375,185	1,429,911	5,805,096
2006	786,241	16.26	96,605	7.00	882,846	14.20	4,836,196	1,379,832	6,216,028
2007	879,036	16.22	118,706	7.65	997,742	14.31	5,420,968	1,550,957	6,971,925
2008	893,065	15.78	105,403	7.19	998,468	14.01	5,659,416	1,465,891	7,125,307
2009	749,879	15.41	81,064	6.36	830,943	13.53	4,865,545	1,275,590	6,141,135
2010	728,320	15.41	86,653	**6.44**	814,973	13.42	4,726,414	1,346,343	6,072,757

[1]Ratio of Romanian tourists in mountain resort divided by the total arrivals of Romanian tourists; [2]Ratio of foreign tourists in mountain resort divided by the total arrivals of foreign tourists; [3]Ratio of arrivals of tourists in mountain resort divided by the total arrivals of tourists.
Source: National Institute of Statistics, Romania.

The length of ski slopes, the lifts, the night lighting or the possibility to produce artificial snow, are important indicators to the development of ski areas. Also, the existence of adequate infrastructure (accommodation, sport facilities, transportation, entertainment etc.) leads to increase the number of tourists.

According to data from the Ministry of Regional Development and Tourism there are 130 certified ski slopes in Romania with a cumulative length of 116 km, most of them being found in Brasov county. Not all of these slopes ensure normal conditions for skiing, although the weather and snow covering are favorable.

A report realized by L. Vanat on international mountain tourism (2011) shows that Romania counts 141 lifts among 44 ski areas, which represents 3.56% of the capacity of France. The French park includes 3685 lifts shared between in 357 ski areas, representing 18% of the international park. If we link the number of ski lifts with the amount of ski resorts, we can observe that for France the ratio is 10.32, against only 3.2 for Romania. The same report shows that the ratio of foreign skiers in Romania mountain resorts is only 5%, when for France it is 28%. Moreover, the number of skier visits in Romania is only 2.19% of total skier visits of France.

Table 3 - Figures about Skiing in Romania and France

Country	Skier visits[1]	No. of skiers (nationals)	Arrivals of international tourists	Proportion of foreign skiers
RO	1,200,000	667,406	1,272,000	5%
FR	54,760,000	12,170,980	74,200,000	28.0%

[1] Average last 5 seasons or estimate.
Source: Vanat (2011).

Of the 44 ski resorts of Romania, only 5 have more than 4 lifts, and none of them has more than 1 million skier visits. Contrasting with Romania, France possesses 233 resorts with more than 4 lifts and 14 of them have more than 1 million skier visits (Vanat, 2011).

Despite the economic crisis, in 2011 in Romania the investment in ski infrastructure was approximately EUR 17.4 mil., and concerned projects financed by the state through the Ministry of Regional Development and Tourism. Regarding the development of tourism products, the program "Ski in Romania" wants to rehabilitate the ski slopes, develop new ski areas with international standards, and develop mountain tourism. A total of 17 projects concerning infrastructure of ski areas are ongoing, aiming at achieving 54 ski slopes, two biathlon tracks, a ski-jump and two recreational facilities (Activity report 2010, Ministry of Regional Development and Tourism).

Among the programs developed by the Ministry of Regional Development and Tourism (www.mdrl.ro), is the Regional Operational Programme 2007-2013 (financed by the state, local budgets, private sources and the European Regional Development Fund), which has a strategic objective "to support and promote local sustainable development, both economically and socially, in the regions of Romania, by improving the conditions of infrastructure and business environment, which support economic growth". This program allows tourism operators to get funding for "creation, development, modernization of infrastructure for natural resources recovery with tourist potential and improving the quality of tourism services", thus stimulating local economic development, creating jobs and using the natural resources in a sustainable manner.

3.2. Some aspects of winter tourism in France

A Western European country, with a population of 65.8 million (National Institute of Statistics and Economics Studies – INSEE, January 2011) and a land area of 674.843 km², France is one of the most developed countries in the world and the world's first tourism destination with 78.95 million international visitors in 2010, 81,4 in 2011 (World Tourism Organization).

Due to the important dimensions of the ski area (124,000 km², which is 28% of the European ski area and 23% of the country area), attractive offers and quality of environment, France is a privileged destination for winter sports, especially alpine skiing and cross-country skiing. Complementary products like: sledge, snowshoe and snowboard are practiced in most winter resorts, even if there are no specific areas (Cabinet Architecture et Territoire, 2005).

Concerning the infrastructure, France bears 230 resorts designed to cross-country skiing (Association Nationale des Centres et Foyers de Ski de Fond et de Montagne – ANCEF, http://www.ancef.com) with a surface of 25,239 km² and 13,000 km of trails.

An important aspect for the development of the winter sport tourism offer in France is the existence of 250 ski schools through France's ski areas, unified in the "Ecole du Ski Français" (French ski school) - the largest ski school in the world, with over 17,000 instructors qualified in all ski disciplines (www.esf.net).

If we cannot use the word "democratization" for winter sports, the amount of tourist arrivals increased considerably during the last forty years. This increase contributed to territory planning with the building of accommodations for the tourists and infrastructures to bring them to the resorts (roads, highways, railways, etc.), and so enable them to practice their favorite sport.

The arrival of winter tourists generates economic growth in these regions, creating jobs but also with many environmental impacts. Initially, only the economic results were seen. New resorts called "integrated ski resorts" were built, especially in the late 1970s, with a lot of architectural and environmental mistakes which took thirty years to be corrected[v].

Today sunny destinations are in severe competition with winter resorts and their development is much more aware of sustainable development - even if not all problems are solved, some of them being the result of the need for customers and/or the efforts to satisfy them, to develop customer loyalty and gain market shares.

Since the little snowy winters of the late 1980s and the evolution of tourism demand noticed during the 1990s, the available activities have been multiplied with the development, especially the snowshoe walks, dog sledding, creation of snowboard parks etc. - and for the most athletic, waterfall ice climbing. The offer designed for children has also been enlarged with the creation of "snow gardens" where children are welcomed and introduced to sliding sports with specific equipment and qualified personnel. Being free, the parents can enjoy the resorts' equipments – and consume.

For the last thirty years, winter sports professionals have been working on improving the available offers and adapting them to the ever-changing tourist behaviors – especially late booking. Over the last few years the sector became more professional and focused on the available services and entertainments, and particularly the ones regarding families (cheaper train fares, shuttle and taxi services in train stations, etc.). Efforts have been made on the training and level of qualification of the staff, the trails for seasonal workers have been secured, the marketing of the ski areas has been improved and there have been major investments in equipment and facilities.

Lately, the tourists have seen new smartphone applications appear with which they can optimize their routes on the trails, get real-time information about the weather, how busy the sites are, etc.

The results obtained, showing a yearly increase of winter tourists of about 2% - the youth being a significant part of it - come from a long-time work with the help of the different actors of the sector, in order to adapt the existing offers and create new products so that winter sports meet the ever-changing customers' expectations – to convince them or gain their loyalty, on the national and international levels.

The National Mountain Resorts Mayor Association (ANMSM, http://www.anmsm.fr/), which federates about 100 mountain resorts in partnership with "Domaines skiables de France" (the Professional Association of ski domains operators), the Agency for the Environment and Energy Management (ADEME, http://www2.ademe.fr/) and Mountain Riders (http://www.mountain-riders.org) created in October 2007 *"The National Charter in favour of sustainable development in mountain resorts"* which "expresses the will of the Mayors of mountain resorts to provide concrete responses to climatic changes in order to ensure the continuation of the local economies and make sure that tourism is sustainable". Each signatory to this Charter for sustainable development benefits from diagnostic tools, decision support or defined their carbon balance using specific software. This charter contains 8 action plans and 130 commitments on various topics like: natural resources, waste, sustainable housing policy, preservation of natural spaces and countryside, management of resources, tourist activities etc. One of the action plans of this charter refers to skiing area and snow sports, taking into account some measures concerning the integration of ski lifts, ski runs, and snow-production installations into the environment. Mountain Riders in collaboration with different partners has developed an Eco guide designed to assess the commitment to sustainable development of mountain resorts. The ski resorts develop specific actions concerning the following topics: transport, energy, development and planning, water, rubbish and waste, social and environmental information and are validated (labels are awarded) according to the assessment criteria.

In spite of this will to develop sustainable tourism, in order to meet the expectations of tourists asking for snow, 49% of French ski resorts (175) are equipped with snow cannons, covering a surface of 3,029 km^2, which represents 12% of the ski area. This percentage continues to grow because tourists want good snow coverage. We can also notice that some ski resorts or credit cards options, etc., offer insurance against the lack of snow. But the production of artificial snow does not contribute to sustainable development.

The installation of pipes and snow cannons need to work the ground with heavy machinery. Flora, fragile in the mountains, suffers from it. The noise produced by the construction and running of the cannons, generally during the night, frightens the (mostly nocturnal) fauna. Water tanks created to supply the installations are not sufficient and about 50% of the water necessary to produce the snow is taken from the drinking water network. We can add to all this the increase of lighted slopes to extend the pleasure of skiers at a time when town and city councils multiply the efforts to reduce the energy used for street lighting.

4. Conclusion

This chapter shows that Romania tries to develop winter sport and the local economy of the mountain regions. The comparison with France today is not very interesting in itself, but the way Romania develops this tourism compared to what was done in France is interesting. In France the interest for wintersport tourism started during the sixties and the winter Olympic Games in Grenoble were obtained by French President C. De Gaulle with the will to turn a region of familial, agricultural economy into a touristic indutrial region. It happened in 1968, when the after WW2 growth was very strong and the purchasing power increased strongly. Now Romania wants to boost wintergames thanks to the European Youth

Olympic Festival (FOTE) in 2013 in a climate of national, and at least European, economic crisis. Even in this context it is interesting to observe that the decrease of winter sport tourism in Romania, which began in 2009, has a stronger impact on domestic tourism than the coming of foreign tourists which grew back again in 2010 after only one year of decrease. And the statistics show that the total number of arrivals and the Romanian tourists decreased more slowly in 2010 than in 2009, definitely emphasizing the vigor of sport tourism whatever the surroundings.

What mistakes were made in France, what is done now to develop the local economy thanks to winter sport and, at the same time, protect the environment and bring some benefit to the population in terms of qualification and long term jobs. That's why comparing two countries at very different levels of their sport winter sport tourism development is interesting. Will the experience in a country be used in another one, what kind of agreement or charter could be brought to protect the people and the environment, or will only the most obvious part be remembered - building accomodation and ski lifts to host the tourists who will spend their money?

How to export the experience, how to initiate a balanced economy, a sustainable development in a new coming country which mainly looks for fast growing incomes thanks to sport tourism?

Notes

[i] Tourists arrival on a worldwide level: 2008, +2.1%; 2009, -3.8%; 2010, +6.6%; 2011, +5%; 2012, +4%. Source UNWTO

[ii] NSAA brings together 321 ski resorts. This underachievement is partly due to the low amount of snowfalls in the country, being the lowest level for 20 years.

[iii] Spring holidays in France now come later than they used to, i.e. after the snow period. This factor would have decreased the number of visits by 50% over this very period. Source: DSF (Domaine Skiable de France, an organ bringing together 236 lift operators in France).

[iv] Zagreb hosts one race for the slalom World Cup every year.

[v] For a study on the impact of winter sports on the development of French mountain areas, see (among other works) P. Arnaud et T. Terret « Le rêve blanc; Olympisme et Sport d'hiver en France Chamonix 1924, Grenoble 1968 », Presses Universitaires de Bordeaux, collection Milon, 1993 et Jeux Olympiques d'hiver : montagne et développement, Revue de géographie alpine n°3 tome LXXIX 1991.

References

Bouchet, P., & Bouhaouala, M. (2009). Tourisme sportif: un essai de définition socio-économique. *Teoros*, 28-2, 2009.

Bouchet, P., & Lebrun, A. (2009). *Management du tourisme sportif. De la consommation à la commercialisation.* Rennes: Presses Universitaires de Rennes.

Cabinet Architecture et Territoire. (2005). *Le positionnement de l'offre Française de sports d'hiver. Note de Synthèse.* Retrieved from http://www.tourisme.gouv.fr/stat_etudes/etudes/territoires/offre_sports _hiver.pdf

Di Cola, G., Costa, C., Bélony, C., & Loze, B. (2008). *Travail décent, développement local et sport.* Genève: Organisation Internationale du Travail.

INSOMAR. (2009). *Consumul de servicii turistice in Romania, Raport de cercetare. Val III.* Retrieved from http://www.mdrl.ro/_documente/turism/studii_strategii/insomar_noiem brie_2009.pdf

Ministry of Environment and Sustainable Development. (2008). *National Sustainable Development Strategy 2013-2020-2030.* Retrieved from http://strategia.ncsd.ro/docs/sndd-final-en.pdf

Ministry of Regional Development and Tourism. (2011). *Activity report 2010.* Retrieved from www.mdrt.ro/userfiles/Raport_activitate_2010.pdf

Nordregio. (2004). *Mountain Areas in Europe: Analysis of mountain areas in EU member states, acceding and other European countries.* Nordregio Report 2004:1, Stockholm. Retrieved from http://www.nordregio.se/en/Publications/Publications2004/Mountain-areas-in-Europe/

Pigeassou, C. (2004). Le tourisme sportif, une réalité sociale aux contours incertains. In C. Sobry (Ed.), *Le tourisme sportif* (pp.33-71). Villeneuve d'Ascq: Presses Universitaires du Septentrion.

Proiect Pisteur. (2010). *Analiza situatiei privind organizarea activitatii de intretinere si salvare pe domeniul schiabil in Franta si Romania.* Retrieved from http://pisteur.eu/download/1_RO_ro.pdf

Sobry, C. (Ed.). (2004). *Le tourisme sportif.* Villeneuve d'Ascq: Presses Universitaires du Septentrion.

Vanat, L. (2011). 2011 International report on mountain tourism. Overview of the key industry figures for ski resorts. Retrieved from www.vanat.ch/RM-world-report-2011.pdf

World Commission on Environment and Development. (1987). *Our Common Future.* Oxford: Oxford University Press.

CHAPTER NINETEEN

MORE THAN FOOD? PROMOTING THE COUNTRYSIDE TO TOURISTS USING LOCAL FOOD PRODUCTIONS IN ITALY

ELISABETE FIGUEIREDO

Abstract

This chapter aims to explore, through a case-study approach, combining content analysis of written promotional materials and a survey directed to rural tourism entrepreneurs, how local food productions are presented and offered to tourists in Campania and Tuscany. It is argued that rural tourism entrepreneurs, namely the ones directly connected with accommodation supply could play a paramount role in using and diffusing particular features of rurality through the mobilization of specific symbols and material elements, which in the tourists' imaginary correspond to the 'typical' countryside. Despite the central position of local food productions in the overall tourism offer and in promoting rural areas as unique destinations, evidence suggests that its character and its connection to local territories are seldom putted in evidence. **Keywords:** Local food, food production, promotional materials, rural tourism.

1. Introduction

Rural tourism entrepreneurs, namely the ones directly connected to accommodation supply, generally have a paramount role in using and diffusing particular images and features of rurality through the mobilization and the effective use of particular signs, symbols and material elements, which in the tourists imaginary characterize the 'typical' countryside (Figueiredo & Raschi, 2011; 2012). Among those elements and symbols, local traditional food products and gastronomy, hold a central position.

Food is an important part of the culture and identity of a territory, reflecting the biophysical specificities of the local environment, the main agricultural productions, activities and traditions as well as the know-how and a particular 'vision of the world' local population has developed throughout the centuries. Local food products and local gastronomy frequently represent key elements in the overall tourism offer, contributing to enhance tourists' experience of the countryside and local communities' development (Bessiére, 1998; Fonte, 2008). Despite this recognition, previous studies suggest that the connection between local food productions and rural tourism activities is still faint (Malevolti, 2003; Renting *et al.*, 2003; Telfer & Wall, 1996; Vieira & Figueiredo, 2010).

Based on a case-study approach, combining content analysis of promotional materials and a survey directed to rural tourism entrepreneurs, this chapter aims to analyze how local food productions are presented, offered and sold to tourists in five municipalities of two Italian regions (Campania and Tuscany). This discussion assumes particular relevance in peripheral regions of Europe – as it is the case of the five municipalities analyzed here – due to the general decreasing economic and social role of agricultural activities combined with a growing investment on tourism activities. Although some results of this study were already published (Figueiredo & Raschi, 2011; 2012) the chapter will focus mainly on unpublished data, related to the connection between local food and tourism activities.

However exploratory in nature and despite the limitations of the study, empirical evidence reveals that regardless the relevance attributed to local food as a promotional asset, its character and its connection to local territories are seldom put in evidence.

2. Local Food Productions and Rural Tourism

Tourism is often presented as the panacea for rural areas socioeconomic problems, particularly in peripheral European regions, where the countryside experienced major transformations mainly in consequence of the declining role of agriculture. These transformations and its diverse consequences have been broadly discussed throughout the last decades (Cloke, 2006; Cloke & Goodwin, 1993; Halfacree, 2006; Marsden, Lowe & Whatmore, 1990) giving raise to the post-productivism paradigm (Marsden, 1995) within rural studies and to the notion of a rural space without productive functions (Figueiredo, 2008). A rural that is "beyond agriculture" (Marsden, 1995) and increasingly portrayed and perceived as a 'consuming idyll', directly opposing 'super productivist' spaces in which the "key spatial practices are consumption-oriented, notable leisure (…)" (Halfacree, 2006: 57).

Although some dimensions of the post-productivism theories might be contested (Evans *et al.*, 2002) it is increasingly evident the political and social perception and valorization of peripheral rural areas of Europe as leisure places and the growing demand for rural tourism destinations as well, particularly from urban dwellers (Bell, 2006; Halfacree, 2006). The current tourism-oriented consumptions of the rural are based on strongly positive images and feelings on the countryside (Bell, 2006; Perkins, 2006) which are apparently increasingly hegemonic and 'global' (Bell, 2006; Cloke, 2006; Halfacree, 2006; McCarthy, 2008) due to the diffusion of certain symbols and signs of rurality which seem ever detached from the materiality of rural territories. These images and symbols are mainly (although not exclusively) conveyed through promotional materials and means used by the tourism industry and rural tourism establishments (RTE) and contribute to form the background to current and increasing rural commodification processes (Figueiredo & Raschi, 2012; McCarthy, 2008; Perkins, 2006).

Tourism promotional materials include a diversity of means (internet, guide-tours, brochures, business cards, leaflets, postcards) and tools (words, videos, pictures) (Choy *et al.*, 2007). Although "based on local characteristics and therefore 'authentic', these promotional elements are often sculpted to be more attractive and assertive" (Figueiredo & Raschi, 2012: 23), by using affective, cognitive and conative elements to shape a destination image (Choy *et al.*, 2007) contributing to shape tourists' decision making. RTE promotional materials frequently utilize images and features of rurality, mobilizing and using particular signs, symbols and material elements of the rural territories in which they operate.

Among the symbols and material elements, local traditional foodstuffs and gastronomy generally hold a central position as pull factors in the promotion of tourism destinations (du Rand *et al.*, 2003; du Rand & Heath, 2006; Horng & Tsai, 2012). Taking into account the diversity of meanings that are normally attached to local and regional food (Brunori 2007) and without intending to reproduce in this chapter the discussion on this topic, it should be emphasized that local and regional food is understood here mainly as "the expression of a local community" circulating through "(short distance) traditional circuits" (Brunori 2007: 11). This is rather different from 'locality food' and 'localist food', as demonstrated by the author and supposes that foodstuffs are consumed, even by the tourists, in the area in which they are produced.

As many authors (Béssiere, 1998; Fonte, 2008; Fonte & Papadopoulos, 2010; Horng & Tsai, 2012; Montanari & Staniscia, 2009; Sims, 2009) demonstrate, food is a relevant part of the culture and identity of a territory reflecting material and immaterial aspects, such as the biophysical conditions, local environment, main agricultural productions, activities and traditions as well as a particular 'vision of the world' and the know-how local populations have developed throughout the centuries. As Bessière (1998) points out, agricultural products and the ways they are transformed, prepared and presented are part of the culture and tradition that are closely linked to the territory. Food is therefore more than just food (more than just nutrients) as it places people "in a social universe and a cultural order" (Bessière, 1998: 24). Food can be considered a patrimony (Fonte, 2008) and a social and cultural construction (Bessière, 1998).

Local food products and gastronomy frequently represent key elements in the overall tourism offer, contributing to enhance the tourists' experience (Boyne *et al.*, 2003; Cohen & Avieli, 2004; Montanari & Staniscia, 2009; Renko *et al.*, 2010; Telfer & Wall, 1996; Vieira & Figueiredo 2010). However, as du Rand and Heath (2006) explain, both from institutional bodies and researchers, the attention to the role of local food in tourism activities and experiences, is relatively recent. As Renko *et al.* (2010: 311) emphasize, food study in the tourism social science was until recently "simply ignored or taken for granted". Nowadays the relevance of foodstuffs for tourism, particularly regarding rural areas is recognized, not only because – as mentioned above – food is part of the culture and heritage of territories – but also due to the value it adds to the image of a particular destination (du Rand *et al.*, 2003, Renko *et al.*, 2010); to the potentialities it presents in terms of destination differentiation and competiveness (Bessière, 1998; du Rand & Heath, 2006; Renko *et al.*, 2010); and to the potential contribution it can give to rural development, especially in peripheral areas (Brunori & Rossi, 2000; Renting *et al.*, 2003; Sims, 2009, Tregear *et al.*, 2007).

Several authors pointed out the mutual advantages that RTE and local food producers may obtain from strengthen the links between them (Boyne *et al.* 2003; Brunori & Rossi 2000; Telfer & Wall 1996; Vieira & Figueiredo, 2010), particularly, as mentioned, by enhancing the overall tourism products and experiences and by providing economic stimuli to preserve local agricultural productions (Boyne *et al.*, 2003; Montanari & Staniscia, 2009). Despite this recognition the connection between local food productions and rural tourism activities is still faint (Malevolti, 2003; Renting *et al.*, 2003; Telfer & Wall, 1996; Vieira & Figueiredo, 2010), due to several factors, ranging from the inadequacy and inexistence of local networks between tourism entrepreneurs, farmers and other stakeholders (du Rand & Heath, 2006; Vieira & Figueiredo, 2010); to the lack of knowledge among tourism operators and tourists on local food character (Malevolti, 2003; Vieira & Figueiredo, 2010). Also the insufficient ability on the supply side in providing local productions (Vieira & Figueiredo, 2010) and the lack of effective marketing and communication strategies (du Rand & Heath, 2006; Vieira & Figueiredo, 2010) are often pointed out as a major constraints in building fruitful connections between local food productions and rural tourism activities.

3. Methodology

The study was exploratory in nature therefore the use of research questions seemed more appropriate than the test of hypotheses. The following research questions were addressed in the study:

1. How the promotional materials used by the RTE do present the local food productions?
2. Which productions are more frequently promoted and offered to tourists?
3. What is the relevance attributed by the RTE owners/managers to local features, particularly to food productions, in promoting their establishments and local communities?
4. Which productions are more often demanded by the guests?
5. What is the relevance attributed by the RTE to the establishment of links with local farmers and producers?
6. Which are the main constraints and opportunities identified by the RTE owners/managers in offering, using and selling local food productions?

The five municipalities (Table 1) studied are representative of the broader changes in the Italian countryside. Although characterized by a large variety of rural environments in consequence of historical, environmental and socioeconomic diversities (Figueiredo and Raschi, 2012), in recent years many agrarian systems and rural areas in Italy faced major transformations. Among these, the reductions in farmers' incomes and the declining role of agriculture and forest are especially relevant, resulting in the abandonment of 15 to 20% of farmland and in losses in socioeconomic dynamics in rural territories. However, as Fonte (2008) refers, this declining situation somehow helped to preserve some traditional characteristics, such as local food culture.

Table 1 – Number and type of tourism establishments

Region	Province	Municipality	Agro Tourism	Room rental and B&B	Hotels	Holiday houses
Tuscany	Siena	Rapolano Terme	15	1	4	2
	Arezzo	Chitignano	1	1	1	1
		Ortignano/ Raggiolo	1	1	0	1
TOTAL			16	3	5	4
Campania	Benevento	San Marco dei Cavoti	5	10	0	1
		San Giorgio la Molara	4	1	0	0
TOTAL			9	11	0	1

The selection of case studies was based on previous research as well as on their diversity in terms of tourism development, agricultural activities and socioeconomic contexts. Despite the differences, mainly regarding landscape and natural characteristics, some similar demographic and socioeconomic features and trends can be identified: heavy depopulation processes in the last five decades, generally low levels of literacy among local population and severe ageing processes, which are common features to a large part of the Italian countryside and other southern and peripheral European rural areas (Figueiredo & Raschi, 2012).

San Marco dei Cavoti and San Giorgio la Molara are located in a remote part of Campania region, in the southern part of Italy, in which agriculture is still a relevant activity and tourism is not much developed. Ortignano/Raggiolo and Chitignano lay in a mountain area of Tuscany (central part of Italy) rich in abandoned chestnut and beech forests. Agriculture possesses a residual role as well as tourism. Rapolano Terme is located in an area which can be considered as the *typical Tuscany*, where the landscape is dominated by castles and farmhouses spread among cereal fields, olive plantations and oak groves (Figueiredo & Raschi, 2012). Here, due to the presence of geothermal springs and to the proximity of Siena, tourism has some relevance, while agriculture is declining.

In a first phase, the promotional materials of 50 RTE (all the existing in 2008) were analyzed, including agro-tourism, room rental and bed & breakfasts, hotels and holiday houses (Table 1). Content analysis (both qualitative and quantitative) of the written parts of the materials (websites, business cards, leaflets) was performed[i]. Particularly regarding local food productions, categorization of the content of the promotional materials involved the identification of the products promoted and their description (words used and its relation with local territories). The content analysis performed indicated that local food productions were used in promotional materials in a more consistent way than other dimensions of rurality.

Based on the previous findings and to better understand the liaisons between rural tourism and local foodstuffs a survey was directed to all the owners/managers of the 50 RTE, in 2010. 42 valid responses were obtained. The survey included mainly questions related to the relevance attributed to local foodstuffs in promoting the RTE and in attracting guests; to the food productions more often demanded by and sold to the guests; to the links between the RTE and the local and regional stakeholders and to the main opportunities and constraints identified in using and selling local food productions to guests. Due to the small number of respondents, data from the survey was analyzed using descriptive procedures.

4. Results

As shown in Table 1, Bed & breakfast establishments are the most frequent type of accommodation in the Campania municipalities. In Tuscany, despite the lower relevance of agriculture, agro-tourism establishments are dominant. In both regions RTE are generally of small dimension (52% possess less than six bedrooms and 38% less than six beds), which partially explains the low number of guests in 2009 (28.5% of the RTE received less than 50 guests). In Campania, the majority of guests are from Italy, while in Tuscan municipalities guests are equally from Italy and other countries.

All the Campania RTE began operating after 1995, which was directly connected to the availability of European Union (EU) funds. In fact, all the establishments in the two municipalities benefited from EU funds (from 45 000€ to 100 000€). Although in Tuscan municipalities the majority of the RTE began operating also after 1995, only a few (five out of 26) had financial support (less than 66 000€). These findings are related to the main motivations to open the RTE: in Campania the 'opportunity to restore the houses' and in Tuscany the *'possibility of starting a business'*.

The majority of the owners/managers of the RTE have between 36 and 55 years old. 22 are females and 20 are males. 21 are born in the same municipality where the RTE is located and 12 in the same region. The majority possess educational qualifications equivalent to high school and 12 a university diploma. 28 have other professional occupations besides the RTE. The establishment is the main source of income only for 8 respondents, 6 of them from the Tuscan municipalities. For the majority, the RTE revenue represents less than 25% of the overall family income. These data confirms the small dimension of the establishments and help to further explain the results obtained.

Data from the analysis of promotional materials shows a relatively strong connection with local agriculture productions, olive oil, wine and vegetables being the most promoted in Tuscan municipalities and meat, cheese, vegetables and wine in Campania. These products are promoted through a variety of words which symbolize a 'certain way' of growing and preparing local productions. 'Traditional' is the word more frequently used to presented local food and cuisine in the promotional materials in both regions, followed by 'typical', 'genuine' and 'natural'. In Tuscan municipalities, the word 'Tuscan' and the expression 'della terra' (from the land) are also used, while in Campania there is no active use of any symbols or words explicitly connected to local culture and territoriality (Figueiredo & Raschi 2011; 2012)

Regarding the food products actually served and/or sold to guests, data from the survey (Table 2) show that the majority of the 34 RTE, which serve or sell any type of foodstuffs, either produce it themselves (particularly the agro-tourism units) or buy it from local farmers and/or retailers. However the number of RTE that buy some of the products also from large supermarkets is relatively high. The results presented in Table 2 also corroborate the above mentioned regional differences in terms of products used and sold in the RTE.

This evidence also indicates that RTE value the connections with local farmers and/or retailers. In fact, 28 respondents declared touse and to foster this type of liaisons. The advantages of these connections are mainly identified by the respondents as: to 'help local community development', 'to have more guests' and 'to increase the services and products offered to guests'. Nevertheless, the small number of farmers and retailers (2 to 3) with whom the RTE have connections, emphasizes the small dimension of the establishments as well as the faint impact of these links in local socioeconomic fabrics.

Table 3 shows the results regarding the perception of the advantages and constraints of buying foodstuffs from local producers and farmers. The advantages perceived are superior to the constraints identified. Among the advantages, the 'better quality' and the 'authenticity' of the products together with the 'support to local economy' stand out. The 'higher price' and the 'irregularities' in the supply are the more frequent constraints identified by the respondents.

Table 2 – Food products used and sold in the RTE and their origin (number of RTE)

Food Products	Campania						Tuscany					
	Self production	Local regional farmers/shops	large supermarkets	Self production and local farmers/shops	All	Does not Use	Self production	Local regional farmers/shops	Large supermarkets	Self production and local farmers/shops	All	Does not Use
bread	4	8	1	0	0	2	2	6	1	1	1	8
milk	3	4	7	0	1	0	0	2	9	0	0	8
cereals	4	0	9	0	0	2	1	4	5	0	0	9
olive oil	5	2	0	0	0	8	10	5	2	0	1	1
wine	3	4	0	0	0	8	5	5	2	0	1	6
fruits	3	6	1	1	1	3	1	5	6	0	0	7
chestnuts	2	0	0	0	0	13	3	0	2	0	0	14
vegetables	6	1	0	0	0	8	8	2	3	2	1	3
aromatic herbs	6	0	1	0	0	8	6	2	0	1	0	10
cheese	4	3	3	0	0	5	0	4	5	1	0	9
yogurt	2	0	6	0	0	6	2	0	6	0	0	12
ham/salami	5	2	4	1	0	3	0	3	3	2	2	9
pasta	6	0	1	0	0	8	4	1	4	1	0	9
honey	0	10	2	0	0	3	4	8	0	0	0	7
jam	9	1	4	0	0	1	5	3	3	1	0	7
sauces	6	0	0	0	0	9	10	1	0	0	0	8
mushrooms	1	4	0	0	0	10	2	5	3	0	0	9
cow meat	3	3	0	1	0	8	0	4	2	0	3	10
ep and goat meat	3	4	0	0	0	8	0	2	2	1	3	11
pork meat	5	2	0	0	0	8	0	3	2	1	3	10
cakes and sweets	8	2	4	0	0	1	9	1	0	1	0	8
eggs	5	1	0	0	0	6	5	2	3	0	1	11
poultry	5	1	0	0	0	6	5	2	3	0	1	11

Table 3 – Perceived Advantages and Constraints of Buying Foodstuffs

Advantages of buying local food products	Campania	Tuscany
better quality	11	8
better flavor	9	4
certification	5	7
authenticity	11	8
support local economy	10	7
mantain traditional agriculture	5	6
Convenience/proximity	5	5
guests preferences	8	6
lower price	2	0
Obstacles to buying local food products	Campania	Tuscany
higher price	5	6
bad presentation	0	1
inferior quality	0	0
Irregularities in supply	3	6
no invoicing	1	2
insufficient production	0	2
bad hygienic standards	1	0

Regarding the perception of the most relevant aspects to attract guests to RTE, results (Table 4) demonstrate that local and RTE agricultural activities and food and wine products are amongst the items less valued, particularly in Rapolano Terme and in the southern municipalities. It is particularly surprising that in Rapolano Terme where the larger number of agro-tourism establishments is located, only 43% of the RTE attributed relevance to these aspects in attracting guests. 'Local landscape', 'local traditional architecture', 'local natural elements' and (in the Tuscan case) 'proximity to main cities and monuments'[ii] are the most valued attributes in attracting guests to the municipality as well as to the establishment.

Content analysis of promotional materials, although evidencing a greater emphasis on the 'immersion' in 'nature' and in 'green' to characterized the establishments and its surroundings, also highlights local food productions and gastronomy as relevant features of the destinations. Somehow, this finding indicates a relative inconsistency between the promotion and the effective use and recognition, by the RTE, of foodstuffs and gastronomy as major attractions of the destination.

Table 4 – Most Relevant Aspects to Attract Guests to RTE

Features	Tuscan Municipalities			Campania Municipalities	
	Rapolano Terme	Chitignano	Ortignano/ Raggiolo	San Marco dei Cavoti	San Giorgio La Molara
Local landscape	100	100	100	76.9	100
Local traditional architecture	81	100	100	76.9	100
Architecture of RTE	85.7	50	100	61.5	100
Local natural elements	90.5	100	100	59.2	100
Local agricultural activities	40	100	66.7	53.8	100
Agricultural activities in RTE	57.1	0	66.7	23.1	66.7
Local culture and festivities	52.4	0	100	100	66.7
Local tourism activities	73.8	100	100	30.8	100
Activities in RTE	90.5	100	100	27.3	66.7
Services in RTE	90.5	100	100	45.5	100
Local traditional wine/food products	85.7	0	100	84.6	66.7
Wine/food products in RTE	42.9	0	66.7	15.4	33.3
Proximity to main cities and monuments	100	100	100	30.8	33.3
Availability of transport connections	85.7	0	66.7	15.4	33.3

The majority of the respondents consider that guests 'can tell the difference between local food products and industrialized ones', mainly in terms of quality and flavor, frequently 'asking for information about the origin of the products' and looking 'for tasting local foodstuffs'. Table 5 displays the data regarding local food products more often demanded by the guests either to taste or to buy.

Table 5 – Food Products More Often Demanded by Guests

Food Products	Campania	Tuscany
bread	11	9
milk	3	1
cereals	2	3
olive oil	15	25
wine	7	23
fruits	2	1
chestnuts	0	4
vegetables	7	10
aromatic herbs	3	5
cheese	15	21
yogurt	0	2
ham/salami	14	17
pasta	5	9
honey	9	11
jam	8	7
sauces	4	3
mushrooms	0	9
cow meat	12	17
sheep and goat meat	13	7
pork meat	12	9
cakes and sweets	14	11
eggs	2	4
poultry	2	4

Regional differences in terms of main food productions are, again, evident. Wine, olive oil and cheese being more demanded by the guests in Tuscan RTE and meat (especially pork and sheep/goat) and bread being more often required in Campania municipalities. These are, as mentioned above, the products also more frequently used in the promotional materials.

5. Conclusion

This chapter uncovered the use of local food productions and its promotion by the RTE in five municipalities of two Italian regions, by analyzing textual information in promotional materials and, mainly, data obtained from a survey to owners/managers of RTE. Based on the assumption that local food productions are a relevant part of the rural tourism offer and experience – due to its connection to biophysical, economic and cultural character of local communities – as well as an important aspect of the local identity, as discussed in the literature review section, this chapter argued that food is 'more than food'. Food is a patrimony and therefore its promotion and active use by the RTE can contribute to enhance local agricultural activities and local economies contributing to local development, particularly in peripheral rural areas (Brunori & Rossi, 2000; Renting *et al.*, 2003; Sims, 2009, Tregear *et al.*, 2007; Vieira & Figueiredo, 2010).

The empirical evidence analyzed in this study demonstrates that RTE owners/managers are aware of the relevance of local food to the promotion of the establishments and to enhance the tourists' experience. In fact, food products are intensively used by all the RTE as a way of promoting the establishments. The relation of food with local territories' identity, activities and culture is also emphasized in the promotional materials analyzed, through the use of words as 'traditional', 'typical', 'genuine', 'natural', 'flavor' and, in Tuscany, 'Tuscan' and 'from the land'. These results are in line with the evidence provided by Malevolti (2003) and Vieira and Figueiredo (2010) regarding the most valued features of local food productions by the tourists. However, these words and symbols are mainly connected to a 'global' image of the countryside (Bell, 2006; Cloke, 2006; Halfacree, 2006; McCarthy, 2008) than to truly specific local attributes.

In the Tuscan municipalities a larger number and variety of local features, including foodstuffs, are mobilized to promote the RTE and rurality with a stronger reference to the 'Tuscan' character of these features. Yet, "Tuscan(y)' is a worldwide brand not only representing the region from which it derives, but also for the 'Italian countryside' and Italy, by presenting a certain type of landscape" (Figueiredo & Raschi, 2012: 39), gastronomy and food productions as 'from the rural'. In this sense, the apparent 'locality' of the symbol 'Tuscan(y)' can certainly be argued. Empirical evidence suggests that, despite the abundant use of food productions in the promotional materials, the respondents attributed a minor role (when compared with other features) to the local agricultural productions and foodstuffs as pull factors in attracting guests, revealing a discrepancy between the promotion and the effective use of (and importance attributed to) local features.

Despite the use of relative 'global' symbols in promoting local food, the products effectively used and sold by the RTE, and also more often demanded by the guests, reflect the regional differences between the municipalities, as well as the relevance attributed by tourists to traditional foodstuffs in the overall rural tourism experience, which is in line with the studies of Boyne *et al.* (2003), Montanari and Staniscia (2009); Sims (2009) and Vieira and Figueiredo (2010), among others. These products – olive oil, wine and vegetables in Tuscan municipalities and meat, cheese and wine in Campania – are mainly from self-production (which is particularly evident, and not surprisingly, in the agro-tourism units in Tuscan municipalities) or bought from local producers or retailers. The reasons pointed out by the respondents to buy locally are related with the 'better quality' and the 'authenticity' of the products and to 'the support to local economies', corroborating some of the findings of Sims (2009) and Vieira and Figueiredo (2010). The generally 'higher price' of local food products and the 'irregularities' in the supply are the main constraints identified in buying locally, again confirming the evidence produced by Vieira and Figueiredo (2010).

As presented in the previous section, the RTE analyzed possess a small dimension, evidenced by the small number of bedrooms and beds, as well as the low number of guests received during the previous year. The small dimension is also emphasized by the limited number of connections that the RTE establish with the local producers, farmers and retailers. Although limited in number, the advantages of these liaisons are valued by the respondents, particularly as a way to help local economies and to contribute to local development; to attract more guests and to expand the offer of local productions. These findings are in line with the studies of Boyne *et al.* (2003), Brunori and Rossi (2000), Montanari and Staniscia (2009), Telfer and Wall (1996) and Vieira and Figueiredo (2010).

Although further research is needed, particularly considering the limitations posed by the small number of case studies analyzed, the small dimension of the RTE and its consequences in terms of services, activities and, especially, food products offered to guests, together with the limited number of connections to local agents, indicate the faint contribution of tourism activities to local development in the municipalities analyzed. This is particularly evident in Campania, where rural tourism is a relatively recent activity that, despite have been largely subsidized by public funds, possess up to now only a small economic impact on local communities' development. This evidence corroborates the studies of Malevolti (2003), Renting *et al.* (2003), Telfer and Wall (1996) and Vieira and Figueiredo (2010).

Acknowledgements

This research was partially funded by CNR (National Research Council, Italy) by the *Short-term Mobility Programme* (contract 140.4, 2008), by FCT – Portuguese Foundation for Science and Technology through a sabbatical grant for a three month visit to Italy, in 2010 and by C.E.S.I.A. – Academia Dei Georgofli, Firenze, Italy. To these institutions, the author wishes to express her gratitude. The author also wishes to thank Antonio Raschi, from IBIMET-CNR, for his cooperation.

Notes

[i] Procedures of this content analysis are explained in detail in Figueiredo and Raschi (2011, 2012).
[ii] Rapolano Terme is located near the city of Siena and not far from Florence. Chitignano and Ortignano/Raggiollo are located in the vicinity of Arezzo and Cortona.

References

Bell, D. (2006). Variations on the rural idyll. In P. Cloke, T. Marsden, & P.H. Mooney (Eds.) *Handbook of Rural Studies* (pp.149-160). London: Sage.

Bessière, J. (1998). Local development and heritage: Traditional food and cuisine as tourist attractions in rural areas. *Sociologia Ruralis*, 38, 21-34.

Boyne, S., Hall, D., & Williams, F. (2003). Policy, support and promotion for food-related tourism initiatives: A marketing approach to regional development. *Journal of Travel & Tourism Marketing*, 14(3/4), 131-154.

Brunori, G. (2007). Local food and alternative food networks: A communication perspective. *Anthropology of food* [(http://aof.revues.org/index430.html), Accessed March 2010].

Brunori, G., & Rossi A. (2000). Sinergy and coherence through collective action: Some insights from Wine Routes in Tuscany. *Sociologia Ruralis*, 40(4), 409-423.

Choy, S., Lehto, X.Y., & Morrisson, A. (2007). Destination image representation on the web: Content analysis of Macau travel related websites. *Tourism Management*, 28, 118-129.

Cloke, P. (2006). Conceptualizing rurality. In P. Cloke; T. Marsden, & P. H. Mooney (Eds.) *Handbook of Rural Studies* (pp. 18-27). London: Sage.

Cloke, P., & Goodwin, M. (1993). The changing function and position of rural areas in Europe. *Nederlandse Geografische Studies*, 153, 19-36.

Cohen, E., & Avieli, N. (2004). Food in tourism: attraction and impediment. *Annals of Tourism Research*, 31(4), 755-778.

Evans, N., Morris, C., & Winter, M. (2002). Conceptualizing agriculture: A critique of post-productivism as the new orthodoxy. *Progress in Human Geography*, 26(3), 313-332.

Figueiredo, E. (2008). Imagine there's no rural – The transformation of rural spaces into places of nature conservation in Portugal. *European Urban and Regional Studies*, 15(2), 159-171.

Figueiredo, E., & Raschi A. (2011). «Un' immensa campagna avvolta dal verde» - reinventing rural areas in Italy through tourism promotional images. *Journal of European Countryside*, 3(1), 1-20.

—. (2012). Immersed in Green? Reconfiguring the Italian Countryside through Rural Tourism Promotional Materials. In K. Hyde, C. Ryan, & A. Woodside (Eds.) *Field Guide for Case Study Research in Tourism, Hospitality and Leisure* (pp. 17-44). Bingley: Emerald.

Fonte, M. (2008). Knowledge, food and place. A way of producing, a way of knowing. *Sociologia Ruralis*, 48(3), 200-222.

Fonte, M., & Papadopoulos, A.G. (2010). (Eds.) *Naming Food after Places - Food relocalisation and knowledge dynamics in rural development*. London: Ashgate.

Halfacree, K. (2006). Rural space: constructing a three-fold architecture. In P. Cloke, T. Marsden, & P.H. Mooney (Eds.) *Handbook of Rural Studies* (pp. 44-62). London: Sage.

Hong J-S & Tsai C-T. (2012). Culinary tourism strategic development: An Asia-Pacific perspective. *International Journal of Tourism Research*, 14, 40-55.

Malevolti, I. (2003). *Prodotti tipice locali tradizionali e turismo rurale.* IRPET - Instituto Regionale Programmazione Economica Toscana.

Marsden, T. (1995). Beyond agriculture? Regulating the new rural spaces. *Journal of Rural Studies*, 11, 285-296.

Marsden, T., Lowe, P., & Whatmore S. (1990). (Eds.) *Rural Reestructuring – Global Processes and their Responses.* London: David Fulton.

McCarthy, J. (2008). Rural geography: Globalizing the countryside. *Progress in Human Geography*, 32(1), 129-137.

Montanari, A., & Staniscia, B. (2009). Culinary tourism as a tool for regional reequilibrium. *European Planning Studies*, 17(10), 1463-1483.

Perkins, H.C. (2006). Commodification: re-resourcing rural areas. In P. Cloke, T. Marsden, & P.H. Mooney (Eds.) *Handbook of Rural Studies* (pp. 243-257). London: Sage.

du Rand, G.E., & Heath, E. (2006). Towards a framework for food tourism as an element of destination marketing. *Current Issues in Tourism*, 9(3), 206 – 234.

du Rand, G.E, Heath, E., & Alberts N. (2003). The role of local and regional food in destination marketing: A South African situation analysis. *Journal of Travel and Tourism Marketing*, 14, 97-112.

Renko, S., Renko, N., & Polonijo, T. (2010). Understanding the role of food in rural tourism development in a recovering economy. *Journal of Food Products Marketing*, 16(3), 309-324.

Renting, H., Marsden, T.K., & Banks, J. (2003). Understanding alternative food networks: Exploring the role of short food supply chains in rural development. *Environment and Planning,* 35(3), 393-411.

Sims, R. (2009). Food, place and authenticity: Local food and the sustainable tourism experience. *Journal of Sustainable Tourism*, 17(3), 321-336.

Telfer, D., & Wall, D. (1996). Linkages between tourism and food production. *Annals of Tourism Research,* 23(3), 635-653.

Tregear, A., Arfini, F., Belletti, G., & Marescotti, A. (2007). Regional foods and rural development: The role of product qualification. *Journal of Rural Studies*, 23, 12-22.

Vieira, C., & Figueiredo, E. (2010). Fruitful Liaisons – articulation between regional food productions and tourism activities. In I. Darnhofer, & M. Grötzer (Eds.), *Building Sustainable Rural Futures - The added value of systems approaches in times of change and uncertainty - Proceedings of the 9th European IFSA Symposium,* (pp. 1647-1660). Vienna: Universität für Bodenkultur.

INDEX